WITHDRAWN

Three Mughal Poets

HARVARD COLLEGE
LIBRARY
CONTRACT

Three Mughal Poets

MIR · SAUDA · MIR HASAN

by Ralph Russell and Khurshidul Islam

STAFFORD LIBRARY
COLUMBIA COLLEGE
1001 ROGERS STREET
COLUMBIA, MO 65216

Harvard University Press · Cambridge, Massachusetts

1968

6904352

DANIEL BOONE
REGIONAL LIBRARY
COLUMBIA, MO.

DISCARD

891.439
R917t

© Copyright 1968 by the President and Fellows of Harvard College
All rights reserved

Library of Congress Catalog Card Number 68-15643
Printed in the United States of America

Publication of this book has been aided by a grant from the Ozai-Durrani Fund

UNESCO COLLECTION OF REPRESENTATIVE WORKS
INDIAN SERIES

This work has been accepted in the Indian translation series of the
United Nations Educational, Scientific and Cultural Organization
(UNESCO). It was recommended for publication by the Committee
on Far Eastern Literature set up to advise UNESCO in this field by
the International Council for Philosophy and Humanistic Studies, and
by the National Academy of Letters of India (Sahitya Akademi).

FOREWORD BY ANNEMARIE SCHIMMEL

"The names of Khwaja Mir Dard, Mir Hasan, Sauda and Mir are some of the most distinguished and honoured on the bead-roll of Urdu literature." Thus writes Ram Babu Saksena in his *History of Urdu Literature*, 1927. He is no doubt right, but unfortunately the names of these great poets of the eighteenth century, not to mention many lesser writers, are almost completely unknown not only to the average Western reader but even to students of Islamic culture; for the history, especially the cultural history, of Muslim India has been deplorably neglected by Western scholars during the last two centuries.

As early as the year 711 Sind, the lower Indus valley, was conquered by the Muslims. This is the same year in which another troop of Muslims crossed the Strait of Gibraltar to conquer Spain, while yet another Muslim army entered Transoxiana. Yet most of the scholars who specialised in Islamic studies found the Indian subcontinent, with its different languages, outside their realm of interest; and for students of Indian culture proper—of the Vedas and Upanishads, of Yoga and bhakti-mysticism, and of Buddhism—the Muslim conquest of India seemed to be only a transient phase in the long history of the subcontinent, a conquest that brought in elements completely alien to the essence of the indigenous Indian religio-social systems they were studying. As for the general reader in Europe and America, he probably knows, for example, that the wisdom of the Upanishads has deeply influenced Western, and especially German, idealistic philosophy since the beginning of the nineteenth century, after Anquetil Duperron's Latin translation of these mystical treatises appeared in 1801 under the title *Oupnekhat, id est secretum tegendum*. But he is perhaps not aware that the Persian translation of the Sanskrit original on which Anquetil based his translation (he was primarily a scholar of Persian) had been prepared by a Muslim, the heir apparent of the Mughal Empire, Prince Dārā Shikoh, who, in 1659, was executed by his brother Aurangzeb for religious as well as political reasons.

John Milton in *Paradise Lost* had Adam look, in the beginning of time, "to Agra and Lahor of Great Moghul," since the empire of the Great Mughals (1526–1857) was, like the Safavid Kingdom in Iran, a famous and fabulous country in the eyes of the Western reader, who became acquainted with some of its strange and fascinating aspects through the travel accounts of Bernier, Tavernier, Manucci, and others. Mughal India was for him a fairyland beyond the imagination of any European, who was limited to admiring the silks and muslins of unsurpassable beauty that were imported by the British East India Company, together with other luxury goods and precious spices. A good example of the influence of the travel books on European art is a work of jewellery produced between 1700 and 1708 at the court of King August of Saxonia by three court jewellers and their most skilful craftsmen. Representing the court of Aurangzeb on the emperor's birthday, it was made of gold, *email*, and jewels, on a scale of 142 to 114 centimetres, and even the most minute details of the dresses and ornaments on the dozens of tiny figures correspond exactly to the descriptions in the classical travel accounts.

But this is a unique example of influence, and though one might have admired the splendid spectacle of the Mughal court and perhaps know something about its administration, no one had any idea of the literary activities that had been developing in India for centuries. They reached their height, strangely enough, just at the time of the decline of the Mughal Empire, in the eighteenth century, when, after Aurangzeb's death in 1707, the anti-Muslim forces started destroying the empire from within and from without. The battle of Plassey, half a century after Aurangzeb's death, marked the beginning of a new period in India, that of British colonial rule, and exactly one century later, in 1857, even the nominal remnants of the once so powerful Mughal rule were abolished.

Interest in the literature of the subcontinent, whether Persian or Hindustani, has never been great in the West. Even Sir William Jones, the famous herald of Oriental lyrics in Europe during the latter part of the eighteenth century, concentrated mostly on translating classical Persian and Sanskrit poetry, even during his stay in Fort William. Muhammad Sadiq, in his *History of Urdu Literature*, attributes a strong interest in the development of Urdu literature to the British orientalists of Fort William in Calcutta, headed by John Gilchrist. However, they had no influence on the native writers, since at Fort William "Urdu prose was artificially cultivated by a few scholars working under official instructions." More-over, the British were anything but interested in Urdu literature—a general attitude that became apparent in the Macaulay scheme of 1835, concerning the introduction of the British educational system in India. Once the Persian language, which for centuries had served as the language of administration, higher education, historiography, and poetry, lost its official character in 1837, Urdu did become, in 1842, one of the examination subjects of Fort William College. However, the interest of those who did not share the prevailing contempt for everything Indian—an attitude that had replaced the romantic dreams of India as the home-land of everything good, at least in the minds of the ruling group—turned more to the regional languages than to Urdu. For example, there was Sir Bartle Frere, who contributed to the development of Sindhi literature by providing the language with a proper alphabet. Also, the languages of present Pakistan—Sindhi, Pashto, and Panjabi—were care-fully studied, in the middle of the nineteenth century, by the German missionary and philologist Ernst Trumpp, who even included some dia-lects of Kafiristan in his penetrating research, but who had not the slight-est sympathy with the literature in such vernaculars. In fact, he rather despised every utterance of mystical poetry. As for Joseph von Hammer-Purgstall, the indefatigable Austrian translator and writer, his scholarly reliability was unfortunately not as great as his literary activity. He did, however, publish several articles on Hindustani literature, and drew the attention of the Europeans to the *Haft Qulzum*, published in Lucknow in 1814, the last section of which was analysed and translated, on Hammer's request, by Friedrich Rückert with unsurpassable eloquence in 1828. This was one of the earliest introductions to the poetical and rhetorical art of Persian and, to a certain extent, of Urdu writers.

The only real specialist in the field of Hindustani literature during the nineteenth century was the Frenchman Garcin de Tassy, the favourite pupil of Silvestre de Sacy, who started teaching Hindustani at the École des Langues Orientales in Paris in 1828 and published a large number of translations, books, and articles on the subject. But, as J. Fück says in his *Die arabischen Studien in Europa*, Garcin de Tassy is a rather lonely figure in the long history of Oriental studies in Europe. On the other hand, since his assiduous activity in this realm was wider than it was deep, he never managed to give the study of Indian Islam the prominence it deserves within the field of Islamology. There was also, of course, the German translation of the most successful work of Urdu theatre, Amānat's *Indar Sabha*, written in 1853 at Wājid Ali Shāh's court in Lucknow, and translated with numerous annotations by Friedrich Rosen in 1892. But again this is a case unique in the history of orientalism. (Curiously enough it inspired one of the most successful German operettas, *Im Reiche des Indra*, by Paul Lincke.)

On the whole the interest in Urdu literature was deplorably small, and the universities rarely offered courses in the language. Just as Turkish literature had been considered, during the entire nineteenth century and to some extent up to the 1930s, a weak transformation of Persian poetry and a far echo of the greater and purer melodies that Hāfiz, Nizāmi, Rūmi, and Jāmi had sung long ago, Urdu literature was treated, if at all, as an unattractive imitation of classical Persian models.

There can be no doubt that the traditional material of Persian poetry has indeed been inherited by the Urdu-writing poets, many of whom write in Persian as well. But to criticise this fact means to misunderstand completely the character of classical Oriental poetry. It has often been said, and may be repeated, that the ideal of the Persian poets, especially of the *ghazal* writers, was not to sing their personal feelings and ideas in a new and very individualistic form, to invent unheard-of situations, or to pour out their hearts in what we used to call *Erlebnislyrik*, but rather to express their feelings according to certain established intellectual structures, yet combining symbols and words in such an artificial and ingenious way that the resulting poem far surpasses the model. Classical Persian poetry is, as it were, comparable to the art of the goldsmith or jeweller, who uses a given pattern which he means to surpass in beauty. The poet thus handles words and symbols even more daringly and skilfully than his predecessor, adorning them with the golden thread of rhythm and rhyme, and setting them together according to the rules of harmonious expression. One may also compare the poet in classical style to the painter of miniatures or the calligraphy artist, who creates according to an accepted pattern of lines and colours, and yet seeks, by means of a slight movement of his brush or his pen, to give the whole picture a personal and new touch, even if he paints Majnūn in the wilderness for the hundredth time. Such poems or single verses may, at first sight, look simple, but their true beauty is revealed only through careful analysis of the manifold elements hidden within them. The greatest works of this poetic art have the simplicity of the letter *alif*, the straight line emerging from the pen of the master calligrapher, or the harmony of a single sound produced by a *tabla* player on his instrument, both of which reveal not only the skill acquired in long years of untiring exercise but also the age-old tradition which is necessary for perfection.

Like the Turkish, Urdu poetry has inherited from Persian the highly developed play on words, which can add inimitable charm by the clever use of the Arabic, Persian, and Indian elements of the poetical language, each of which bears not only its simple meaning but also different accessory notions. From this stems the peculiar art of oscillation between mystical and profane meanings, or between sensuality and spirituality, which is so typical of classical Islamic poetry. The development of Islamic mysticism, especially in Iran, and its influence on Persian lyrics have been treated by many scholars, and anyone who has read Hāfiz' poetry knows that it is just this glittering ambiguity which makes these verses so charming, intricate, and, in a certain respect, untranslatable. "The word is a fan behind which a pair of beautiful eyes may be seen." So Goethe described the art of veiling and unveiling in Persian poetry. Who knows whether the wine is real or is the wine of love? Who knows whether the beloved is a handsome young boy, wearing his silken cap awry on his head, his curls hanging down beside his moonlike face, or whether this description is only a symbol of the Divine Beloved, whose beauty surpasses everything and is yet to be expressed only in terms of human attributes? And the cruelty of the beloved, a favourite subject of all poets, may apply to an earthly being—the young, cruel Turkish soldier of so many poems—or to a *parda* lady, or to the divine power whose inscrutable acts man can but accept silently, patiently, even gratefully.

From its Persian ancestors Urdu poetry too has inherited the complete system of mystical expression and traditions that had become, at least since the thirteenth century, so popular on the subcontinent, where the role of the mystical orders was decisive for the widespread expansion of Islam. The influence of Maulānā Jalāluddīn Rūmī (1207–1273), the greatest of Persian-writing mystical poets, on the development of mystical poetry and literature, from the Bosporus to the borders of East Bengal, cannot be overrated. Likewise, the works of his spiritual predecessor Farīduddīn ʿAttār must have been popular with the mystics of the subcontinent, judging from the numerous allusions to his symbolism. Through 'Attār's and Rūmī's work, the figure of Husain ibn Mansūr al-Hallāj, mostly called by his patronymic Mansūr, or "the Victorious," has become one of the central figures not only in Urdu but also in Sindhi and Panjabi literature. This martyr-mystic, who was executed in Baghdad in 922, has been made the symbol of the consuming fire of love. He is contrasted with the dry theologians who preach from the pulpit the barren outward theories of the faith, whereas Hallāj, on his impaling stake, teaches mankind—through the daring affirmation *anā' l-Haqq*, or "I am the absolute Truth"—the mystery of divine love and of all-embracing unity, which can be realised only through martyrdom.

The suffering lover is one of the central themes and perhaps the one central subject of Persian, Turkish, and Urdu poetry, and it makes no difference whether the model of the lover be a mystic like Hallāj or one of the great legendary heroes of Islamic epic literature. There is Farhād, the stonecutter, for example, who worked for years and years in order to pierce the rock so that he might win his beloved Shīrīn, and is at last treacherously deceived by the false news of her death, so that he dies in despair. Then there is Majnūn, the madman of Arabic love stories, who lived in the deserts, surrounded by gazelles and wild animals, the birds building their nest in his dishevelled hair—the lover who yearns for his beloved Laila and yet, after years of longing, realises that Laila is within himself, that the beloved is not distinct from himself but is the very core of his heart.

While Majnūn tells every living being the name of his Laila, and even addresses the shy antelopes by her name, most of the lovers in classical poetry prefer not to tell the name of the beloved object. The fear of divulging his or her name is a motive as popular in Turkish poetry, from Sultān Jem to Nedim, as in Iran, for the poets have not forgotten the punishment which was inflicted upon Hallāj for having openly proclaimed the secret of Unity, and since in magic practices the name itself is the person, telling the name of the beloved is considered unpardonable treason.

A great part of the traditional imagery of Islamic poetry is based upon the Quran, which relates the stories of the Prophets. This holy book has become, as Massignon put it, the textbook of the *Weltanschauung* of every Muslim. Small wonder, then, that allusions to Quranic verses are dispersed throughout the whole body of Persian and Arabic poetry, so that a real understanding of numerous verses is impossible without a knowledge of the Quranic expressions that are hinted at. Besides the pre-eternal covenant between God and man (Sura 7/171), which is one of the favourite subjects of classical poetry and should always be kept in mind when the word *yesterday* occurs in a poem, it is the Quranic legend of creation, of man's role in the universe, that has been repeated through the centuries by the poets and mystics who have interpreted the words of the holy book—sometimes in very strange verses. Just as they may depict the lover as a humble creature, completely left to the mercy of his beloved, so, on the other hand, do they stress the fact that man is the *ashraf ul-makhlūqāt*, the noblest creature, before whom the angels prostrated themselves, and who was ordered to act as vicegerent of his Lord. It is man who was honoured with the burden that heaven and earth refused to carry (Sura 33/72), whereas he willingly took it from the hand of his Creator. A poet like Mir echoes the famous verses of Hāfiz, who wrote, in the great ghazal *Dūsh dīdam* . . . (Yesterday [that is, on the day of the pre-eternal covenant] I Saw the Angels Knocking on the Door of the Tavern), the typical line, "Heaven could not bear the burden of the trust—thus the lot was cast for me, the madman." This burden or trust, the *amānat* mentioned by the Quran, has been interpreted by the mystics as a burden of love. One may compare Gertrude Bell's rendering of Hāfiz' line: "For Heaven's self was all too weak to bear/the burden of His love God laid on it." But it has also been interpreted by Muhammad Iqbāl, for example, as the burden of personality, of individuality. Mir, in his verses about man as the "noblest of creatures" and about the pre-eternal burden, is faithful to the traditional interpretation, but gives a new, and quite unexpected, view of the value of human life.

Among the numerous inherited *topoi* of Persian-Urdu poetry we might mention also the constant tension between the poet or lover, on the one hand, and the theologian, the *shaikh* or *pīr* of the Sufi order, on the other. Pre-formed at the confrontation of Hallāj and the theologian, of gibbet and pulpit, this relation of the ecstatic lover and the representative of the established theological or mystical tradition is one of the constantly recurring themes of poetry, from Hāfiz, with his mockery about the shaikh who enters the tavern, to Muhammad Iqbāl, who gives the old motif a new and practical dimension by applying it to the fossilised theologians of his own time.

The task of the true poet was to fill with new life the patterns and forms of the hundreds of traditional topoi and symbols, and to make the truth of the symbols he used a part of his own life, through his own experiences. Mir, the pathetic lover, is a fine example of this highest achievement of the art of poetry. But it would be wrong to see Urdu poetry only as the elaborate art of ghazal-writing. Other forms of expression, also inherited from the Persian, developed amidst the peculiar circumstances of literary life on the subcontinent during the eighteenth and early nineteenth centuries. Satire, of course, was composed all over the world, and both the pre-Islamic Arabs, who were masters in poignant satirical verses, and the Persians, who excelled in the art of exaggeration both in their encomiums and in their derisive poetry, contributed to this very human genre. In Urdu the art of satire reached its culmination with Sauda, from whose poems and colourful descriptions we may reconstruct a picture of life in Delhi and Lucknow during the eighteenth century. The ease and wit of his expression, and his sharp criticism of the political and social evils of his time, have made him a favourite amongst those who enjoy that kind of literature, while his qualities as a poet have established him as one of the best satirists of the Islamic world.

While Sauda critically highlighted the weak points of his society, his contemporary Mir Hasan succeeded in transforming the old form of the *masnavi*, the narrative poem in distichs, by giving it a romantic flavour, combining reality with fairy tale, and blending Indian and Islamic tradition, thus remaining faithful to that of the oldest stories of the *Thousand and One Nights*, which had reached the Arab countries long before on their way from the Indian motherland. Mir Hasan's lovely story *Sihr ul-bayān* has influenced almost every later work of this kind in Urdu literature, and we find some traces of its plot even in the *Indar Sabha*.

Thus the three poets represented in this book are to a certain extent representative of three different facets of eighteenth-century literary expression: Sauda, a critic of his society and an able satirist; Mir Hasan, who transformed lovely and frightening dreams into enchanting poetry; and Mir, the deeply melancholy lover who aptly used the whole treasure house of inherited imagery and symbolism, giving the words a soft personal touch out of his own bitter experiences.

Although the bibliography lists the extant editions of Mir's, Mir Hasan's, and Sauda's works (and we know that new attempts to publish

the works of these and other Urdu poets are being made in India and in
Pakistan), we thought it would be useful here to add the Urdu original of
the translated verses. Ibrahim Allahabadi, of Delhi, is responsible for the
calligraphy. We hope one day to publish a bilingual anthology of Urdu
poetry. Meanwhile, this book—the product of the collaboration between
a European and an Indo-Muslim scholar—shows some of the greatest
Urdu poets in their historical setting, and we are confident that it will
help to give the Western reader some real understanding of classical
Urdu poetry. If the authors have succeeded in transmitting at least a
spark of the love they feel for their subject, we should be more than
happy.

AUTHOR'S PREFACE

Some thirty to forty years ago an Oxford don is reported to have said that the mention of India was enough to empty the smallest lecture hall in Oxford.[1] His statement was perhaps exaggerated, but that relatively few people in the West felt any great interest in India and its culture was certainly true in those days. This is no longer the case. In recent years the desire to know more about India—India and Pakistan since the partition of 1947—has markedly increased and is still increasing. This book is addressed to those who share that desire. It is an attempt, which so far as we know has not been made before, to introduce to the English-speaking reader the work of three great poets of one of the major modern languages of the Indian subcontinent—namely, Urdu. We have not assumed in the reader any previous knowledge of the subject. All that we *have* assumed in him is a readiness to make that minimum mental effort which is required of any man who wants to understand and appreciate the literature of a people and an age which are not his own.

Urdu is one of the most developed of the dozen or so major modern languages of the Indo-Pakistan subcontinent, but it differs from most of the others in that it is not the language of a single, continuous, well-defined geographical area, as, for example, Bengali is the language of Bengal. Its real homeland is the western part of the state of Uttar Pradesh[2] and the country round Delhi, for it is on the native speech of the people of this region that literary Urdu is based; but its speakers are to be found all over India and Pakistan, and are particularly numerous in the area comprising West Pakistan and the great northern Indian plains up to the western border of Bengal. It is spoken especially by Muslims—though by no means exclusively by them—and its literature has for the most part a Muslim background. We do not mean by this that it is primarily a

---

[1] The dictum of the Oxford don was often quoted by the late Edward Thompson. It stands at the head of his sketch *A History of India* (London, 1927).

[2] Its name before independence was United Provinces. The initials of the old and the new names conveniently coincide, and the state is still commonly called "U.P.," as it was long before it received its present name.

religious literature, but simply that, like the Arabian Nights, it portrays the life of a people who profess the religion of Islam. The language developed to approximately its present literary form early in the eighteenth century, and the three poets with whom this book deals were among the first to write it in this form. During the greater part of their lifetime the acknowledged centre of Urdu was Delhi, though in later years the city lost its exclusive importance as the one great centre of the literature. Urdu is today one of the major languages listed in the Indian Constitution, and is one of the two official languages of Pakistan.

Urdu is thus one of the most important languages of the subcontinent. But it does not necessarily follow that its literature is worth the attention of the English-speaking reader. If it is, he may ask, why has he not heard of it before?

To this very natural question there is no simple answer. But the explanation lies mainly in the history of Britain's relationship with India. The beginning of British rule in India is often dated from the Battle of Plassey in 1757, which made the British the real rulers of Bengal. By this date the fame of Mir and Sauda, the first of the great poets of modern Urdu, was already established; but until nearly half a century later the great centres of Urdu literature still lay outside the area of British rule, and it is not surprising that only a very few Englishmen should have been acquainted with it. When at the beginning of the nineteenth century the British extended their power as far as Delhi, it might have been expected that a knowledge and appreciation of Urdu literature would have become more widespread; but an attitude was now rapidly becoming dominant which was to prevent this even more effectively than geographical remoteness had done—that of the early Victorian age, when Englishmen were profoundly convinced that in contemporary England human civilisation had reached its highest development, and that while further progress would continue along the lines which England had laid down, Englishmen now had little to learn from the past or from other nations less favoured by God than Victorian England. It was Macaulay who gave classic expression to this outlook. In his view a knowledge of English sufficed to provide for every important cultural need. "Whoever knows that language," he wrote, "has ready access to all the vast intellectual wealth, which all the wisest nations of the earth have created." Certainly the literature of India and other Asian countries had in comparison nothing to contribute—"no books on any subject which deserves to be compared to our own." "A single shelf of a good European library . . . [is] worth the whole native literature of India and Arabia." The quotations are taken from his Minute on Indian Education, written in 1835.[3] In it he is mainly concerned to belittle the value of Arabic and Sanskrit, the classical languages respectively of the Muslims and the Hindus. It is interesting that Persian, the language of Omar Khayyam and of other poets greater than he, which had for centuries been the language of diplomacy and culture not only in India but throughout a large part of the Muslim world, is not even referred to, while the modern languages of India ("the dialects commonly spoken among the natives") are dismissed as being "poor and rude." This is not the place to assess Macaulay's Minute as a whole, but there can be no doubt that the attitude it expresses is one which precludes any sympathetic interest in Indian literature. And that attitude did not die with the Victorian age; it has continued up to our own day to influence English opinion deeply. This is not our view alone; it is also that of the Scarbrough Commission appointed by the British Foreign Office in 1944 to investigate the state of Oriental and other studies. Its report, published in 1947, quotes from Macaulay's Minute as the expression of "a traditional exclusiveness which tends to disregard and even look down upon culture which has little in common with our own," and considers this exclusiveness to be "the chief reason why these studies have not prospered."[4]

So far as India is concerned, direct subjection to British rule and the rise of a movement for national independence led to a tension which also limited the development of British interest in Indian culture and reinforced the effect of the Macaulay outlook. The result has been that while the British, throughout the period, recognised the importance of the Urdu language for administrative purposes—for example, Urdu in the Roman script was, until independence, the official language of the Indian Army—the literature of Urdu aroused very little interest. Only relations of equality and mutual respect between nations enable them to appreciate

[3] Macaulay's Minute is included in the volume *Selected Speeches*, ed. G. M. Young (London, 1935). The extracts quoted here are to be found on pp. 350, 351, 349, and 348, in that order.
[4] Para. 25, in *Report of the Interdepartmental Commission of Enquiry on Oriental, Slavonic, East European and African Studies* (London, 1947).

truly one another's culture, and it is only recently that such relations have been established between Britain and the Indo-Pakistan subcontinent. Now that they have been, work can begin in earnest to introduce to English-speaking readers literatures which, if hitherto little known, are all the same worth their reading.

Those who attempt this task may draw encouragement from the fact that they are not breaking entirely fresh ground. The literatures of India are Oriental literatures, and differ in many ways from those of the West. But experience has already shown that the differences are not too great to prevent the English-speaking reader appreciating them. The Bible, the Arabian Nights, and the Rubaiyat of Omar Khayyam are all works of Oriental literature, and successive generations of English-speaking readers have been moved, inspired, and entertained by them. It is worth stressing that the chief reason for this has been that they have approached these works with respect, knowing of the power they have exercised over millions of readers before them and expecting to experience something of this power themselves. There are things in them which they do not understand or appreciate, but they generally assume (and for the most part correctly) that this is because of an insufficient knowledge of their background, and they do not allow these things to stand in the way of their enjoyment. All of which is only another way of saying that the Macaulay spirit is dormant when they approach these books.

Unfortunately it is not only the Macaulay spirit which hinders a true appreciation of Indian literature. It is matched by an opposite tendency, smaller but more vocal, voiced by those who proclaim the glories of Indian literature in tones that are often more royalist than the king. Such enthusiasts have done something to counteract the Macaulay outlook; but they have also done a good deal of harm by strengthening the erroneous impression that Indian literature is something of an entirely different order from that of the West. The two opposed outlooks have more in common than at first sight appears. Both exaggerate what they believe to be the peculiarly Indian elements in the literature, with the difference that while the one finds these elements strange, incomprehensible, and repulsive, the other finds them exotic, mysterious, and attractive. Both have kept alive ideas of "the mysterious East"—ideas that "East is East and West is West and never the twain shall meet"—and such ideas have now been so widely held, and for so long, that the very words Eastern, Oriental, Indian, and so on now carry something of these connotations with them. An unduly heightened consciousness of difference between East and West is traditional with us now. Had it not been so, it would have been realised long ago that many "peculiarly Indian" features of Indian literature are in fact not peculiarly Indian at all, and that still less are they mysterious once their background is understood.

This is certainly true of the eighteenth-century Urdu literature with which this book deals. Its atmosphere is markedly different from that of eighteenth-century English literature, and this is indeed partly due to the fact that the one is English and the other Indian. But a much greater part of the difference arises not from the national but from the social and historical setting. Eighteenth-century English literature is already unmistakably modern; eighteenth-century Urdu literature is still essentially medieval, and it differs from contemporary English literature only about as much as medieval European literature does. Realisation of this fact does not, by a long way, remove all the difficulties of understanding it, for a medieval literature also presents problems to the modern reader; but it does at least change his conception of the nature of these difficulties, and he can at any rate safely banish the idea that in approaching Urdu literature, he will be dealing with another race of men who were the product of a national tradition entirely alien to him, and whose ways, despite every effort on his part, are therefore likely to remain inscrutable to him. Our own experience of teaching Urdu literature to English and European students shows that once the historical setting has been explained, the main obstacles to an appreciation of the literature are overcome. That is why we have devoted the first chapter of this book to a description of that setting.

It may be helpful here to say something of the plan of the chapters which follow. We have tried wherever possible to let the literature speak for itself, with only the minimum of comment, and this aim has largely determined the arrangement of the chapters. Although on the title page the poets are named in the order that comes naturally to anyone acquainted with Urdu poetry, we begin, in Chapter 2, with the satirist Sauda, for it is to his work that a knowledge of the historical setting is most directly relevant. Next comes Mir Hasan, whose long romantic poem offers very little difficulty to the English reader, and prepares the way for the more directly realistic love poetry of Mir. And Mir is taken last.[5]

This part of the book was the most difficult to write. Since Mir is the greatest poet of the three, and in our view one of the great love poets of world literature, we have done our best to enable the reader to appreciate him. But the task was not an easy one. Most of Mir's best poems are in a form known as the *ghazal*, and the ghazal was the product of a long tradition which had evolved set conventions affecting both its form and its content. These needed to be fully explained, and even when that had been done, there remained the task of presenting the ghazal itself. Ideally, this meant translation, but the extreme conciseness imposed by the ghazal form, and the wealth of suggestion and allusion packed into each of its lines, confront its translator with difficulties so great that we had originally felt them to be insuperable. However, friends who read our first draft (and to all of whom our sincerest thanks are due) nearly all insisted that the attempt should be made, and we have now made it—with what success we must leave it to the reader to decide.

In general, direct translation of continuous passages has been only one of our means of presentation. We have used it more in Chapter 2 than elsewhere, for Sauda's poems go very well into the sort of verse which Nevill Coghill has done so well in his translation of Chaucer's *Canterbury Tales*. While we have not aimed at a close and literal adherence to the Urdu, we would claim that our English version taken as a whole does reproduce fatihfully the spirit and substance of the original. Elsewhere we have given abridged prose versions of the original poems—a method suggested partly by Rex Warner's admirable presentation of Greek stories in his *Men and Gods* and *Greeks and Trojans*. We would stress that in such poems we have taken care not to introduce any matter of our own. For example, in the abridged prose version of Mir Hasan's narrative poem which takes up the greater part of Chapter 3, we have not departed from the original in any way, and there is no detail of incident or description and no line of dialogue which does not occur in the original work. The same point holds good of the other poems thus handled.

---

[5] Throughout the book we have used their names without diacritical marks. The *i* of Mīr corresponds roughly to the *ee* sound in *meet*; the *au* of Saudā approximates to the *ou* of *loud*; and the *a*'s in Hasan to the unstressed *a* in *above*.

We must hope for a reader of fairly catholic tastes, one who, to elaborate the point by familiar examples, enjoys literature as diverse as Rabelais, the Arabian Nights, and the English metaphysical poets. If the coarseness of Rabelais puts him off, so will the coarseness of Sauda; if the Arabian Nights' naive delight in fantasy and disregard of the complexities of characterisation offends his sophisticated taste, he will not find much to admire in Mir Hasan; and if the ingenious conceits of the metaphysical poets seriously impair their appeal to him, so will similar features of Mir's poetry. But if he likes all these things, we can hope that he will like these three poets of Mughal India too.

This book is not, in the deplorably narrow sense which the words have come to bear in academic circles, a "scholarly work." But we hope that it may interest the scholar as well as the general reader, and we have therefore added footnotes in which those who wish to do so may find the basis on which the book has been built and check for themselves the validity of what we have written. Further, it would perhaps be prudent to forewarn scholars who bring specialist knowledge to the reading of the book that since it is not primarily addressed to them, they will not necessarily find in it discussions of the questions which particulary interest them. Our theme demands some treatment of eighteenth-century Mughal history, some account of Islamic mysticism, and some discussion of the role of convention in literature; but none of these themes receives the full, balanced treatment which would have been its due had we been studying it in its own right. On the contrary, we have deliberately excluded everything relating to these themes which does not have a direct bearing on the understanding of eighteenth-century poetry. In other words, our treatment of them is partial and incomplete, but it is avowedly and deliberately so.

Most of the footnotes are our own, but additions have been made by Professor Annemarie Schimmel, representative of the Ozai-Durrani Fund at Harvard University, whose name is well known to Islamic scholars in both the West and the East. All such additional notes are followed by the initials A.S. Dr. Schimmel also supplemented our bibliography with entries of works in French, German, and Italian. We gratefully acknowledge her help and encouragement.

It has not seemed desirable in a work of this kind to give in the text full transliterations of the names and the Urdu words that occur. In general we have confined ourselves to marking the long vowels where these occur in the body of the word. (Final vowels may be assumed to be long.) Full pointing is, however, provided in the footnotes, bibliography, and glossary. Urdu words are italicised at their first occurence, but not thereafter.

The map on p. 27 is reproduced by permission of Oxford University Press from *An Historical Atlas of the Indian Peninsula* by C. Collin Davies.

I must end on a more personal note. It is twelve years since Khurshidul Islam and I began work on this book. The conception of the work was chiefly his, and his unfailing enthusiasm was the main force which carried it to completion and enabled us to produce a first version by 1958. Up to that time we had worked in the closest collaboration, selecting, reading, and discussing together every line of the poetry we were attempting to present, and modifying the final text until we were both completely satisfied with it. Since then circumstances have made it impossible to continue this close cooperation, and a good deal of rewriting, especially in the last three chapters, has had to be done by me alone. The translations of the verses quoted in these chapters are also mine, and it has not, for the most part, been possible for me to discuss them with my coauthor. Hence, while these chapters follow the general lines agreed between both of us when we wrote the first version, their detailed elaboration is mine, and I alone bear the responsibility for their inadequacies.

My especial thanks are due to Miss Hilary Davey for her help in the final stages of preparing the book for the press.

Ralph Russell

Harlow, England
March 1968

CONTENTS

Three Mughal Poets

CHAPTER ONE

The Eighteenth-Century Background

MIR, SAUDA, AND MIR HASAN were the poets of a society very much like that of medieval Europe. The great majority of its members were peasants, and in the last resort it was on the wealth they produced that society lived. The social organisation was a hierarchy. At the summit stood the king, from whom all power and authority derived, and to whom all his subjects, high and low, owed allegiance. He had a corresponding obligation to protect them and to promote their welfare, and in order that he might have the means to do so, the peasants gave up to him a proportion of their crop. Next in order to the king came the great nobles; by the king's authority they received in various forms a part of the social wealth, and they were bound in return to perform the customary services which he could demand of them—in particular, to render him military aid whenever he called upon them. In Mughal India a noble's rank was expressed in terms of the number of cavalry which the king could call upon him to provide; he was a "commander of five thousand," or whatever the figure might be. The cavalryman found his own horse, arms, and equipment. In addition to providing for the welfare of the people, the king and the nobility were expected, through patronage, to make provision for the intellectual and cultural life of society.

In theory this social organisation was seen as one which enabled all members of society to work in harmony for the common happiness of all. God had given each man his capacities and set him in that station in life for which those capacities fitted him; He had defined the rights and the responsibilities of every class of men, and so long as every man—be he noble or peasant—conscientiously performed the duties of his station, society would prosper. These duties involved, in medieval eyes, a good deal more than what modern man regards as the civic virtues. In modern societies the general view is that every man's life is his own, and that society should interfere with it as little as possible; he accepts, not altogether gladly, that certain minimum positive demands must be made of him—that he must pay his taxes, for example—and that society must forbid by law activities which are seriously harmful to it. But provided he performs his minimum social obligations and refrains from breaking the law, he regards the rest of his life as his own affair, and society need not and should not be concerned with it. Such a conception is quite foreign to the medieval way of thinking. Medieval society demanded of its members what modern society may only hope from them: it required of every man a much more positive conception of his social duties, and over and above that, the observance of a whole way of life which it held to be as much society's concern as the individual's. A king or a noble had to be more than an efficient statesman, administrator, and commander in war. He also had to have all the attributes which the word "noble" in all its senses still implies. He was supposed to be a man of inborn dignity, a natural leader of men, a soldier personally skilled in all the arts of war and as distinguished for his personal bravery as for his high birth. He had also to be a widely cultured man, abreast of the arts and sciences of his time, a liberal patron of learning and culture, and one qualified both by taste and by training to appreciate what he patronised. The man of learning had to master his heritage and study to develop it further. The poet had to be well versed in his craft, and have something of significance to say. The soldier had to keep his horse, his arms, and his equipment in good order, and fight with courage, skill, and devotion in the service of his lord. The peasant had to till his land well and pay promptly and honestly that share of his produce which was his contribution to the ordered running of society.

Society was actively concerned with every important aspect of men's lives. In this respect, the most striking contrast between modern and medieval ways appears in the attitude toward love and marriage. In medieval society love and marriage are two quite separate things, and medieval love poetry, whether of Western Europe or of Mughal India, is hardly intelligible unless this fact and its main implications are understood. In Mughal India, in respectable Muslim families, marriage was a matter with important social implications, and it was generally arranged between the parents of the young man and the young woman. The *parda* (purdah) system was strictly enforced, and bride and bridegroom normally saw each other for the first time during the celebration of the wedding. Love was seen as a danger to ordered social life, and was persecuted accordingly. It is important to realise that the unfortunate lovers themselves shared this view of love. The character of Urdu love poetry is determined by this background.

In general, the force of convention was extraordinarily powerful in medieval societies and pervaded almost every department of life. A medieval society was essentially a static one. Political changes may have been many and violent, but they took place within a system of society which could endure unchanged for centuries together. The medieval ideals were correspondingly static. They envisaged no change to disturb the eternal order of things: all that was required with the passage of time was to elaborate and make more precise principles which in their general application had been known for generations; and in this way conventions were formed which had all the force of an age-old tradition behind them.

The literature and the literary life of society were markedly affected by this atmosphere. In eighteenth-century India the aspiring poet would as a matter of course approach a poet of already established reputation and ask him to accept him as his *shāgird*. The word is used in various senses—of pupil, disciple, and servant—and though the first is in this context the most appropriate English equivalent, the other connotations are by no means wholly irrelevant. The relation of the shāgird to his *ustād*, or master, resembled that of a vassal to his overlord, and society expected him to behave accordingly, acting not simply as his pupil in the art of poetry but as one under general obligation to him, bound to submit to his authority and, so to speak, to uphold his cause. In consultation with his ustād he would choose a *takhallus*, or poetic name. This would consist of a single word, and might or might not coincide with some part of the poet's real name. Every poet had to have one, for some of the poetic forms in which he would have to write prescribed the introduction of the takhallus into the final verse. The poet would generally, though not always, be known by his takhallus. Mir was a takhallus, and so was Sauda.

Mir Hasan was the poet's real name; his takhallus was Hasan. The guidance which an ustād gave to his shāgird consisted in "correcting" all his verses, and the word bore an all-embracing sense. The ustād would correct not only defects in metre and language, but also alter verses in any other way or simply delete them, in order to bring his shāgird's work into conformity with his own taste and judgement. A shāgird might with due respect question a correction and defend his own version, but the attempt would generally be a hopeless one unless he could produce authority for what he had written—that is, quote some parallel from the work of a classical poet. This characteristically medieval emphasis on precedent and authority was very marked in the eighteenth-century Mughal literary world.

When the young poet was considered to have acquired the necessary skill, he could take part in mushāiras. These were gatherings at the house or court of some eminent scholar or poet or noble—many nobles were in any case also poets—to which poets would be invited to recite their own work. Such assemblies had their own traditional procedure. Often the invitation would include a line of verse, and all who participated would be required to come with a poem incorporating this line, written in the same metre and using a rhyme scheme in harmony with it. The guests would be seated on the carpet and a candle would be passed round from one to another. As the candle came before him, each would recite his verse. The audience responded in terms of the elaborately courteous etiquette which tradition required. Polite exclamations of praise would greet a good line, and the poet would bow and salaam in acknowledgement. Criticism could also be expressed or, more commonly, delicately implied. A courteous request to the poet to repeat a line often indicated that there was felt to be some defect in it, and a poet quick enough to detect the fault and versatile enough to correct it extempore might do so. A poet whose verse was greeted with general approval in these assemblies might regard his apprenticeship as being at an end, though convention would require him throughout his life to treat his old ustād with all the respect due from a former shāgird.

The taste for poetry was (and still is) very widespread, for Indians do not suffer from that "successfully cultivated distaste for poetry"[1] of which the English have, with some justification, been accused, and a good

---

[1] Thompson, *History of India*, pp. 32–33.

poet would rapidly win fame. People would eagerly seek access to gatherings where it was known he was going to recite, and in various other ways his reputation would spread beyond his own city. There was as yet no printing, but in Mughal India, as in every country where Islam has spread, the art of calligraphy was highly appreciated and widely practised, and a great man might commission a good calligrapher to prepare him a copy of a favourite poet's verse. Or the poet himself might have a copy made for presentation to a patron. In the India Office Library in London there is a manuscript copy of Sauda's collected verse which was presented by the author to Richard Johnson, the British Assistant Resident at the court of Oudh during the last years of Sauda's life.[2] Of Mir it is said that his verses were so highly esteemed that men travelling to other parts of the country would have a few of them copied on a sheet of paper and take this to present to their host when they reached their destination. Such were some of the ways in which a poet's fame would spread far afield. Mir often speaks with pride of the spread of his own fame:

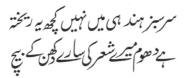

My poetry grows green not only in the northern plains.
In all the Deccan too the praises of my verse resound.

(II.258.17)

The metaphor is aptly chosen, for the great north Indian plain is some of the most fertile land in the world, and the metaphor suggests how abundantly his fame flourished.

A famous poet would not generally find it difficult to win the patronage of a great noble, who would relieve him from the anxiety of finding a livelihood, and enable him to devote his time to poetry. There is a modern prejudice against patronage which almost takes it for granted that no poet dependent on it can possibly write anything worth-while. "I can conceive of no system," says Macaulay, "more fatal to the integrity and independence of literary men than one under which they should be taught

2 See T. F. Blumhardt, *Catalogue of the Hindustani Manuscripts in the Library of the India Office*, No. 146 (London, 1926), pp. 76–78. The inscription reads, "Mr. Richard Johnson, the gift of ye author Mirza Soudah."

to look for their daily bread to the favour of ministers and nobles. I can conceive of no system more certain to turn those minds which are formed by nature to be the blessings and ornaments of our species into public scandals and pests.''[3] There is no doubt that one of the effects of patronage in all ages has been to encourage sycophancy, but there is equally no doubt that it alone made possible the greatest works of literature and art that we possess, works produced by men whose integrity and independence were apparently in no way impaired by it. Patronage was to medieval society the normal, accepted way of providing for the development of learning and culture, and the relationship between the poet and his patron was, like every other medieval relationship, prescribed by long usage. Nothing in it sanctioned anything in the nature of censorship. The poet might be expected to write odes on state occasions, just as the modern British poet laureate is, and the result, in both cases, cannot often be rated as great poetry. But for the rest the poet was free to write as he felt inspired, and rather than the poet being expected to write what his patron would approve, it was the patron who was expected to appreciate what the poet wrote.

Great nobles would often welcome the opportunity to become patrons of famous poets, for their social prestige would be enchanced accordingly. There is nothing in the writings of Mir, Sauda, and Mir Hasan to suggest that patronage restricted their freedom of expression, and much, both in their writings and in traditional stories about them, which shows on the contrary that they wrote as they pleased—and not only wrote as they pleased, but in matters where poetry was concerned, spoke very much as they pleased too. There is a story that the Mughal Emperor once asked Sauda how many poems a day he composed. ''When I am in the mood, about three or four couplets,'' Sauda replied. ''And I can compose four complete poems as I sit in the lavatory,'' said the Emperor proudly. ''Yes,'' said Sauda, ''and they smell like it.'' A Macaulay might well find Sauda's Rabelaisian directness offensive to his sense of propriety; but he could hardly argue from it that patronage had been ''fatal to his integrity and independence.'' On another occasion the Emperor had it conveyed to Sauda that he was prepared to confer on him the title of poet laureate. Sauda's comment was, ''What difference will His Majesty's title make?

[3] From Macualay's speech of 1841 on copyright, in *Selected Speeches*, p. 160.

If anything makes me poet laureate, it will be my own poetry."[4] Many similar stories are told of Mir as well, and it is striking that such incidents never resulted in a breach between the patron and the poet unless the poet himself chose to make it the occasion for one. Any ending of the relationship between them generally had other causes: in the eighteenth century the most common was the abrupt changes of fortune which would often deprive a patron of the means to pay the poet's stipend.

The medieval stamp is evident not only on the literary life of society but also on the literature itself. Convention, authority, precedent— these things ruled in the domain of poetry as they did elsewhere. There was a limited number of forms, most of them strictly and minutely defined, within which all poetry had to be written, and relatively detailed prescription extended to content as well as to form. Before he could use these forms, a poet had to master a complex system of prosody, from which no departure was permitted, and know how to handle an enormously elaborate "science of rhetoric," as it was called, in which figures of speech, subdivided into "figures of thought" and "figures of words" are analysed in amazing (and to our way of thinking quite pointless) detail, and rules for their use are laid down.

The three most important poetic forms were the ghazal, the *qasīda*, and the *masnavi*, and of these the ghazal was the most highly developed.[5] Urdu took all of them from Persian, as English took the sonnet from Italian. The ghazal is a short lyric, in which themes of love predominate. (The word is derived from a root which means approximately "conversation between lovers.") Its form is bound by strict rules. The authorities on poetics vary as to the number of couplets it may contain:

[4] The anecdotes of Saudā and the Emperor are from Muḥammad Ḥusain Āzād, *Āb i Ḥayāt* (14th printing, Lahore, n.d.), p. 149. Many modern critics are inclined to dismiss Āzād's stories as mere gossip, and therefore of no account. In our opinion this is too sweeping an attitude. At the time when Āzād wrote (*Āb i Ḥayāt* was first published in 1879), he had access to written and oral sources which we no longer possess today, some deriving from the accounts of men who had personally known the poets of whom he wrote. Where his anecdotes do not conflict with more reliable evidence and are consistent with the picture which emerges from a study of the poet's own work, there is no reason to reject them absolutely, even though means of positive substantiation may be lacking and points of deta'l, on occasion, demonstrably false. At the very lowest assessment Āzād's anecdotes are of value in showing the sort of impression their personalities made on their contemporaries.

[5] For detailed definitions of the ghazal, qasīda, and masnavi see, e.g., G. D. Pybus, *Urdu Prosody and Rhetoric* (Lahore, 1924), pp. 59–60, 61–62, 63; Mirzā Muḥammad 'Askarī, *Āīna i Balāghat* (Lucknow, 1937), pp. 17, 19–21, 22; Najm ul Ghanī, *Bahr ul Faṣāhat* (Lucknow, 1926), pp. 69–80, 80–92, 104–112.

there seems to be general agreement on a prescribed minimum of five, but the maximum is variously stated as eleven, seventeen, or some other figure. As a general rule each couplet must express a complete and independent thought, though it is permissible within the ghazal to connect several of the couplets to form a single statement. The unity of the poem is one not of content but of form, and is achieved by a common metre for all the couplets and a strict rhyme scheme (AA, BA, CA, DA, etc.), which may not be varied. The rhyme is almost always a double one (though this is not obligatory), its two parts being known as *qāfia* and *radīf*, terms which English writers on the subject have translated respectively as rhyme and end rhyme.

Their meaning can be illustrated from Flecker's poem *Yasmin*, which he calls "A Ghazel," though it does not in fact conform to all the rules of the ghazal, at any rate as the form is defined in Urdu.[6] In the rhymes "head, Yasmin," "said Yasmin," "shed, Yasmin," and so on, "head," "said," and "shed" are qāfia (rhyme), and the recurring word "Yasmin" is radīf (end rhyme). Flecker's use of the name "Yasmin" is an easy, if effective, solution to the difficulty of finding a double rhyme. In Urdu, where rhymes are more plentiful than they are in English, such simple devices are rarely resorted to. End rhyme of three, four, five, or even more syllables are not uncommon. Thus Mir, the greatest eighteenth-century exponent of the ghazal form, writes to his mistress:

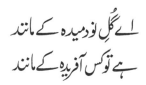

Perhaps the flower in spring compares with you—
Yet what created thing compares with you?   (I.63.19)

Skilfully used, this double rhyming can be most effective.

Finally, the last couplet of the ghazal must introduce the takhallus of the poet. While in the ghazal themes of love predominate, these may treat either of earthly love between human beings or of the mystic love of the worshipper for the Divine Beloved. Many lines are capable of

[6] See *The Collected Poems of James Elroy Flecker* (London, 1916), p. 158. It is also included in *The Century's Poetry* (1837–1937), ed. D. K. Roberts (Harmondsworth, 1938), II, 298.

either interpretation. But many ghazals include lines on themes which have no conceivable connection with love—a practice that the poet could perhaps justify within the terms of the definition of the ghazal by the argument that even lovers talk of other things besides love. In general, the only thing which gives unity to the poem is its form. There is generally not even a unity of mood between the independent couplets that compose it: the mood may vary in one and the same ghazal between tragedy and broad humour.

The qasīda, which may be roughly translated as "ode," is defined in similar detail and with similar divergencies between the different authorities. Sauda is the greatest master of this form in our period. Some authorities prescribe a minimum of 7 couplets, others of 15, and yet others of 21. No definite maximum is prescribed by most authorities, though some limit it to 170 couplets. At all events it is a fairly long poem. Its rhyme scheme is the same as that of the ghazal. Most qasīdas are odes in praise of the poet's patron or of some other potentate, and are divided into parts, each of which has its technical name. The manuals of rhetoric divide qasīdas into two main classes: those which have a "preamble" (*tamhīd* or *tashbīb*) and those which do not. The permissible themes of the preamble are laid down: the poet may extol his own greatness, or describe the beauties of spring, or write of love or of the transience of the things of this world, or lament his illfortune. The preamble is followed by a second part in which the poet turns towards his main theme. The third part is devoted to singing the praises of the person to whom the qasīda is addressed; the fourth states the poet's request to him; and the fifth and last calls down the blessings of heaven upon him. The qasīda is, of all the classical forms, the least appealing to modern taste even in India and Pakistan, and nowadays qasīdas are rarely read and still more rarely written. Even in former times the qasīda was judged mainly as a *tour de force*, a form in which it was the poet's object to demonstrate his complete command of language and of the full range of rhetorical device rather than to express any deeply felt experience.

The masnavi, for which the name of Mir Hasan is most famous, is the least strict of the classical forms, for all that is prescribed is its rhyme scheme. It is a fairly long poem, rhyming AA, BB, CC, DD, and so on, like Chaucer's *Prologue*. It may be on almost any theme, but in Urdu the largest single class of masnavis consists of love stories.

A number of other forms similarly prescribe little more than the rhyme schemes. For example, there is the *mukhammas*, a form that Sauda frequently used. This is a poem consisting of stanzas of five lines each, the first four of which must employ the same rhyme. Often the fifth lines of the stanzas also rhyme together (AAAAX, BBBBX, CCCCX, etc.).[7]

These were the major forms in which Mir, Sauda, and Mir Hasan wrote their poetry. To the modern reader it might seem that the conventions by which they were bound must seriously hamper the poet's expression, and it is perhaps true that except for the masnavi, they exercised a tyranny which only a real poet could break. The general pressure of cultural opinion against any departure from established standards made originality difficult, and the strict conventions tended to encourage a preoccupation with form at the expense of content, and a refinement and overelaboration of rhetorical devices to the point where verse becomes nothing more than a display of technical virtuosity. But the greatest poets made themselves the masters and not the servants of this complex machinery, and used it to good effect. Mir made the ghazal, in many ways the strictest of all the classical forms, his chosen medium of expression, and only rarely violated its canons, but the freshness and vitality of what he has to say are not impaired by it.

To this somewhat generalised description of medieval society and its literary life must be added some account of the particular medieval society to which Mir, Sauda, and Mir Hasan belonged—that is, of the Mughal Empire, an empire which had been, not long before their time, one of the most splendid known to world history.[8]

Nominally, the Mughal Empire had been founded in 1526, for it was in that year that Bābur, the ruler of a kingdom based on Kabul in Afghanistan, invaded India, and by defeating a greatly superior enemy force at Pānipat, some fifty-five miles north of Delhi, established a titular sovereignty over the greater part of the north Indian plain. But its real

[7] For the mukhammas see Pybus, p. 66 (which, however, gives a false impression); 'Askarī, p. 23; and Najm ul Ghanī, pp. 96–98. The poem of Saudā summarised below, pp. 64–68, is a mukhammas.

[8] For the account of the Mughal Empire we have used a number of books, ranging from short, popular accounts to full-length histories. See the bibliography below. We have, however, often given our own interpretation to the facts which they present. Extracts from Mīr's narrative are translated, with some abridgement, from his Persian work *Zikr i Mīr*, ed. 'Abdul Ḥaq (Aurangābād, 1928).

founder was Akbar, Bābur's grandson, the third and greatest of all the Mughal emperors. He came to the throne in 1556, and during his long reign of forty-nine years he not only established Mughal power in fact as well as in name, but brought the Empire to the zenith of its achievement. By the time of his death in 1605 it comprised Afghanistan, all of northern India, and territories extending south to a boundary which would roughly correspond with a line drawn across the country from modern Bombay, in the west, to Cuttack, in Orissa, in the east. Within this vast territory Akbar established over the years a peace and prosperity which made later generations, living in a period when the Empire was dissolving in anarchy, look back to his reign as to a golden age, in which all the medieval ideals had been largely realised. It has been well said that in such circumstances "what passes for a memory is in fact an aspiration,"[9] but in this case idealised memory was much closer to historical fact than it has usually been.

Akbar himself came close to being the ideal medieval king. He came to the throne when he was only thirteen years old, and quickly showed himself to be a brilliant statesman, a most able administrator, and a fine soldier. He was a generous patron of the arts and sciences, and a great builder. He possessed, too, the personal qualities which a medieval society looks for in its king. He was a man of great physical strength, of strong will and commanding personality, brave to the point of foolhardiness, an excellent horseman, and not only proficient in all the skills of war but also, to a wholly exceptional extent, well-versed in all the learning of his day. "All . . . authorities agree in stressing the wideness of his interests and his eagerness for concrete facts; nothing came amiss to him in art or sport, in mechanics or theology, in metallurgy or natural history; and when the facts were in doubt, he was quick to devise experiments for their ascertainment."[10]

If, however, Akbar's empire enjoyed peace and prosperity, it was not because all classes gladly fulfilled their social duties, working in harmony with one another, but because Akbar mastered the problems which in real life arise in every medieval society. The greatest of these was to ensure that the allegiance which the nobility owed to the crown should be

9 H. W. C. Davis, *Medieval Europe* (London, 1911), p. 23.
10 See W. H. Moreland and A. C. Chatterjee, *A Short History of India*, 3rd ed. (London, 1953), p. 213.

real and not merely formal. For the nobles effectively controlled great resources of wealth and manpower, and if opportunity arose, they could use them to throw off their allegiance and act in disregard of the king's authority. It had to be the king's constant effort to prevent such opportunities arising, and all the time to strengthen his position as against theirs by every means open to him. One of the foundations of Akbar's greatness was the substantial success he achieved in doing this. He began by playing off one palace faction against another to the detriment of both; then, having made himself master in his own house, he set out to reduce the nobility as a whole to real and permanent submission. He knew how to estimate his own strength realistically, and set himself at each stage only such aims as he had the strength to achieve. Some of his vassals were left to enjoy virtual independence in their own domains, as long as they acknowledged the Emperor's authority and refrained from active opposition to his interests. But where he felt strong enough to enforce a more absolute submission, he was quick to do so. One of his basic policies was to combine the maximum conciliation with the maximum threat of force. He demanded from his nobles a real and absolute submission, but he was prepared to reward it on a scale which made submission offer better prospects than rebellion did. In this way he ensured that only the most unyielding persisted in resistance to him, and that against these he was able to bring overwhelming force.

As a result, the nobility during Akbar's reign was more effectively under the control of the crown than at any other period in the Empire's history. His nobles were, in effect, employees of the crown, and even the greatest of them were appointed, transferred, and dismissed entirely at the Emperor's discretion. Their services were recompensed on a scale which enabled them to live a life of great magnificence; but the obligations were correspondingly great, and no effort was spared to prevent any evasion of them. Some of the nobles were not assigned to a particular territory. Their duty was to appear regularly in attendance on the Emperor, to maintain a prescribed force in readiness, and to be prepared to undertake any task the Emperor might assign them; and these tasks might be of the most varied kinds—military, judicial, or purely administrative. Those who were assigned to particular territories governed them on the Emperor's behalf, and not in virtue of any right of their own. They too were paid, wherever possible, direct from the imperial treasury, and where this was the case they had no claim whatever on the land or on the produce of the land or on the land revenue paid by the peasantry in the areas to which they were assigned. In other words, they had no direct control either of the wealth or of the manpower of their territories.

It is true that Akbar could not apply this system as universally as he would have wished, and the *jāgīr* system was also not uncommon. Under it a noble would be paid not directly from the treasury but by an assignment on the revenue of a village or group of villages estimated as adequate to defray the legitimate expenses of his position. The nobles preferred this system, because it gave them a greater measure of independence. For precisely the same reason the Emperor disliked it, and resorted to it only with reluctance. The nobility was not hereditary. In practice the sons of a great noble would be appointed during his lifetime to an appropriate place in the imperial hierarchy, but in theory neither wealth nor office could be inherited, and in this way, too, the Emperor's position was strengthened. Actually, the noble's main obligation was to maintain a cavalry force appropriate to his rank. Under Akbar the highest ordinary rank was that of a "commander of five-thousand"; commands of larger numbers were reserved for princes of the imperial family.

Akbar could not have maintained such firm control over his nobles had he not taken steps to win the active support of the rest of his subjects, of the merchants and the peasants in particular. The merchants benefited directly by the abolition of inland transit dues and other similar levies, and by the maintenance of a currency "very much superior to that of contemporary European sovereigns."[11] The peasants' interests were safeguarded by vigilance to prevent any unauthorised demands being made upon them and by the most careful attention to just assessment and collection of the land revenue. "The essence of his system . . . was that each unit of area sown was charged with a sum of money (varying with the crop) calculated to represent the average value of one-third of the produce . . . and this sum was collected at harvest, with an allowance for any area on which the crop had failed to mature."[12] Revenue officials were required to pursue a policy of agricultural development; they could advance loans to the peasant to meet the expenses of new development and could vary the rates of revenue charged so as to offer inducements for the

[11] See S. M. Edwardes and H. L. O. Garrett, *Mughal Rule in India* (London, 1930), p. 218.
[12] See Moreland and Chatterjee, *History of India*, p. 226.

ploughing up of waste land or increasing the area sown to particularly valuable crops. Actual performance no doubt fell short of the high standards which Akbar prescribed, but still the peasantry prospered, and it is known that their condition was very much better than that of the peasantry in the rest of India, south of the Mughal boundaries.[13]

Some of these measures of Akbar ran directly counter to the interests of the nobles. For example, it had been they who had benefited from the levies on both merchants and peasants which were now forbidden. But even where their interests were not directly attacked, the indirect effect was to weaken their position considerably. The people saw the Emperor as the author of their prosperity, and rebellious nobles were thus deprived beforehand of any popular support.

The prosperity of the countryside was matched by that of the towns. Contemporary European travellers were greatly impressed by their size: their accounts describe both Agra and Lahore as being bigger than London, and Delhi at a slightly later period is said to have been nearly as big as Paris. Not only was Akbar in his day one of the richest monarchs in the world, but the standard of living of his subjects in all probability compared favourably with that of contemporary England under Elizabeth.[14] It was Akbar's reign and those of his successors Jahāngīr (1605–1627) and Shāhjahān (1627–1658) that produced the great gardens and the impressive buildings in red sandstone and white marble which are today the most tangible memorials of Mughal times. The Shalimar gardens in Kashmir, the Taj Mahal at Agra, and the Red Fort and the great mosque (the Jama Masjid) at Delhi are among the most famous of these. The last two were built by Shāhjahān, in whose reign the outward magnificence of the Empire reached its height. The famous Peacock Throne, which was made by his command, is a fitting symbol of this magnificence. It "was made of pure gold, studded with gems . . . the inner roof was enamelled, the outer covered with rubies and other jewels; twelve pillars of emerald supported the roof, which was surmounted by the figures of two peacocks, ablaze with precious stones. Between the peacocks was a tree set with diamonds, rubies, emeralds and pearls;

[13] Cf. *ibid.*, pp. 244–245.
[14] For the size of the towns see W. H. Moreland, *India at the Death of Akbar* (London, 1920), pp. 13–15; Edwardes and Garrett, p. 237. For Akbar, "the richest monarch in the world," see Edwardes and Garrett, p. 307. For standard of living, see T. G. P. Spear, *India, Pakistan and the West,* 2nd ed. (London, 1952), p. 110.

three jewelled steps led to the Emperor's seat, which was surrounded by eleven jewelled panels, of which the middlemost bore as its central gem a splendid ruby." [15]

The great age of the Empire extends over a century and a half, from 1556 to 1707, and spans the reigns of four emperors—Akbar, Jahāngīr, Shāhjahān, and Aurangzeb. Under the first three its capital city was Agra, but Shāhjahān planned to move the capital to Delhi, where he built what was practically a new city, named Shāhjahānābād after him; and the move was made shortly after his death. In this period the fame of Delhi spread far beyond the borders of India. It became "a great and imperial city . . . with anything between one and two million inhabitants . . . the largest and most renowned city, not only of India, but of all the East from Constantinople to Canton. Its Court was brilliant, its mosques and colleges numerous, and its literary and artistic fame as high as its political renown." [16] Such was Delhi at the height of its glory, and such to all outward appearance it remained until in 1739 catastrophe overwhelmed it. In that year the Persian king Nādir Shāh invaded India, crushingly defeated the Mughal armies, entered Delhi without resistance, and after a brief occupation returned to his kindom carrying with him "the accumulated treasures of eight generations of emperors." [17]

These events dealt the Empire a blow from which it never recovered; but 1739 does not mark the beginning of its decline. That had begun much earlier. Symptoms can already be discerned shortly after Akbar's death, and become plainly evident in the second half of Aurangzeb's reign. After Aurangzeb died, the Empire began to break up rapidly, and had Nādir Shāh's invasion come years earlier, the result would almost certainly have been the same. But 1739 showed in a few short weeks, and with unmistakable clarity, how rotten the state of the Empire had become, and what were the factors which had made it so. The story is worth telling in some detail, for it formed part of the early memories of all three[18] of the great eighteenth-century poets, and though in later years the personalities change, the forces which produced the catastrophe

15 Edwardes and Garrett, pp. 339–340.

16 Percival Spear, *Twilight of the Mughuls* (London, 1951), p. 1.

17 William Irvine, *Later Mughals*, ed. Jadunath Sarkar (Calcutta, 1922), II, 375.

18 This is true only if we accept the year A.H. 1140 (A.D. 1727–1728) as the date of Mīr Ḥasan's birth. Some authorities give the date as A.H. 1151 (A.D. 1738–1739). The point is discussed more fully in the first note to Chapter 3 below.

continued to operate throughout the century. The events which led up to the invasion need not concern us here, but for many months before it took place, the imperial court was aware of the imminent danger and did virtually nothing to prepare against it. The frontier province of Afghanistan had for years been neglected; it was left to the care of incompetent governors, and as a result of the intrigues of factions at court hostile to the governor and his friends, was starved of the funds necessary to effective defence. Even the Panjāb, the province which lay between Afghanistan and Delhi itself, was similarly treated. It had a strong and capable governor, but he was prevented from preparing a defence in any way adequate against so formidable an enemy as Nādir Shāh.[19] This was because he did not belong to the party dominant at court and was therefore feared (probably quite justifiably) as a potential rival. The result was that Nādir Shāh overran both Afghanistan and the Panjāb with comparative ease, and by January 1739 he had occupied Lahore. As he advanced, complete lawlessness spread everywhere among the population, for people no longer felt any deep loyalty to the Empire, and as authority broke down or became preoccupied in preparing resistance, men seized the opportunity to make themselves their own masters.

Meanwhile the Delhi court, having procrastinated until it could do so no longer, prepared to face the invader. The governor of the Deccan provinces, Nizām ul Mulk, the most able soldier and statesman in the Empire, had been called to Delhi and nominally given full powers to meet the threat. But in reality he was far from being in supreme control. At the court itself it was not he but a faction led by another leading noble, Samsām ud Daula, which was dominant, and Sa'ādat Khān, governor of the province of Oudh, represented yet a third centre of power. The mutual quarrels of these three were soon to prove disastrous to the Empire as a whole.

The imperial forces were given orders to move out to meet the invader as early as December 2, 1738, but they remained encamped outside Delhi for over a month, and when at last they did move, spent nine days in covering the fifty-five miles to Pānipat. Here they halted another nine days for the coming of the Emperor, who had at last heeded the unanimous

[19] The account of Nādir Shāh's invasion is based upon Sarkar's concluding chapters to Irvine's *Later Mughals*.

advice of his generals that he should join the army in person. The army then moved on another twenty miles to Karnāl, and there waited again for the coming of Sa'ādat Khān of Oudh. It was at length decided to entrench there, to surround the camp with a mud wall, and so to await Nādir's attack.

The imperial camp was huge—twelve miles in perimeter, according to one authority—and contained a total population of perhaps a million men, of whom only 75,000 were combatants. As against this, Nādir's army numbered about 55,000, and the total population of his camp about 160,000. One-third of this figure were servants, "but these were all mounted and some of them completely armed, so that they could take part in plunder and the defence of their baggage."[20] Thus the Persian force was very much more mobile and effective. It was able to hem in the imperial army completely, and within a few days all its food supplies were exhausted and there was nothing to eat.

The Indian side continued to show its incompetence when battle was ultimately joined. Sa'ādat Khān came out to battle first, with utterly inadequate preparation and against the advice of both Nizām ul Mulk and Samsām ud Daula. Samsām ud Daula's contingent later moved out to his support. Both forces were drawn upon the Persian artillery and suffered appalling casualties. Samsām ud Daula was mortally wounded; Sa'ādat Khān surrendered and was taken captive to Nādir Shāh. The Indian camp followers saw that their troops were leaving the field of battle and at once plundered their own camp so thoroughly that when the dying Samsām ud Daula was brought back, his servants had to borrow a small tent to shelter him in. Meanwhile Nizām ul Mulk, the ablest general on the Indian side, had remained completely passive. A contemporary historian suggests that this was because he hoped Sa'ādat Khān and Samsām ud Daula might be killed and his own position in the Empire thereby strengthened. The Emperor's contingent too had made no move. Nādir refrained from attacking them, and allowed them to retire within their walled camp.

The same evening Nādir told his prisoner Sa'ādat Khān that his aim was now to extract an indemnity from the Emperor, make peace, and return home. Sa'ādat advised him to send for Nizām ul Mulk and settle peace

[20] *Ibid.*, II, 338.

terms with him, and he himself wrote to the Emperor to the same effect. Nizām ul Mulk accordingly appeared in the Persian camp the next day with full powers to negotiate. After a long discussion it was agreed that Nādir should be paid 5 million rupees as the price of his withdrawal, of which 2 million were to be paid at once and the rest by instalments, the whole sum being paid over by the time the Persian army had been withdrawn as far as Kabul. But agreement on these terms was short-lived. Soon after the battle Samsām ud Daula died of his wounds, and a quarrel at once began over the question of who was to succeed him in the post of Imperial Paymaster. Nizām ul Mulk at first secured the appointment of his son, but this so inflamed a rival candidate that he at once left the Emperor's camp and announced his intention of going over to the enemy, and in order to bring him back, it was necessary to reverse the decision and, for the moment, to give the office to Nizām ul Mulk himself. Meanwhile the news reached Sa'ādat Khān, who was still in Nādir Shāh's camp; Sa'ādat had himself hoped to get the post, and his reaction now was to go to Nādir at the first opportunity and persuade him to repudiate the terms of the proposed indemnity. He said that Nizām ul Mulk had tricked him, and that if he would march on Delhi he could secure 200 million rupees in cash and jewels alone—forty times the amount of the indemnity agreed with Nizām ul Mulk.

To show that he was in earnest, Sa'ādat Khān volunteered to bring all his troops and property into Nādir's camp, and this was done. Nādir made no overt move for several days, but all this while his blockade of the imperial camp continued, on the ground that no indemnity had yet been paid. When the camp was reduced to such extremity that for five days the soldiers had had nothing to eat, Nādir again summoned Nizām ul Mulk for discussions. He went, knowing nothing of what had happened since the first agreement had been made, and was now confronted with the demand for 200 million rupees and told that he would be held captive until he agreed to this demand. Nizām ul Mulk protested that to raise so vast a sum would be absolutely impossible and that even Shāhjahān, at the height of the Empire's glory, had never amassed more than 160 million rupees in the imperial treasury. But Nādir Shāh was adamant, and he completed his strangle hold two days later when the Emperor visited him and was similarly detained as a virtual captive. The next day all the important nobles were instructed to come over to Nādir's camp, and the imperial army, still hemmed in by the Persians, was left without leaders. But they were now told that they were free to go where they pleased, and the camp broke up. Few of them escaped to safety. Roving bands of Persian soldiers plundered them without restraint, and so did the peasants, who were now in open insurrection.

The news of the imperial defeat at Karnāl reached Delhi within two days. It had been totally unexpected, and the whole city waited apprehensively to see what would happen. Twelve days later Nādir's advance party, which included Sa'ādat Khān, reached the capital, and on March 9, a little less than a month after the battle, Nādir Shāh himself rode in. That same night Sa'ādat Khān got the reward of his treachery. Nādir sharply rebuked him for not having raised the large sum which he himself had said could be extorted from Delhi, and told him that if he did not raise the money quickly, he would be personally beaten. Knowing that he could not possibly raise the sum, and unable to face the humiliation which awaited him, he committed suicide.

Nādir Shāh had not been in Delhi two days when, late in the afternoon of March 10, the Delhi populace rose against the Persians. There are conflicting accounts of the immediate cause of the rising, but once it began, it spread rapidly and Persian soldiers were everywhere set upon and killed by the people. Only the poorer classes took part in it. It seems that they alone, when the odds were overwhelmingly against them, showed a readiness to resist the invader and despoiler of their country.

Attacks on the Persian soldiers continued in full force until three o'clock in the night, slackened a little, and then revived again at daybreak. A conservative estimate is that 3,000 Persians were killed in the course of them. Nādir Shāh had at first refused to believe reports of what was happening; but he now took ruthless measures to crush the rising. At dawn on the 11th he armed, and rode to the Golden Mosque in Chāndni Chauk (then, as now, one of the main streets of the city), where he enquired in what parts of the city the rising had occurred, and then unsheathed his sword as the signal for general massacre in those districts. The killing began at about 9 A.M. and lasted till 2 P.M., when the Emperor sent the highest nobles of the Empire to intercede, and Nādir was persuaded to give orders for the massacre to end. It is estimated that some 20,000 people had been killed. Houses had been looted and burned, men put to the sword regardless of age, and women made captive. Many had killed their wives and daughters to save them from dishonour, while others committed suicide by throwing themselves into the wells. For some days afterwards the corpses lay in the streets, for no one dared to touch them, and the stench became intolerable. Nādir then gave permission for them to be removed. But Delhi's sufferings were not yet at an end. On Nādir's orders all the granaries were sealed and guarded, and bodies of cavalry were posted to prevent anyone entering or leaving the city. Famine broke out, and even when after some days Nādir permitted people to go out of the city to buy food, they had to encounter bands of Persians who for thirty to forty miles around were plundering and looting on the highways and in the villages.

Meanwhile the systematic plunder of the capital was taking place. The Emperor had to give up all the crown jewels, the famous Koh-i-Nūr diamond, and the Peacock Throne. The nobles and their ladies were also compelled to surrender enormous wealth, and finally all the well-to-do citizens of Delhi were ordered to contribute half their property. Torture was used to compel them to do so. The total spoils thus accumulated were certainly not less than 150 million rupees, and may have been considerably more. In addition the booty included some hundreds of elephants and many thousands of horses and camels.

Finally, after two months in Delhi, Nādir Shāh was ready to depart. He now restored full power to the Emperor, and in exchange, all the Mughal territory west of the Indus was ceded to him and lost to the Empire for ever. In addition he could claim much territory east of the Indus by right of conquest, and though it continued to be governed by Mughal officers, Nādir's right to the revenue was not disputed. Then he set out on his return home. The peasantry rose in the rear of his returning army and plundered what they could from his baggage train.[21] Some idea of India's loss may be gained from the fact that on his return to Persia, Nādir remitted the revenue of the whole kingdom for three years.

By modern standards we do not know much of the lives of the eighteenth-century Urdu poets. But we do know that in 1739 Sauda was already a grown man, that Mir was sixteen or seventeen years old, and that

21 *Ibid.*, II, 374.

Mir Hasan was a boy of eleven or twelve.[22] Sauda and Mir Hasan were both born in Delhi; so far as we know, they had always lived there, and presumably were still there in 1739. Mir was born in Agra, but we know that he had come to the capital a year or more before the invasion, and it is not impossible that he had stayed on there, though it is more likely that he had returned to Agra.[23] Thus it is probable that Sauda and Mir Hasan personally experienced the occupation of Delhi, and possible that Mir did also. At any rate Mir's personal fortunes were deeply involved. For about a year his main source of income had been a monthly allowance from Samsām ud Daula, and when he was killed at Karnāl, this abruptly stopped. We know too that all three men continued to live in Delhi after 1739, though in Mir Hasan's case it was not for long—perhaps for another three or four years. Sauda stayed till 1757, and Mir remained longest of all, for he lived there from about 1740 to 1760, and again, after a prolonged absence, from 1772 to 1782. Thus all three saw with their own eyes the contrast between the capital as they had known it in their boyhood and as it became after the invasion. On the two older men in particular this contrast made an unforgettable impression, as their writings show, and it was deepened by experience of the misfortunes which continued to befall Delhi almost without respite during the years they lived there. Moreover, to all three of them Delhi was not like any other city; the fall of Delhi was to them the fall of a whole civilisation, and one so catastrophic that they felt that the whole universe in which they lived was different. Thus Mir writes:

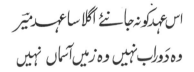

---

[22] One cannot be more precise, because the dates of their birth are known (or, in Mīr Ḥasan's case, estimated) only in terms of the Muslim calendar. The Muslim year rarely falls wholly within the Christian year, and strict accuracy nearly always demands that the A.D. equivalent be given as, e.g., 1738–1739, as long as the exact birthday, or at least the month of birth, is not known. In this book we have given dates throughout in terms of the Christian calendar. Where our sources give the Muslim date alone, we have given the Christian equivalent in the way just described; but one occasionally finds important dates given both in Muslim and in Christian terms, and in such cases we have assumed (though one cannot vouch for this) that the precise Christian year was known to the writer, and had adopted his date. G. S. P. Freeman-Grenville, in *The Muslim and Christian Calendars* (London, 1963), gives the detailed correspondence of dates.

[23] Qāẓī 'Abdul Vadūd's article in *Ma'āṣir* (Jan. 1956), p. 170.

This age is not like that which went before it.
The times have changed, the earth and sky have changed.

(II.290.16)

Some of the forces which brought about the fall of the Mughal Empire
have already shown themselves clearly in the story of 1739. To begin
with, an Emperor who no longer possesses any real authority is alike unable to command that active good-will of the mass of his subjects which
Akbar had enjoyed, and to control the great nobles. Further, all effective
power is in the nobles' hands, and they act only in their own interest, so
blinded by mutual jealousies that even when all are threatened by a common danger, they cannot or will not combine against it.

This state of affairs had developed well before 1739, and it was to continue throughout the century until in 1803 the British occupation of
Delhi put an end to the anarchy and, in effect, to the Empire too. The
shift of the centre of power from the crown to the warring factions of the
nobility was not due solely to the individual weaknesses of successive
Emperors, important though this cause was. It was also an indirect consequence of the increased burdens laid upon the peasantry after Akbar's
death. The magnificence of Shāhjahān's reign was founded upon this increased exploitation, and it was continued under Aurangzeb in order to
pay for the ceaseless warfare which, from early in his reign, became an
almost permanent feature in the life of Mughal India. In this way the
crown alienated the support of the most numerous class of its subjects,
and this necessarily resulted in an increased relative strength of the
nobility. So long as the Emperors remained personally strong and capable,
this fundamental weakness in their position was to some extent concealed. But Aurangzeb's immediate successor was the last who possessed
any real ability, and from 1712 successive Emperors diminished in
political stature until they were in fact much less powerful than the great
nobles nominally subordinate to them.

One of the clearest signs of the Empire's decline was its disintegration
into virtually independent dominions. In some of the most important
provinces this happened without any overt conflict between the provincial
governors and the central power. While the emperors were strong, no
governor was allowed to govern his province for a term of more than four
years, but from 1707 onwards in many of the key provinces a different

picture emerged; the exceptionally long rule of a governor led to the founding of a dynasty, and the governorship was handed down from father to son. True, the governorship was not formally hereditary, but each succeeding governor did in fact arrange to be appointed as such by the emperor. These virtually independent dynasties date in Bengal from 1707, in the Panjāb from 1713, in Oudh from 1723, and in the Deccan provinces from 1724–1725.

As the provinces one by one fell away from the Empire in all but name, the territory under imperial administration progressively dwindled until it comprised little more than the area around Delhi. Within this shrinking area violent struggles developed between rival nobles for the spoils of high imperial office, leading more than once to armed clashes in the streets of the capital itself and to atrocities against emperors and other members of the imperial family who were the pawns in their struggles. Up to 1753 some of the rulers of the provinces were sometimes among the contestants. In 1748 Safdar Jang, the governor of Oudh, succeeded in becoming Vazīr,[24] or chief minister, of the Empire, and in holding the post until 1753; the Emperor then dismissed him, but it took a six-months' civil war to compel him to relinquish office.

However, the disruption of the Empire was not the work of the nobility alone. Plebeian movements of revolt also played an important part. As the crown increasingly lost the support of the people, and as the lawlessness and disorder produced by the fighting between rival powers in the land laid increasing burdens upon them, the peasants learned to look after their own interests and refused to give up their produce except when confronted with a force they could not oppose. Thus in 1758 the Vazīr, accompanied by the Emperor in person, had to mount a regular military campaign in the country west of Delhi in order to exact tribute from the villages. "In this region the sturdy villagers from behind their mud walls frequently offered stout resistance and fought the Vazīr; they could be subdued only by . . . artillery . . . On 19th September, when the Emperor and Vazīr were . . . following two different routes, the people of Bhiwani, matchlock in hand, shut their sovereign out of their village, while the local robber population carried off many . . . carts laden with baggage from both divisions of the imperial army."[25]

[24] The "Vizier" of the Arabian Nights.
[25] Jadunath Sarkar, *Fall of the Mughal Empire*, 2nd ed. (Calcutta, 1950), II, 120–121; cf. also II, 288–290.

The more adventurous peasant people went further than self-defence, and plebeian movements of which the peasantry formed the backbone arose in a number of areas to wage active warfare against their common enemies. Of these the most remarkable was that of the Sikhs in the Panjāb. The Sikhs had originated as a popular religious sect in the sixteenth century, and the community still has this character. But in the eighteenth century it was social discontent which rallied to their standard the Panjābi peasantry and the poorer classes of the town population,[26] and made them in the latter half of the century the strongest power in the Panjāb. Their movement was also an expression of the growth of national feeling, and many Sikhs to this day regard their community as the natural leadership of the Panjābi nationality. In no other movement is this blend of social, religious, and national elements as evident, but in all of the plebeian movements which combined with those of the aristocracy to disintegrate the Empire, these three elements were perhaps present in varying degrees.[27]

This internal disintegration was hastened by the external pressures to which the Empire was subjected—from the south, the northwest, and the east—and it was these which in the end decided the Empire's fate. The threat from the south was the first to develop, in the form of one of the part-national, part-religious, and part-social movements of which we have spoken. Akbar had begun the expansion of the Empire beyond the northern plains into the Deccan, and his successors contined the process. It began to meet determined resistance from the Marāthas, a predominantly Hindu people whose homeland, Mahārāshtra, corresponds to the modern Indian state of that name, and comprises, very approximately speaking, the western half of the Deccan. They were among the earliest of the modern Indian peoples to develop a strong national consciousness, and under their great leader Shivaji they began a determined struggle to free themselves from Mughal rule. The second half of Aurangzeb's reign was occupied with almost continuous war against them, but without lasting success. By about 1720 their power was paramount in the Deccan,

---

[26] *Ibid.*, I, 425.

[27] In our view the standard histories overstress the religious aspect of these movements, with a consequent underemphasis on the national and social aspects. Yet these same histories to some extent provide the data and the estimates to support our view. Thus, on the Sikhs, see Irvine, I, 72–84, and esp. 82–84. On the Marāthas see esp. Edwardes and Garrett's striking statement in *Mughal Rule*, p. 127.

and when in 1724–1725 the six Deccan provinces of the Empire virtually seceded, Mughal power outside northern India came to an end. But the Marāthas did not rest content with control of the Deccan. From 1720 they began to push northwards, and became a factor of ever increasing importance in the affairs of northern India. They demanded and received for themselves or their nominees the governorship of imperial territories, fought as mercenaries in the struggles between the north Indian powers, and raided and pillaged far and wide on their own account. Their power steadily increased until 1761, when they were crushingly defeated by the Afghan king Ahmad Shāh Abdāli, invading from the northwest. But they returned by 1771, and from that date until their defeat by the British in 1803, were the real rulers of what remained of the Empire.

From the northwest, in 1739, came the invasion of Nādir Shāh, which has already been described. On Nādir's death his mantle fell upon Ahmad Shāh Abdāli, who succeeded to Nādir Shāh's Afghan territories and to the Mughal provinces which had been ceded to him. He too was a constant menace to the Empire, invading in 1748, when he was repulsed; in 1757, when he occupied and plundered Delhi as thoroughly as Nādir Shāh had done; and in 1760. On this last occasion he stayed in India a full year, preparing for a full trial of strength with the Marāthas. In January 1761 he defeated them so overwhelmingly that for ten years they ceased to be a significant force in northern India; but he himself withdrew to Afghanistan shortly afterwards. After that, in repeated incursions, he never got farther than the Panjāb, where the Sikhs were in permanent revolt against his and every other authority, and in 1767 he had virtually to admit defeat at the hands of this "entire nation in arms,"[28] as they have been called, and retire permanently to his own kingdom.

In the East, in Bengal, the British established themselves by their victory at Plassey in 1757. But Bengal had already ceased in all but name to be a province of the Empire some fifty years earlier. Like the Marāthas and the *de facto* independent rulers of great provinces like Oudh and the Deccan, the British were still *de jure* subjects of the Mughal Emperor, and in this period they did not pursue a strongly aggressive policy against the Emperor. That was to come later.

Together, the working of these internal and external forces destroyed the Empire, and it was during the process of its destruction that Mir,

[28] Sarkar, II, 296.

Sauda, and Mir Hasan lived their lives. The picture of the Empire which they saw before them towards the middle of the century, when they were young men, is somewhat as follows: To the west, all the territory beyond the River Indus had been lost since 1739. The Panjāb had for years been either virtually independent or subject in varying degrees to Nādir Shāh or to his Afghan successor, Ahmad Shāh Abdāli, though the Sikhs were increasingly making themselves the real power in the land. South of that, Rājputāna was in the hands of its various chiefs, many of whom were in turn subordinate to the Marāthas. South of that again, Gujarat was under Marātha control. Moving eastwards from there, the Marāthas were supreme practically all the way across the peninsula up to the southern limit of the north Indian plain. In the plain itself, beginning in the east, Bengal and Bihar had long been virtually independent of the Empire and were soon to pass under British control. West of them lay Oudh, also virtually independent, and west again, between Oudh and the River Ganges, territories settled in the sixteenth century by immigrants from Afghanistan, and now constituting the kingdoms of Rohilkhand and Farrukhābād. Beyond them, but to the south of Delhi, was the Jāt kingdom, built up by peasant chieftains who began as little more than highwaymen on the Delhi-Agra road. The territory under the direct control of Delhi had shrunk to a comparatively small dominion around the capital itself.

It might be concluded that, thus left to itself, Delhi must have enjoyed comparative peace. But this was not so. On the contrary, no other city had to endure so much as Delhi did. The reason was that Delhi was the imperial capital and normally the seat of the emperor; and although lacking in all real power, the emperor was nonetheless constitutionally the supreme authority, and no power was legitimate unless formally derived from him. And so it was not only the invasions of Ahmad Shāh Abdāli that Delhi had to fear. Within India itself every aspirant for power sought the control of Delhi and of the emperor's person. The city was repeatedly occupied by the armies of contending powers, and occupation almost always meant looting, burning, and extortion upon its citizens. Even in the short-lived intervals of peace, there prevailed misery, uncertainty, and lawlessness.

The history of the years 1753–1757—years in which both Mir and Sauda were in the city—well illustrates what it meant to live in Delhi in

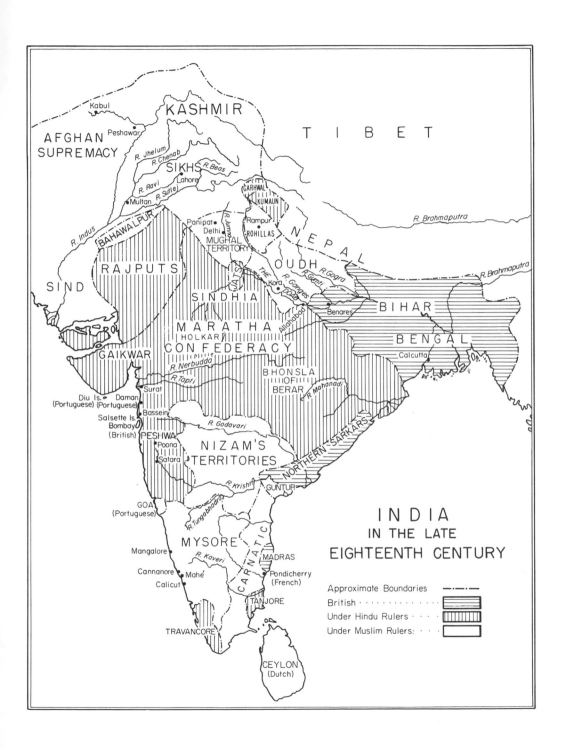

Kabul

KASHMIR

AFGHAN
SUPREMACY

Peshawar

T I B E T

R. Jhelum
R. Chenab

SIKHS
R. Beas

Lahore
R. Ravi
Multan   R. Sutlej

GARHWAL
KUMAUN

R. Brahmaputra

R. Indus

BAHAWALPUR

Panipat
Delhi

R. Jumna

Rampur
ROHILLAS

N E P A L

MUGHAL
TERRITORY

RAJPUTS

OUDH
R. Gogra

R. Brahmaputra

SIND

SINDHIA

The Koro DOAB

R. Ganges
R. Gumti

M A R A T H A

Benares

BIHAR

HOLKAR

Allahabad

C O N F E D E R A C Y

BENGAL

GAIKWAR

R. Nerbudda

Calcutta

R. Tapti

BHONSLA
OF
BERAR

R. Mahanadi

Diu Is.   Daman
(Portuguese) (Portuguese)

Surat

Bassein

R. Godavari

Salsette Is.
Bombay
(British)   PESHWA

NIZAM'S
TERRITORIES

Poona

Satara

NORTHERN SARKARS

GOA
(Portuguese)

R. Krishna

GUNTUR

R. Tungabhadra

MYSORE

CARNATIC

I N D I A
IN THE LATE
EIGHTEENTH CENTURY

Mangalore

R. Kaveri

MADRAS

Cannanore   Mahé

Calicut

Pondicherry
(French)

Approximate Boundaries

British

TANJORE

Under Hindu Rulers

TRAVANCORE

Under Muslim Rulers

CEYLON
(Dutch)

that age. In March 1753 Safdar Jang, who held simultaneously the governorship of Oudh and the office of Vazīr of the Empire, was dismissed
from office by the Emperor and "given leave" (that is, commanded) to
return to his province. This was the result of the intrigues of a hostile
faction, and he refused to comply with the Emperor's orders. The result
was civil war, which lasted from March until November. Both Safdar
Jang and his rivals, led by the sixteen-year-old Imād ul Mulk, called in
outside help. Safdar Jang's main allies were the Jāts, and in the course of
the fighting he instigated them to plunder old Delhi, where, in contrast
to the new city built by the Emperor Shāhjahān, only the poorer sections
of the population lived. The Jāts did their work so thoroughly that they
added a phrase, *Jāt gardi*—"Jāt affliction" or "Jāt invasion"—to the
vocabulary of Urdu, and in later days their excesses ranked in Delhi
people's memory with those of Abdāli's invasions. Imād ul Mulk relied
upon the Marāthas, who were ready to sell their armed support to anyone
who could pay a high enough price; and it was thanks mainly to them that
Safdar Jang was defeated and Imād, at the age of seventeen, made Vazīr in
his place. Before being invested by the Emperor with the robe of office,
Imād had sworn on the Holy Quran never to betray him. That same
morning he deposed him and enthroned one of the princes in his place.
The deposed Emperor was thrown into prison, together with his mother,
and was later blinded by having a red-hot needle drawn across his eyes.[29]
   In Mir's first collection of ghazals there is a verse which seems to be a
direct reference to this event:

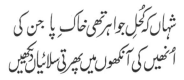

I lived to see the needle drawn across the eyes of kings
For whom collyrium ground with pearls was dust beneath their feet.

(I.103.4)

The verse contains a characteristic play on words. Collyrium, made
usually of ground antimony, was used by men and women alike to tinge

[29] Sarkar does not mention the blinding, but Shaikh Cānd, in *Saudā* (see the first note to
Chapter 2 below) writes of it on p. 8.

the eyes with, both because this was considered to make them more attractive and because it was believed to have medicinal properties, enhanced if the collyrium were mixed with ground pearls. Collyrium was applied with a large, blunt needle, and it was this same needle that could be heated red-hot and used to blind a man. So that the first line of the couplet could refer equally to the applying of collyrium and to the blinding—the sort of conceit which, like the English Elizabethans, Mir's contemporaries loved.

The new Vazīr was desperate for money. Much of his inherited personal fortune had been spent in the civil war against Safdar Jang, and the support of the Marāthas had been gained by the promise of a huge subsidy which he had no means of paying. He was not capable of establishing good order in the areas nearest to Delhi and so ensuring a flow of revenue from which he could meet his needs; he therefore resorted to levying forced contributions from all except those who had the armed strength to resist. The imperial family was the first to suffer, from confiscation of estates and of treasure and jewellery. Attempts were made to extract money from the nobles and the rich, and when this plan failed for lack of the necessary power to enforce it, from the traders, artisans, and common people in the markets. This too produced little result: the bazaars were closed in protest, and thousands of people assembled under the palace windows protesting to the Emperor. He, to his credit, supported them, threatening to fast to the death if Imād persisted in his measures, and Imād had for the moment to drop the idea. But he made a further attempt only two months later, seizing and beating the citizens in order to compel them to pay. This continued for six weeks, until public outcry compelled the abandonment of this attempt as well.

Meanwhile the Marātha armies stayed close to the capital, and it was clear that they would not withdraw until their promised subsidy was paid. For eight months, from June 1754 to February 1755, they moved about in the villages round Delhi, living off the country, looting the villagers, and robbing travellers, pilgrims, and even high imperial officials. Much of the normal grain supply of the city was cut off, and scarcity and high prices added to the misfortunes of the people. Only after Imād had alienated to them sufficient land (including crown land and some of the privy purse estates) to provide for the payment of his debt to them, did they at last withdraw.

This was not all. In the territory around Delhi lay estates whose revenue was earmarked for the maintenance of the Emperor and his family, and for payment of the palace servants, the imperial artillery, and the palace guards. But this revenue was now appropriated by the Vazīr, and the imperial family itself had to suffer extreme hardship in consequence. Contemporary historians speak of occasions when imperial princesses went three days together without food, and of the Emperor having to go about on foot because no conveyance could be provided for him. The palace servants and guards went unpaid for years at a time—in 1754 their pay was already three years in arrears—and had to live as best they could. It was not surprising in such circumstances that they paid little attention to the Emperor's needs and no longer regarded themselves as bound to perform duties for which they were not paid. The soldiers in particular resorted to the most desperate measures in order to live. They rioted continually in the capital and even in the imperial fort itself. They attacked and plundered the houses of the wealthy; chased, stoned, and manhandled the high officials responsible for paying them; and on one occasion forced their way into the Vazīr's house and carried off the meal which had been prepared for him. When an Imperial Paymaster died in 1756, they refused to allow him to be buried until they had received some satisfaction. In the same year they blockaded the fort and prevented even food and water going in until they had gained their demands. This general lawlessness was sometimes encouraged by the imperial officials. Thus the Vazīr himself, unable to raise the money to pay the soldiers, is accused by contemporary historians of encouraging them to plunder the property of the well-to-do. In 1757 the chief of the Delhi police was widely believed to be in league with gangs of armed burglars, shielding them in return for a share of their spoils.

When in 1757 Abdāli again invaded India, Imād could not offer even the slightest resistance, and all Delhi trembled at the news of his approach. Those who had the means to do so evacuated their families to Jāt territory, and then followed themselves. A force of the Marāthas barred their way, and acting on orders from Imād, turned them back, but not before extorting money from them. The Jāts also took full advantage of those who sought refuge with them, knowing that the refugees were in no position to resist their demands.

On January 28, 1757, Abdāli rode into the capital. As he did so, his escort dispersed to loot the markets and houses, but Abdāli was concerned to see that whatever spoils Delhi could be forced to give up should come to him, and severe punishments soon put an end to the individual enter-prise of his soldiers. Attention was first concentrated upon the nobility. Their servants, and where necessary they themselves, were, without distinction of sex, subjected to torture to compel them to disclose their buried hoards of treasure, and the houses of those who had fled from the city were broken into and looted. Next, the entire population was systematically despoiled: the city was divided into sections, and a regular staff appointed to levy contributions house by house. Many died under torture, which was everywhere used to extract the very maximum that could be extorted. This process lasted for sixteen days. A few more days were taken up in commandeering the necessary transport to carry away the spoils to Afghanistan.

It was at this time that Sauda left Delhi, and though there is nothing to indicate that he intended at this stage to leave the city permanently, in point of fact he never returned. Mir, however, stayed on for another four years. The most summary account of these years shows that Delhi's suf-ferings were far from over. It was given a short respite for a month while Abdāli's armies campaigned in the country south of Delhi, looting, raping, killing, and burning, until water contaminated by the corpses of their victims caused an outbreak of cholera in their camp. They now made all possible haste to return to Afghanistan. During the last days, when Abdāli was halted near the capital, arranging the final details of the with-drawal, Delhi was again plundered by hordes of his soldiers. But at last, early in April, the march back to Afghanistan began. The Afghans carried away with them an enormous booty. For Abdāli's goods alone 28,000 transport animals were needed, and his cavalry marched on foot, loading their booty on their horses.

When Abdāli departed, he left as his plenipotentiary in Delhi Najīb Khān, an Indian Afghan who had actively assisted him in his invasion. In June, Imād, again aided by the Marāthas, returned to drive him out. He succeeded, but Delhi had to endure siege and famine for a month before Najīb would surrender. The following year the Marāthas threatened to put Delhi to plunder if tributes which Imād owed them were not paid, and did in fact plunder the northern suburbs before Imād, for the moment, bought them off.

By early 1760 the Marāthas were at the height of their power, and had even ventured to attack Abdālī's Indian domains. But this provoked Abdālī to invade once more, and in January 1760 he and his Indian ally Najīb defeated the Marātha army ten miles north of Delhi. This time Abdālī did not enter the city, but made his camp some miles to the south. According to Mir, this did not save it from looting and atrocity.[30] It was quite near enough to Abdālī's encampment for his soldiers and those of Najīb to make their way there in considerable numbers, and Mir describes what they did:

> In the evening Rāja Nāgar Mal [Mir's patron at the time] left the city, and in due course safely reached the forts of Sūraj Mal [ruler of the Jāt kingdom]. I stayed behind to look after my family. After evening, proclamation was made that Shāh Abdālī had granted security to all, and that none of the citizens should be in any fear. But night had scarcely fallen when the outrages began. Fires were started in the city and houses were burnt down and looted. The following morning all was uproar and confusion. The Afghans and Rohillas [Najīb's soldiers] started their work of slaughter and plunder, breaking down the doors, tying up those they found inside, and in many cases burning them alive or cutting off their heads. Everywhere was bloodshed and destruction, and for three days and three nights this savagery continued. The Afghans would leave no article of food or clothing untouched. They broke down the walls and roofs of the houses, and ill-treated and tormented the inhabitants. The city was swarming with them. Men who had been pillars of the state were brought to nothing, men of noble rank left destitute, family men bereft of all their loved ones. Most of them roved the streets amid insult and humiliation. Men's wives and children were made captive, and the killing and looting went on unchecked. The Afghans humiliated and abused their victims and practised all kinds of atrocities upon them. Nothing which could be looted was spared, and some would strip their victims even of their underclothing. The new city [Shāhjahānābād] was ransacked.

---

[30] Contemporary histories, it seems, do not speak of the looting of Delhi on this occasion, and Sarkar's account (II, 161) naturally follows theirs. However, from the fact that Delhi was spared the occupation and systematic plunder which had taken place under Abdālī's own direction three years earlier, it does not necessarily follow that it was left unmolested, and we see no reason to doubt that Mir's account is, in essentials, reliable.

On the third day some sort of law and order was introduced, but the officer in charge himself completed the work of despoliation; and when at last the looters were driven out of the new city, they simply turned their attention to the old, where they put countless people to the sword. For seven or eight days the tumult raged. Nobody was left with clothes to wear or with enough food even for a single meal. Many died of the wounds they had received, while others suffered greatly from the cold. The looters would carry off men's stores of grain and then sell it at an extortionate price to those who needed it. The cry of the oppressed rose to heaven, but the king [Abdāli], who considered himself a pillar of true religion, was quite unmoved. Large numbers of people left the city and fled into the open country, where many of them died. Others were carried off by force to the invader's camp. I, who was already poor, became poorer . . . My house, which stood on the main road, was levelled with the ground.[31]

A year of suspense and uncertainty followed, as Abdāli and his Indian Afghan allies on one side and the Marāthas on the other mustered their full strength for a clash which all could see would be more fateful in its consequences than any event since 1739. The result was anything but a foregone conclusion. The Marātha force which Abdāli had defeated was only a fraction of their total strength, and as the year went by and they moved up from their main bases in the Deccan, it sometimes looked as though they, and not Abdāli, were likely to win the coming battle.

Mir was in particular agitation and distress during this year. In July the Marāthas occupied Delhi. Mir left the city about the same time. "I have suffered many hardships in this city," he told his patron. "Perhaps I may find peace and comfort elsewhere."[32] He continues: "I set out, taking my family and dependants with me. I did not know where I was going, but set out, trusting in God to lead me. After walking all day and undergoing great hardship, we had covered ten to twelve miles. We spent the night under a tree in the courtyard of an inn. In the morning Rāja Jugal Kishor's[33] wife passed that way, and seeing our plight, took us along with her to Rasāna, and did all she could to make us comfortable." After some

[31] *Ẕikr i Mīr*, pp. 85–88.
[32] *Ẕikr i Mīr*, p. 90.
[33] A highly placed noble and a former patron of Mīr.

time he settled in Kumbher, in the Jāt kingdom; but there was nobody there who could make any permanent provision for him. He relates an experience of this period at some length: [34]

One day when I was sitting wondering where my next meal was coming from, I had the idea of going to visit Āzam Khān, the son of Āzam Khān the elder, who had once been a great noble and was a good and generous man. At any rate, I thought, it will pass a pleasant hour or two. Accordingly I went and sought him out in Sūraj Mal's stables, where those who had been ruined in Delhi were now living. God bless him! he enquired tenderly after me. I told him all that had happened to me, and all who were present listened in shocked distress. Then when the hookah was set before me I recited [a verse of Urfī [35]] and one or two others appropriate to the occasion, until I was myself moved to tears. After a while I noticed that Āzam Khān seemed worried. I asked him what was the matter. "It is nothing," he replied. "No, tell me," I said, "What is it?" He said, "I was thinking how when you used to visit me in Delhi I would have all kinds of sweets brought in and we would sit and eat them together. And now I haven't even crude sugar to make you a drink of sherbet." "All those things," I replied, "were for happier days. For my part, as you well know, I am not a slave to my belly. And times change. That was a time for sweet things, and this is a time for bitterness." As we were conversing a woman came in at the door bearing a tray on her head. She came to Āzam Khān and said, "Sa'īd ud Dīn Khān's sister sends you these sweets with her blessing." As he turned back the tray cover, Āzam Khān's face lit up; turning to me he said, "I have long grown used to fasting: there have been days when I have not had so much as a piece of bread or a mouthful of water, let alone such luxuries as sweets. You are my guest. These are for you. Give me a little and send the rest home." "There is too much here," I said, "I shall not know what to do with it all." "Your son Mir Faiz Ali will know how to use it," he replied. In the end, at his insistence, I allowed him to send a large dish of the sweets to my house, and it was on them that we lived for the next two days.

[34] *Ẕikr i Mīr*, pp. 91–93.
[35] A Persian poet, born in 1555–1556 in Shīrāz, court poet of the Mughal Emperor Akbar, who became famous through his high-styled qasīdas. 'Urfī died in 1590–1591. (A.S.)

Not long after this he resumed his connection with his old patron, Rāja Nāgar Mal, and both remained in the Jāt country. Mir explains why: "Delhi in those days was little better than a wilderness, which every six months was laid desolate afresh. Besides, a man cannot wander from place to place forever. In the Jāt country there was peace, under a prosperous ruler, and we settled down there under the shadow of his protection." [36] His words do not exaggerate. He had himself experienced the plunder by the Afghans in January. In July came the Marāthā occupation, and in January 1761, after their crushing defeat of the Marāthas at Pānipat, the Afghans again moved in to loot whatever was left to be looted. Mir saw the effects when he visited the city a little later:

> The scene of desolation filled my eyes with tears and my mind with the most solemn thoughts. At every step my distress and agitation increased. I could not recognise the houses and often lost my bearings. Of the former inhabitants there was no trace, and no matter whom I enquired about, I was told that he was not there and nobody knew where he might be found. The houses were in ruins. Walls had collapsed. Cloisters and wineshops alike were deserted . . . Whole bazaars had vanished. The children playing in the streets, the comely young men, the austere elders—all had gone. Whole quarters were in ruins, their lanes desolate. Everywhere was a terrible emptiness . . . All at once I found myself in the quarter where I had once lived. I recalled the life I used to live, foregathering with my friends in the evenings, reciting poetry, and living the life of a lover—weeping at nights for the love of beautiful women, writing verse to them, and passing my days in the company of those whose long tresses held me their captive, and knowing no peace when I could not be with them . . . In those days I had really lived. And what was there now ? Not a soul whom I even recognised and with whom I could hope to pass a pleasant few minutes in conversation. I came away from the lane and stood on the deserted road, gazing in stunned silence at the scene of desolation, and filled with abhorrence at what I saw. And there and then I made a vow that as long as I lived, I would never come this way again. [37]

36 *Z̲ikr i Mīr*, p. 95.
37 *Z̲ikr i Mīr*, pp. 99–100.

Mir left Delhi soon afterwards, and it was ten years before he returned. But wherever he went, he saw the decay of the civilisation he loved. In this same year of 1761 he revisited his native city of Agra after an absence of more than twenty years, and stayed there for four months. Agra had not suffered as much material destruction as Delhi had, but the city seemed empty to him. "On two or three occasions," he writes,[38]

> I went right through the city, meeting scholars and holy men and poets, but none could give peace to my restless heart. I said to myself "Great God! This is that city where in every other street were fine houses and gardens, inns, cloisters, mosques, schools and seminaries, and where scholars and doctors of law, divines and learned men, saints and mystics, physicians and teachers and poets and writers were seen on every hand. But now I see no place where I could rest in peaceful enjoyment, and no man in whose company I could rejoice." I saw a scene of dreadful desolation, and grieved deeply.

No sensitive man could live in such an age and not be deeply influenced by all he saw happening around him; and the writings of Mir, Sauda, and Mir Hasan show how each in his own characteristic way reacted. All feel a deep regret at the passing of Mughal glory, and a life-long attachment to Delhi, which even in its decline symbolised for them all that was most precious in the values of Mughal India. It was these values which they sought to uphold, inspired by the idealised memory of their own child-hoods and what the Empire had been in their fathers' and grandfathers' day. Their methods differ. Sauda uses his power as a satirist to pillory those who contribute to the general decline in civilised standards, whether in personal or social life. Mir Hasan condemns by silence, with-drawing from the decadent world around him and holding up before men's eyes a picture of one moulded nearer to his heart's desire. In Mir the keynotes are a deep, personal sorrow and an unshakable determination to uphold in his poetry the principles in which he believed with all his heart and which guided his own life. But at this point we can turn direct to the poets' works and leave it to the reader to make his own appraisal.

[38] *Zikr i Mīr*, p. 104.

The Satires of Sauda

AN AGE LIKE THAT OF eighteenth-century Mughal India calls aloud for a satirist, and in Sauda it found one.[1] He was not a satirist alone. His collected verse is a bulky volume, including poems in all the main classical forms, and all have played their part in making him one of the great names in Urdu literature. Traditionally he is assessed not only as a great satirist but also as one of the only two Urdu poets to achieve real distinction in the difficult form of the qasīda. But it is his satires which today arouse the greatest interest, and these alone will be discussed here.

Sauda was of noble descent on both sides of his family, and was born and brought up in Delhi. His father died when he was still quite a young man, and he inherited a considerable fortune. But he was generous, and liking the good things of life, his money was soon spent. Even so, he never seems to have experienced any great hardship. He made his name as a poet quite early in life, so impressing his ustād that he used to tell people that Sauda could have said of him what the Persian poet Sāib (1601–1676) said of his ustād:

[1] Sources for this chapter are Shaikh Cānd, *Saudā* (Aurangābād, 1936), which is still the only substantial study of the poet; and Saudā's *Kulliyāt* (collected verse). No satisfactory edition of the *Kulliyāt* exists. The most recent is that of 'Abdul Bāri Āsī, 2 vols. (Lucknow, 1932). Unfortunately, despite the better arrangement of the poems and the very much greater clarity of the text, Āsī's edition is inferior in many respects to some of its predecessors, notably in that he has taken it upon himself to expurgate Saudā's verse of what he regards as obscene and objectionable matter, following an earlier edition "from which," to quote his complacent words, "these thorns had been cleared" (p. 18 of his Introduction). We have therefore preferred an earlier edition—that prepared by Momin's pupil, Mīr 'Abdur Raḥmān Āhī, and printed at Delhi in A.H. 1272 (A.D. 1856). *Kulliyāt* in the notes below means this edition. The edition is not easily accessible, and all but a few of the verses we quote are included in Khurshidul Islam's selection *Kalām i Saudā* (Aligarh, 1965). We have therefore added the references to this selection, abbreviated in the notes below as *Kalām*.

Respect commands my silence, but the truth is
My master is not fit to be my pupil.

Both his noble birth and his fame as a poet gave Sauda access to the
courts of the nobility and ensured him a life of material comfort. We do
not know who his first patrons were, but when he left Delhi in 1757, he
had for some time been attached to the court of Imād ul Mulk, the Vazīr
of the Empire whose political crimes have already been described. Imād
seems, however, to have known and fulfilled his obligations as a patron,
and there is nothing to suggest that Sauda found any cause for dissatisfaction with him in this respect. Subsequent patrons provided equally
well for him. From 1757 to about 1770[2] he lived at Farrukhābād, under
the patronage of the chief minister of the kingdom, and from then to his
death in 1781 at the court of the Governors of Oudh, who were then the
most generous patrons of Urdu literature in Mughal India. Richard
Johnson, the British Assistant Resident at the court of Oudh, who is said
to have known Urdu well and to have appreciated Urdu poetry, was
among those whose acquaintance he made there.

His attitude to his patrons was, as we have seen, a healthy one. He was
a great poet, and his obligation to society, which he fully accepted, was to
practise and perfect his art. Society's obligation to him was, through the
institution of patronage, to assure him the means of doing so. What he
received from his patrons was his due; he owed them appreciation and
respect, but nothing more than that. He maintained this attitude all his
life, as a story of his last years shows.[3]

Sauda was living under the patronage of Āsaf ud Daula, the Governor
of Oudh. Āsaf ud Daula was once out on a hunting expedition and the
news came that he had killed a lion. Sauda at once celebrated the
occasion with a couplet:

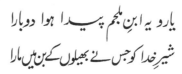

See, Ibn i Muljam comes to earth again
And so the Lion of God once more is slain.

[2] To be more precise, some time between A.H. 1183 (A.D. 1769–1770) and A.H. 1185
(A.D. 1771–1772). Cf. Shaikh Cānd, pp. 55–56.
[3] See Āzād, Āb i Ḥayāt, p. 169.

The point of the verse is in the play on the words "the Lion of God."
Lion of God is one of the titles of Ali, the cousin and son-in-law of the
Prophet, and Ibn i Muljam was the name of the man who assassinated him.
Āsaf ud Daula was a Shia, a sect of Muslims which holds Ali and his
family in special veneration, and to be compared, even in jest, with Ali's
assassin, was something he was not likely to appreciate. Āsaf ud Daula
heard of the verse, and on his return said to Sauda, "Mirza,[4] I hear you
have compared me to the murderer of the Lion of God." Sauda was quite
unabashed. He laughed and replied, "Well, it was a fair comparison. The
lion *was* God's, not yours or mine."

This independent spirit is one of his many attractive qualities. There
is nothing complicated about his character. He enjoyed life without any
inhibitions, and he liked others to enjoy it too. He thought he was a good
poet, and took a pride in being so. But he was not an arrogant man, and
made no pretensions to qualities which he knew he did not possess. "I am
not the fairest flower in the garden, nor am I a thorn in any man's path,"
he wrote of himself. "I am neither famous for virtue nor notorious for
vice . . . I seek nobody's favours, and want nobody to seek mine. People
may think well or ill of me as they please : I act as my nature prompts me."[5]

Acting as his nature prompted him meant, among other things, giving
free rein to a quick wit and an exuberant, often Rabelaisian, sense of
humour, as many stories of him show. On one occasion a friend of his
brought a young poet to see him. The poet had long been anxious to meet
Sauda, and had hopes of persuading him to be his ustād. After Sauda had
listened to a few of his verses, he asked him what takhallus he had chosen.
"Umedvār," he replied, meaning one who hopes for, or expects, or
aspires to something. Sauda smiled and said,

ہے فیض سے کسی کے شجر ان کا باردار

اس واسطے کیا ہے تخلّص امیدوار

Someone has made him fruitful : need he tell us
Why he has made Umedvār his takhallus?

---

4 "Mirzā" was the proper courteous form of address for a gentleman of Mughal (as opposed
to Persian) descent.

5 *Kulliyāt*, p. 363, lower margin, lines 18–20; p. 364, centre, line 1; and p. 355, centre,
line 14. *Kalām*, p. 207, lines 1–2, and p. 211, lines 4–5.

Umedvār, like the English "expectant," also means pregnant. The young man was covered in confusion, and decided both to change his takhallus and to look for another ustād.

On another occasion he was visited by a poet named Hidāyat. After the usual formalities Sauda asked him what he was doing these days. Hidāyat replied pompously, "The management of my affairs leaves me but little leisure, but my temperament constrains me from time to time to write some trifling verses, and occasionally I compose a ghazal." "Why waste time on ghazals?" Sauda replied. "You should write satires." Hidāyat was taken aback. "But whom should I satirise?" he asked. "That's no problem," said Sauda. "You satirise me and I'll satirise you." Having shown Hidāyat that he was not impressed by his pompousness, Sauda seems to have been content to leave it at that.[6] Otherwise Hidāyat would have found to his cost that to be the target of Sauda's satire was a painful experience.

One of such targets was Mir Zāhik, the father of the Mir Hasan of this book, and a man whom Sauda regarded as a sponger and detested accordingly. One day Sauda and another poet named Sikandar were at the house of Mirza Sulaimān Shikoh, a son of the Emperor Shāh Ālam, and their host was conversing with them when Mir Zāhik came in. Sulaimān Shikoh, who was well aware of Sauda's dislike for the man, greeted Zāhik politely, asked him to be seated, and had the hookah set before him. He then turned to Sauda and said, smiling, "Won't you recite something for us?" Sauda replied that he had not written anything recently, and then, with a gesture towards Sikandar added, "But he has just written a poem; I'll recite you the first verse":

یارب تو مری سن لے یہ کہتا ہے سکندر

ضاحک کے اُڑا دیوے کسی بن میں قلندر

گھر اس کے تو لڈ ہوا گر بچہ بندر

گلیوں میں نچا تا پھرے وہ بنگلے کے اندر

روٹی تو کما کھاوے کسی طور مچھندر

---

[6] The anecdotes about Umedvār and Hidāyat are from Āzād, *Āb i Ḥayāt*, pp. 170, 171, respectively.

Sikandar craves this boon of the Almighty:
Rouse Zāhik up to lift his spouse's nightie.
And then when she brings forth his monkey-lad
He'll dance it through the streets of Faizābād
And earn his living by an honest trade.

Without waiting to hear any more, Mir Zāhik rose to his feet and threw himself upon the astonished Sikandar, while others rushed in to part them. Meanwhile Sauda stood on one side smiling; the verse was not Sikandar's, but his own.[7]

The incident illustrates both Sauda's character and his satirical style. Within five lines it is suggested that Zāhik is incapable of performing a husband's duties without divine intervention, that he is so apelike that most people would mistake his son for a monkey, that he lives by sponging on others, and that even going the rounds with a performing monkey would be a more honourable way of getting a living. Amidst this shower of insults only the last but one is at all seriously intended. There is a single motive for attack, but the attack is made with any and every weapon that comes to hand.

This method can be disconcerting to one whose ideas of literary polemic are based on the modern conventions that an opponent must be treated fairly and courteously, that personalities should be avoided, and that anything not strictly relevant to the point at issue should be excluded from the argument. But these are quite irrelevant to the satire of Sauda's day—and indeed to that of most countries and most ages up to quite modern times.[8] Sauda enjoyed all and more of the license that is

---

[7] Shaikh Cānd, pp. 82–83.

[8] The comedies of Aristophanes in ancient Athens, the polemics of Luther against the Pope, and the attacks of Milton on Salmasius illustrate in different countries and different ages that this was so. Thus E. H. Gombrich and E. Kris, in *Caricature* (Harmondsworth, 1940), p. 8, write, "Some of the woodcuts against the Pope which he [Luther] ordered Cranach to make are today hardly reproducible . . . they are illustrated libels, debasing the opponent as crudely as possible." Milton in his polemics addresses Salmasius as "busy puppy," "you slug you," and "you silly loggerhead." Another work against an anonymous opponent has such passages as: "'Salmasius will make the trumpet blow a deadly blast.' You announce a new kind of harmony; for to the terrors of that loud-sounding instrument no symphony bears so close a resemblance as that which is produced by accumulated flatulency." And: "Take away, O ass! those panniers of airy nothingness; and speak, if you can, three words that have an affinity to common sense; if it be possible for the tumid pumpkin of your skull to discover for a moment anything like the reality of intellect." Milton, *The Prose Works*, ed. J. A. St. John (London, 1848), I, 15, 17, 232, 242, respectively.

still granted to the modern political cartoonist, who may ridicule the personal appearance and habits of his target, though these have nothing to do with the point of his cartoon. The atmosphere of his satires is the atmosphere of the open-air political meeting, where speaker and heckler are all the time trying to score off each other, and the audience thoroughly enjoys every hit that goes home, no matter how irrelevant it may be to the subject under discussion. In the last resort they are not deeply malicious, though that is not to say that they didn't hurt. They did, and they were meant to. Not all of them are personal attacks. Some are sheer clowning, like modern slapstick comedy. One is a ferocious attack on the intolerable heat of the Indian summer.[9] But most of them are, like the verse on Mir Zāhik, directed against people who are specifically named. And if modern taste has grown unaccustomed to this sort of thing, it had at any rate one great advantage, and Sauda did not have to complain, as Swift did, that "satire is a sort of glass wherein beholders do generally discover everybody's face but their own."[10]

One in which the victim is not named lampoons a rich man for his meanness.[11] Sauda introduces his subject:

ہے خدا کا یہ ایک شمّۂ نور

جس سے روشن ہے آسماں کا تنور

کس زباں سے ہو اس کا شکر ادا

نعمتیں کیا کیا ان نے کیں پیدا

میوے ہیں باغ میں زمانے کے

واسطے کھانے اور کھلانے کے

9 Kulliyāt, pp. 138–140. Kalām, pp. 103–104.

10 Swift, A Tale of a Tub and The Battle of the Books (London, 1948), p. 172.

11 Kulliyāt, pp. 141–144. Kalām, pp. 145–151. Passages translated are Kulliyāt, p. 141, upper margin, line 20, to lower margin, line 1, and lower margin, lines 6–13; p. 142, centre, lines 7–8; and p. 144, upper margin, lines 1–4 and 19–20. Kalām, p. 145, lines 1–6; p. 146, lines 4–5; p. 149, line 15, to p. 150, line 11; p. 150, lines 16–17; and p. 151, lines 6–7.

فضل سے اس کے کچھ نہیں ہے کمی

لیک وہ کیا کرے جو ہم ہوں دنی

سُنیو یاروں کروں ہوں میں اک نقل

جس کو باور کرے نہ ہرگز عقل

God filled the world with numberless good things,
That every man might eat and have to spare;
Men live in a vast orchard, fit for kings,
Laden with fruits enough for all to share.
The ordinary man like you and me
Gives thanks that He provides for us so well.
But what is He to do with such as he
Who figures in this tale I'm going to tell?

He goes on to relate how an acquaintance of his once went to visit a rich nobleman. Hardly had he been admitted when the sky clouded over and it began to look like rain. His host at once became extremely agitated, and forgetting even the normal courtesies with which a visitor is welcomed, began to ask anxiously whether he had brought a cloak or shawl which would give him some protection if it should happen to rain on his way home. He replied that he had not, for he had not expected rain when he left home. Shortly afterwards the rain began. The host went and fetched a waterproof and laid it before his visitor, exclaiming against his evil fortune and lamenting that one who had not visited him for so long should be put to all the inconvenience of going home in the pouring rain. The other, who knew that a man of his host's wealth and position could put him up for the night without the slightest inconvenience, was genuinely puzzled at his words and replied:

بولے یہ سادگی سے کیا ہے ضرور

بھیگتا جاؤں گا میں اتنی دور

رکھے خالق سلامت آپ کی ذات

نہ کھلے گا تو میں رہوں گا رات

Why all this agitation, my good lord?
What need to fancy me in such a plight?
I need not hasten home; be reassured.
If it keeps on like this I'll stay the night.

At these words his host turned pale, as though his guest had dealt him a mortal blow, and in even greater agitation he spoke constantly about the rain, sending his servants out repeatedly to look at the sky and see if there were any sign of it clearing up. But when the steady downpour continued, he realised that other measures would be needed. For a while he conversed with his visitor, dwelling at length, for his benefit, on a tradition of the Holy Prophet, which tells how he reproved one of his acquaintances for visiting him too frequently; and when it was time for dinner, he excused himself, saying that he had to go to the lavatory, but telling his guest to send for the steward and order anything he wished. The visitor accordingly did so. The steward came only after being repeatedly summoned, and having at length appeared, said that no food was ready, that there were no provisions in the house, and that the tradesmen had found it so difficult to extract payment for what they supplied that they had all long since refused to deal with the house any longer. Then, warming to his subject, he launched into a long and contemptuous account of his master's unspeakable meanness—this speech forms the bulk of the satire—ending with an incident which was meant to convince his hearer that he could not expect to receive the slightest hospitality at this house:

ایک فرزند یہ رکھے ہے اُلّا غ	سارے گھر کا ہے اس کے چشم و چراغ
اُن لے اک روز یہ حماقت کی	آشنا اپنے کی ضیافت کی
نہ ضیافت کہ حبس میں ہو رنگ رس	اک رکابی طعام و دیگر بس
تس پہ یوں پیش آیا یہ مردود	یاد آیا اُسے چھٹی کا دودھ

اور ماں کو بھی اس کی دیوے طلاق — چاہتا تھا کرے یہ اس کو عاق

تب یہ جورو کے حق میں فرمایا — بارے لوگوں نے آ کے سمجھایا

کاش بھنس مرتا واں یہ ناشدنی — پتھراس کے عوض تو کیوں نہ جنی

میرا بیٹا اور اس قدر ابتر — یارو مجھ سے تو لا ولد بہتر

اس سلیقے سے پر کرتے تھا معاش — اس کا دادا بھی گرچہ تھا عیّاش

رات کو اس پہ یہ مقرر تھا — جو کوئی اس کے گھر میں نوکر تھا

لاتا آٹا کے آگے جھولی بھر — پھرتا وہ ٹکڑے مانگتا گھر گھر

برے تنخواہ میں لگاتے تھے — اچھے چھن چھن کے آپ کھاتے تھے

سو یہ بدبخت دے ہے یوں برباد — پیدا کر گئے تھے اس طرح اجداد

پر یہ مجھ سے بھی نکلا نامعقول — میں تو آپ ہی کو جانتا تھا فضول

اینٹوں تک بیچ بیچ کھاوے گا — گڑے پیسے یہ سب اڑاوے گا

کرتی ہیں یاں ضیافتیں پامال — تھی بزرگوں کی اپنے تو یہ چال

لواتا لیق کے مہینے سے — خوب جو کچھ اٹھا خزینے سے

This fellow has a son, a stupid boy,
But none the less his father's pride and joy.
Do you know what he did, the silly fellow?
One day, feeling particularly mellow,
He asked a friend to lunch—'twas nothing much—
A plate of greens and lentils, or some such.

You should have seen his father's agitation.
You'd think his son had feasted half the nation.
He swore he'd cut him off without a shilling;
Divorce his mother too: *he'd* not be willing
To call her wife who'd borne a son so monstrous!
Then, less infuriated and more pompous,
He called her and proceeded to hold forth:
"O would that you had never given birth!
Or else brought forth a stone! Or else miscarried!
Better by far if I had never married.
Better by far die childless than have one
So utterly unworthy for a son!
His grandsire was a great voluptuary.
But still, he was no spendthrift—no, not he!
He planned his operations like a soldier
And sent his servants, haversack on shoulder,
To beg from door to door for scraps of food,
And bring them back to him; anything good
He'd pick out for himself. Then he would say
"The rest is yours"—and dock it from their pay.
That's how our family fortunes were amassed,
And was it all for this, that he at last
Should leave us naked 'gainst the winter's blast?
I thought *myself* extravagant, but he
In reckless spending outdoes even me.
He'll rapidly exhaust our buried hoards,
Pull down the house, and sell the bricks and boards.
And all for senseless prodigality!
Well, since the thing is done, I'll have to see
Where lies the true responsibility.
His tutor should have taught the boy more sense,
So he shall pay the bill . . ."

The steward concluded by saying that the visitor would get nothing here,
but that his own humble dwelling was not far away and he would be very
welcome to dine there if he wished. The visitor thanked him and returned

home, and the next day came and related the whole story to Sauda, who concludes:

بھیجو یار و اب ایسے عمدہ پر

لعنتِ کردگار شام و سحر

On such a perfect nobleman, I say,
May God send down His curses night and day.

Another satire is on the gluttony of Mir Zāhik.[12] It depicts a number of separate scenes rather than telling a connected story.

گھر میں اب جس کے دیکچی کھڑکے

در پہ اس کے یہ بیٹھے یوں اڑے کے

گور سے پھر جو رستم اٹھ کر آئے

میّت اس کی اٹھائے یا نہ اٹھائے

He only has to hear a saucepan rattle,
And like a soldier digging in for battle,
He'll take up his position by the door.
Nothing can shift him then: that god of war,
Rustam himself, might rise up from the tomb
And try his strength against him. He'd stand firm.
He'd fight to the last breath and never yield
Until his corpse was carried from the field.

It is enough to catch a whiff of food cooking for him to fly to the place and sit there beating his head with both hands in an agony of impatience and looking like a great fly which sits on the food washing its face with its front legs. When food is set before him, he rushes at it as a soldier

---

[12] *Kulliyāt*, pp. 144–147. *Kalām*, pp. 156–161. Passages translated are *Kulliyāt*, p. 144, centre, lines 4–5, and p. 145, upper margin, lines 11–18. *Kalām*, p. 157, lines 2–3; p. 158, lines 2–4; other verses not included in *Kalām*.

rushes to loot a house, feverishly gathering everything up in case anyone
should come and disturb him before he can finish, and his hands flash back
and forth between the plate and his mouth as nimbly as those of a fencer
hard pressed by a determined opponent. So obsessed is he by the thought
of food that it dominates his mind even when he is alone with his wife.
He

جورو اپنی پہ جب کرے ہے نظر

اس سے کہتا ہے تب یہ گیدی خر

کچھ ترے پاس اے حمیدہ ہے

تیری انگیا میں گاؤ دیدہ ہے

یا چھاپے ہیں تونے قُرصِ پنیر

سچ ہی کہہ در نہ ہوں گا میں دلگیر

کچے خوشتک پہ ہاتھ پھیراء جان

کس طرح کی یہ پنجہ کش ہے نان

Fixes his lady's bodice with a stare,
"Tell me," he asks, "What have you got in there?
Are they two loaves? Or two delicious cheeses?"
Or, if his hand should stray into her breeches,
"What's this I feel," he cries, "So soft and warm?
Newly-baked bread?[13] If so 'twould do no harm
To let me eat it. Why do you hide it from me?''

Another satire is directed against an ignorant *hakīm*,[14] or one who
practises the traditional Greek system of medicine as developed by the
Arabs—a system still widely prevalent in all countries which have a large

---

[13] Saudā uses the word *panjakash*. This was a kind of bread bearing the marks of five fingers.
[14] *Kulliyāt*, pp. 151–153. *Kalām*, pp. 137–141. Passages translated are *Kulliyāt*, p. 151,
lower margin, lines 3–6 and 16–20; p. 152, centre, lines 5–9; and p. 153, upper margin,
lines 7–8. *Kalām*, p. 137, lines 1–2, 5–7, and 10–15; p. 141, lines 3–4.

Muslim population. In this case Sauda launches his attack without any general preamble:

صدر کے بازار میں ہے اک دبنگ

عار طبّاؤ طبابت کا ننگ

شکل ہے شیطان کی اور غوث نام

جگ میں ہلاکو کا ہے قائم مقام

قاتلِ ہندو و مسلماں ہے وہ

نسخہ نہ لکھتا کبھو وہ بد سرشت

بھرتے نہ انسان سے دوزخ بہشت

جب سے مریضوں کو دے ہے دوا

کام میں ہے مگر معطّل شفا

There's a hakīm, the mention of whose name
Makes every good physician blush with shame.
Down in the main bazaar you'll find his house;
He looks like Satan, yet his name is Ghaus.[15]
Since he took up his practice people say
Death works while Healing takes a holiday.
None whom he treated ever yet got well;
His patients populate both Heaven and Hell.
Worthy successor to Halāku Khān,[16]
He massacres Hindu and Musalman.

---

[15] Ghaus is a title of a Muslim saint.

[16] Halākū Khān was the grandson of Chingīz, or Jenghiz, Khān, and commander of the Mongol hordes which overran the Muslim 'Abbāsid Empire. When he took Baghdad, he ordered a general massacre of the population of the city and of the surrounding country.

ہو کے کسل مند جو وہ بے حیا

اپنے تئیں آپ کرے ہے دوا

مردہ شو، مولودی و تابوت گر

گھیرتے ہیں آن کے سب اُس کا گھر

دیں ہیں دُہائی وہ بصد قیل و قال

ان میں سے ہر ایک کرے ہے سوال

اپنی دوا آپ تو ظالم نہ کر

میرے کس و کو، کی طرف کر نظر

خوب جو کرتا ہے تو آپ ہی دوا

اور کوئی آپ سا مجھ کو بتا

روزی سے خاطر ہو مری تا کہ جمع

بھیجوں تری گور پہ گل اور شمع

This idiot once felt slightly indisposed;
He dosed himself with his own preparations.
Corpse-washers, mourners, coffin-makers, all
Thronged round his door with earnest supplications:
"You'll kill yourself! How can you be so cruel?
Have pity on our wives and families!
How shall we earn our bread when you are gone?
We need you more than you can realise—
Well, if you must then, tell us someone who
Makes out the same prescriptions as you do,
And we will promise (given what we crave)
Always to keep fresh flowers on your grave."

The poem goes on to describe how a man went to consult him and was given a prescription to take to the druggist to be made up. The druggist took one look at it, and asked the man to describe the hakīm who had given him it. From the description he at once recognised that it must be Ghaus, whereupon he launched into a long diatribe against him (which takes up the rest of the poem), cursing him heartily and quoting numerous instances of his complete incompetence. Sauda concludes:

تھا غرض اس نقل سے یہ مدّعا
تاکہ تو ایسے کی نہ کھاوے دوا

> The moral is, make this a golden rule:
> Don't go for treatment to this bloody fool.[17]

Ignorant, self-important frauds like hakīm Ghaus are the target of a great number of satires. One of Sauda's favourite butts was a "learned" Kashmiri named Nudrat. This man did his best to acquire a reputation for virtue, learning, and poetry alike; but he seems in fact—if Sauda is to be believed—to have been a close spiritual kinsman of

> . . . the peerless paper lord, Lord Peter,
> Who broke the laws of God, and man, and metre.

There is perhaps no other figure whom Sauda attacks so often and so mercilessly in his satires, sometimes in terms which shock even one accustomed to his coarseness. But the best of them is less crude, and concentrates on exposing Nudrat's pretensions to be a great scholar and poet:

فاضلوں کی تو بزم میں ہوتے ہو جاکے شعر خواں
شاعروں پاس آپ کو کہتے ہو نحو و صرف داں
دونوں ہوں جمع جس جگہ پھر تھیں واں جگہ کہاں
بولو جو واں کچھ ان کر سب کہیں تم کو مہرباں
گھوڑے کو دو دو نہ دو لگام منھ کو تنگ لگام دو

---

17 The whole tone of this satire reminds one of Robert Burns' *Death and Doctor Hornbrook*.

Where scholars are assembled, you're a poet;
Where poets gather, a grammarian.
Both claims are false, but how are they to know it?
They can't catch Nudrat! He's too spry for them!
But what when both are met? If you speak there,
These are the words you'll very quickly hear:
    Give your old nag full rein, but curb your tongue! [18]

About satires like these Sauda might well have given his readers the
same advice as Rabelais gave his: "You . . . may not too easily conclude
that they treat of nothing but mockery, fooling, and pleasant fiction . . .
You must open this book and carefully weigh up its contents. You will
discover then that the drug within is far more valuable than the box
promised." [19] What in essence his satires all assert is that it is not too
difficult to fulfil your elementary obligations to your fellowmen and to
society at large, and that if you fail in them, he has the right to tell you so
plainly and to make you smart for it. This down-to-earth approach en-
gages one's sympathies much more than a high moral tone would do. But
in any case Sauda did not like the high moral tone. He knew that it was
all too often the mark of people who could see failings only in other
people, and never in themselves; and he left no one in any doubt about
what he thought of such people: [20]

Pious severely censures me, I hear,
On evidence Abstemious supplied him.
Sauda will not resent that, never fear,
But I would just respectfully remind him:
    That which Abstemious saw fit to do
    For me, he very well may do for you.

I never understood what prompts a man
To ferret out the vices of his neighbours.

[18] *Kulliyāt*, p. 357, upper margin, lines 12–16. *Kalām*, p. 196, line 13, p. 197, line 2. The
last line is a refrain that follows each of the 15 verses.
[19] *Gargantua and Pantagruel*, trans. J. M. Cohen (Harmondsworth, 1955), pp. 37–38.
[20] *Kulliyāt*, p. 355. *Kalām*, pp. 211–212. The translation represents a considerable abridgement of the original, but draws upon most of the stanzas.

Surely a decent human being can
Find a much better object for his labours.
    The rosary was meant for other things
    Than counting up a fellow-creature's sins.

Suppose my every sin a deadly one—
Does that stop *you* living a life of piety?
I sin in my own way, involving none:
Does that in any way corrupt society?
    Does it require the strictures of the pious?
    Ask any normal person free from bias.

I wish this tribe would learn another trade;
But meanwhile let them heed this friendly warning:
I cannot spy; that's not the way I'm made:
I go to bed at night and sleep till morning.
    And yet I also know a thing or two;
    You'd best leave me alone: be off with you!

In another short poem he tells how he was approached by an acquaintance who warned him not to make any man his friend, because there are no friends who prove true once they are put to the test. Sauda records his words and then writes:

يہ دن کے اس سے کہا مسکرا کے مودا نے

شکایت اتنی کسو کی کوئی بیاں نہ کرے

بھلے بُرے کے تجھے امتحاں سے کیا کام

یہ شکر کر کہ جو کوئی تجھ کو امتحاں نہ کرے

I heard him out; then, smiling, said to him:
"It is not good to speak so ill of men.
Who made *you* judge of others? You had best
Thank God that no one puts *you* to the test."[21]

---

[21] *Kulliyāt*, p. 315, centre. *Kalām*, p. 68. The lines translated are *Kulliyāt*, p. 315, centre, lines 13–14. *Kalām*, p. 68, lines 8–9.

The attitude these poems express helps to explain why Sauda was so popular in his day, when people saw and condemned the degeneracy all round them, and wanted to see their feelings expressed, but were too conscious of their own human failings to sympathise with the conventional moralists. The poems also help to correct a false picture of Sauda to which Urdu critics of the Victorian age gave currency and which is still quite commonly presented. This picture represents him as a proud, irascible man, very conscious of his powers as a satirist and always ready to use them at once against anyone who did anything to upset him. This idea of him arises from a failure to understand the conventions of eighteenth-century satire. What has already been said on this point is not special pleading for Sauda. The few satirical poems of Mir and Mir Hasan are in the same convention as his—a fact these critics seem to have overlooked, for none of them draws similar conclusions about their character. The truth is that no such conclusions can legimately be drawn, either about them or about Sauda. Mir Hasan, for example, has always been thought of as a man of gentle and courteous disposition; his contemporaries go out of their way to praise these qualities in him, and no subsequent writer has seen any reason to question their testimony. Yet manuscripts of his verse include a satire written in reply to Sauda's attack on his father, Mir Zāhik, and couched in terms so scurrilous that modern editors do not venture to print it as it stands.[22] The outrageous charges made in verse of this kind have nothing to do with the writer's serious estimate of his adversary. One of Mir Hasan's works is a short account of the Urdu poets,[23] and in it he gives high praise to Sauda, adding in passing that he was a frequent visitor at Sauda's house, and was always treated with kindness and affection.

In Mir's case the evidence is even more substantial. The high regard in which Mir and Sauda held each other is well known. Yet they satirised each other in terms which, if taken at their face value, would lead to quite the opposite conclusion. For example, Sauda was very fond of dogs, and Mir wrote a satire attacking him for this.[24] He used many sticks to beat him with, including the argument that Islam regards the dog as an

---

[22] An expurgated extract is quoted in Maḥmūd Fārūqī, *Mīr Ḥasan aur Khāndān ke dūsre shuʻarā* (Lahore, 1956), pp. 42–43.
[23] Mīr Ḥasan, *Tazkira i Shuʻarā i Urdū*, quoted in Shaikh Cānd, *Saudā*, p. 84.
[24] *Kulliyāt i Mīr*, ed. ʻAbdul Bārī Āsī (Lucknow, 1941), p. 823.

unclean animal, and the suggestion that Sauda's ostentatious love of dogs is nothing but self-advertisement, necessary because he had no other qualities that would attract anyone's attention. Whether Mir really attached any weight to the views of orthodox Islam on the dog is questionable, for he himself had once kept one.[25] And it is quite certain that Mir did not really think that Sauda had any need to advertise himself, for we know that Mir fully shared the current opinion of him as one of the greatest poets of his day. The whole piece is in lighthearted vein, and probably means only that Mir—in common, no doubt, with many others —thought the attention which Sauda devoted to his dogs extravagant, a little ostentatious, and rather ridiculous.

Sauda replied to Mir's attack in a short piece of about the same length.[26] He takes the argument about the attitude of Islam at its face value and replies that he fully accepts that dogs are unclean animals; but after being in contact with them, one only has to bathe to be clean again. He argues that there is therefore no harm in keeping dogs, and goes on to say that there is one dog, however, which a man should on no account cherish, and that is the dog of his own baser impulses. Love for this dog so contaminates a man that no amount of bathing will make him clean. Let those who want to teach others the way they should live preach against all attachment to this dog; and above all let them see to it first that they themselves are free from such attachment—a plain suggestion to Mir that if he is so concerned with godly living, he should first concentrate on correcting his own faults. The whole thing amounts to a mild rebuke to Mir—not perhaps wholly undeserved—for being too ready to tell others what they ought and ought not to do.

Mir is the target of another short satire[27] in which Sauda says that one of the best calligraphers of his day came to him complaining bitterly that Mir was ruining his reputation for him. "How so?" asked Sauda. The man replied that Mir brought him verses of the classical poets to write out, but insisted on "improving" them. When other people saw them, not knowing that Mir was responsible for the changes, they blamed them on the carelessness of the calligrapher. Here again, the serious intention

[25] He preferred cats, however, and this too is made the occasion for a hit at Saudā: "Now if he had kept cats, then I would own / That he had shown himself a man of sense."
[26] *Kulliyāt*, p. 363, lower margin to p. 364. *Kalām*, pp. 207–208.
[27] *Kulliyāt*, p. 316. *Kalām*, p. 170.

is simply to take a hit at Mir for the readiness with which he passes literary judgements, both on the poetry of his own day and on that of the past.

In short, in such exchanges there is on both sides a point of criticism quite seriously intended, but it is accompanied by a good deal more which is not. Serious judgements were another matter. Mir wrote of Sauda as "Pre-eminent among the poets of India . . . and worthy to be called the poet laureate of Urdu."[28] One of the most famous anecdotes about him tells how, when he was asked to name the great poets of his day, he replied without hesitation, "First Sauda; secondly, myself" (adding after a pause that a third poet, Mir Dard, was "half a poet").[29] The names of the two poets—"Mir and Mirza," as their contemporaries called them— were regularly linked together, and they themselves must have approved of the judgement this implies, for they use the phrase in their own writings.[30] There is an anecdote which shows that Sauda did not consider anyone and everyone entitled to attack Mir.[31] He was present on one occasion at a gathering where he was approached by a self-styled poet named Khāksār,[32] who asked him to compose an extempore satire on Mir. To his delight, Sauda agreed to his request. A couplet ostensibly ridiculing Mir's personal appearance was greeted with roars of laughter in which Khāksār joined until, when the laughter showed no sign of dying down, it dawned upon him that the verse described not Mir but himself.

All this shows that one poet might lampoon another in the most extravagant terms without this necessarily implying any real feeling of enmity between them. It does not, of course, mean that such enmity never existed between the satirist and his victim. Probably Sauda cordially detested most of those whom he attacked by name. But even then it is important, before forming conclusions, to distinguish the essential theme of the satire from the rest and to assess its underlying tone.

That Sauda was not at all the arrogant, touchy, waspish person that some have made him out to be is well illustrated by an incident which

[28] Mīr, *Nikāt ush Shuʿarā*, ed. Ḥabīb ur Raḥmān Khān Shīrvānī (Aurangābād, n.d.), pp. 32–33.
[29] Āzād, *Āb i Ḥayāt*, p. 216.
[30] Cf., for example, Mīr, *Kulliyāt*, p. 826, line 11; and Sauda, *Kulliyāt*, p. 155, lower margin, lines 12–13.
[31] Shaikh Cānd, *Sauda*, pp. 78–79.
[32] Khāksār means humble, but the name was hardly an apt one; he thought himself a far better poet than Mīr, and had conferred upon himself the title of King of Poets.

occurred during the last period of his life in Lucknow.[33] There was a man named Ashraf Ali Khān who had spent fifteen years in compiling a selection of Persian verse taken from the works of the great poets. When he had completed it, he took it to Fākhir Makīn, who enjoyed the reputation of being the best Persian poet of the day, and asked if he would consent to look over it. Fākhir Makīn made all sorts of difficulties, but in the end took the selection and began to look through it. Ashraf Ali Khān later heard to his consternation that he was crossing out the verses of even the greatest poets, on the ground that they were meaningless, and was making drastic alterations in others. He at once went to him, and having after much persuasion got the selection returned, went with it to Sauda. He told him of all that had happened, and of how distressed he felt at what Fākhir Makīn had done, and in the end asked Sauda to undertake the revision of the selection. Sauda replied that his knowledge of Persian was not adequate to the task; he felt sure, he said, that a scholar like Fākhir Makīn must have good reason for what he had done; if Ashraf Ali Khān could not bring himself to accept Fākhir Makīn's corrections, he should approach other eminent Persian scholars, and named five whom he considered competent to undertake the task. Ashraf Ali Khān pointed out in reply that Fākhir Makīn held the very poorest opinion of those whom Sauda had named, and again asked Sauda himself to revise his selection. At length Sauda reluctantly agreed. When he began to examine the selection, he was astonished to find what Fākhir Makīn had done. The verses of great classical poets had been mutilated beyond recognition. Sauda then wrote a pamphlet which he entitled "Ibrat ul Ghāfilīn," or A Warning to the Heedless. In it he dealt with all the mistakes that Fākhir Makīn had committed in making his so-called corrections, and then went on to a detailed examination of all the mistakes in Fākhir Makīn's own Persian verse.

Fākhir Makīn heard of this with alarm, and at once took steps to prevent the thing becoming public knowledge. He first sent one of his best pupils, a man with some reputation as a Persian scholar in his own right, to dispute some of the points Sauda had made, but Sauda completely refuted all his arguments. He then took more desperate steps. He sent a gang of young bloods to compel Sauda under threat of violence to accompany them to Fākhir Makīn's house and settle the whole matter with him

---

[33] Āzād, *Āb i Ḥayāt*, pp. 165–168.

there and then. Sauda had no alternative but to submit. On the way there they tried to humiliate him in public by provoking a clash with him, and the dispute was at its height when, fortunately for Sauda, the retinue of Āsaf ud Daula's brother Sa'ādat Ali Khān passed that way. Having ascertained what was happening, he compelled the men to release Sauda, and seating him beside him on his own elephant, went directly to Āsaf ud Daula. He was taking his meal at the time, but Sa'ādat Ali Khān went straight in to him and related the whole incident, expressing his regret that the ruler of Oudh apparently could not prevent such a thing happening even in the streets of his own capital. Āsaf ud Daula was very concerned. He at once came out, and having heard a more detailed account of what had happened, ordered that the rowdies should be expelled from the city and the quarter where they lived razed to the ground, while Fākhir Makīn was to be commanded to appear at once at court, just as he was. It was Sauda who interceded for his adversary, saying that the help already given him was sufficient protection, and that what was after all in origin a literary dispute should be settled by literary means. Āsaf ud Daula deferred to his wishes and Sauda was allowed to go home, escorted as a precaution by some of the Navvāb's own soldiers.

The next day Āsaf ud Daula rebuked Fākhir Makīn sharply before the whole court, and told him in conclusion: "If you possess the poetic talent you claim, compose a verse against Sauda here and now in his presence." Fākhir Makīn replied, "That is more than I can do." "Yes," said the Navvāb, "but you could set these devils on Sauda and let them drag him from his house into the street and humiliate him. *That* was not more than you could do." He then turned to Sauda and indicated that he should speak. Sauda, never at a loss, at once recited a *rubāi* in Persian, which may be freely translated:

> The learned class in every land reveres thy name;
> O crown of poetry, who has not heard thy fame?
> Three errors in two lines! Pray you correct them, friend;
> For "class" read "ass"; for "crown" read "clown"; for "fame"
>   read "shame."

The story is interesting not only because it shows Sauda to have been a modest man, capable of exercising restraint and tolerance even under great provocation, but because it also shows the great honour and respect in which a good patron was expected to hold a great poet.

Most of Sauda's satires are personal, in the sense that they attack particular people, often by name. But in some of them personal merges with social satire, because it is public figures who are under attack. And in addition to these there are others which directly satirise social institutions. In his social, as in his personal, satire Sauda spoke from a standpoint very close to that of the ordinary man. He stood by the medieval ideals of social life, and was not prepared to abandon them, no matter how generally they had ceased to be observed in his own day. He attributed the decay of the Empire to the selfish neglect by men of all classes of the duties to society appropriate to their station; and he therefore saw the remedy in himself doing his duty to society according to his lights, and in persuading or shaming others into doing theirs. As a satirist, he played his part by attacking any departure from the social ideals in which he believed. Like most men of his age, he looked for inspiration to the past, or more accurately, to an unconsciously idealised part, which in fact represented his aspirations for the future. Many passages show how this idealised memory sustained him, so that while the contemporary scene often aroused his anger and sorrow, he did not succumb to pessimism.

In demanding, so to speak, that his social ideals be realised, he did not feel that he was demanding the impossible, for he believed that they had already been realised once before—and only a generation or two before his time. Thus one of his satires contrasts the Delhi of former times with that of his own day.[34] There was a time, he says, when the administration was firm, vigorous, and incorruptible, and the people of the city lived a good life in peace and prosperity, assured that their lives and property were secure. But today the city swarms with thieves and robbers, who go unpunished because the police are in league with them; the danger of assault is always present, so that men go out in the evening to a mushāira fully armed, as though they were going out to battle. Elsewhere he describes the age as one in which

سنتا نہیں ہے درد رعیت کا بادشاہ

The king no longer heeds his subjects' cry.[35]

---

[34] *Kulliyāt*, pp. 136–138. *Kalām*, pp. 130–133.
[35] *Kulliyāt*, p. 338, centre, line 14. (Not included in *Kalām*.)

And in another place he exclaims:

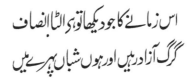

See the perverted justice of this age!
The wolves roam free: the shepherds are in chains.[36]

Sauda raised his voice against all these social ills, and the more effectively because his own conscience was clear. The standards he set for
himself were no less exacting than those he set for others who had a
different part to play in society, and his writings show how seriously he
took the responsibilities of his calling. They also show his confidence that
he was fulfilling them adequately, and reflect the pride and pleasure
which this gave him. He knew that in his age none could surpass him, and
only one—Mir—could equal him, and then only because Mir's superiority
in his own particular field matched his own pre-eminence in his. He
never rested content with what he had achieved, but always tried to perfect still further his mastery of his craft, and to keep himself always ready
to learn. He wrote towards the end of his life[37] that in the forty or more
years since he had made his name as a poet, he had tried all the time to
learn from the great poets of the past as a pupil does from his master, had
never withheld the praise that is the due of good poetry, even though it
was the work of his enemies, and that he still does not regard his own
poetry as incapable of improvement, and will continue as always to
listen attentively to criticism and to accept it where he feels it to be just,
even should the critic be the rawest and most unpractised of poets.

This receptiveness served him well. The mastery of his craft revealed
by his poetry is remarkable, particularly when one considers that Urdu
poetry in northern India was in its infancy when he and Mir entered the
field. He handles with ease the complex metres and figures of rhetoric.
His range of vocabulary is wide, and he never seems to be at a loss for
words, while at the same time he uses his vocabulary with economy,
giving the fullest expression to what he wants to say without wasting any

36 *Kulliyāt*, p. 308, centre, line 6. *Kalām*, p. 107, line 3.
37 Shaikh Cānd, *Saudā*, p. 75.

words. He writes on the most varied themes, particularly in his satires, and uses with uniform ease the range of vocabulary appropriate to each. His satires also show a wide and varied experience of life, a keen power of observation, and an impressive familiarity with the arts and sciences of his day, so that when he lampoons an ignorant hakīm or a self-styled scholar, he can carry the attack into his opponent's own territory. For all these reasons he speaks with the vigorous assurance of one who knows that his own position is unchallengeable. If he enjoyed a life of comfort and even luxury, he regarded this as no more than what was due to him as one of the two greatest poets of the age, each of whom, moreover, had in his own field raised Urdu poetry to a level never before attained. He was satisfied with his own part in the life of his age; he did not feel tempted, as a weaker man might have done, to blind himself to the reality of what he saw around him in case he should be compelled to face also the reality about himself; and he knew he had no need to protect himself from the possibility of counterattack by holding back in his denunciation of the vices and shortcomings of others.

Sauda was never overawed by anyone. Men with a countrywide reputation were attacked by name in his satires. The great religious leader Shāh Vali Ullāh is the subject of one of them.[38] Zābita Khān, the Rohilla chieftain, son of a distinguished father, Najīb ud Daula, who from Delhi had ruled what was left of the Empire with great ability for seven years after the momentous events of 1761, is satirised for his cowardice.[39] One full-length satire is a devastating exposure of Shīdi Faulād Khān, *kotvāl* of Delhi.[40] The duties of the kotvāl of a city correspond very roughly to those of a modern chief of police, though his powers and responsibilities were in many respects much wider. Faulād Khān, however, instead of protecting the property of the citizens of Delhi, was in league with the thieves and shared with them the proceeds of their activities.

In other satires he speaks out against evils too widespread to be attacked through satire against individuals. One pictures the chaos and inefficiency of the imperial army,[41] in which every man tries to evade his obligations and in which the skill, equipment, and courage without which no army

[38] Cf. *ibid.*, p. 86. The poem is given in *Kulliyāt*, p. 108, where, however, no name is mentioned. Some manuscripts describe this as a satire on Shāh Vali Ullāh.

[39] *Kulliyāt*, p. 315.

[40] *Kulliyāt*, pp. 136–138. *Kalām*, pp. 130–133.

[41] *Kulliyāt*, pp. 113–115. *Kalām*, pp. 121–125.

can give a good account of itself in war are all wanting. Finally there are two satires which give so comprehensive a view of the society of his day that they are worth summarising at some length. The first[42] tells how a man approached Sauda and asked him whether he could tell him of any way to earn his living in Hindustan today. Sauda replied:

> Better to keep silent than try to answer such a question, for even the tongues of angels cannot do justice to the answer. There are many professions which you could adopt, but let us see what difficulties will beset you in each of them these days. You could buy a horse and offer yourself for service in some noble's army. But never in this world will you see your pay, and you will rarely have both sword and shield by you, for you must pawn one or the other to buy fodder for your horse; and unless the moneylender is kind to you, you or your wife must go hungry, for you will not get enough to feed you both. You could minister to the needs of the faithful in a mosque, but you would find asses tethered there and men young and old sitting there idle and unwilling to be disturbed. Let the muezzin give the call to prayer and they will stop his mouth, for no one cares for Islam these days . . . You could become the courtier of some great man, but your life would not be worth living. If he does not feel like sleeping at night, you too must wake with him, though you are ready to drop, and until he feels inclined to dine, you may not, though you are faint with hunger and your belly is rumbling. Or you could become his physician; but if you did, your life would be passed in constant apprehension, for should the Navvāb sneeze, he will glare at you as though you ought to have given him a sword and buckler to keep off the cold wind. You will live through torture as you watch him feed. He will stuff himself with sweet melon and cream and then fish, and then cow's tongue, and, with it all, fancy breads of all kinds; and if at any stage he feels the slightest pain in his stomach, then you, you ignorant fool, are to blame, though you were Bū Ali Sīna himself.[43] Why not become a merchant then? But if you do, you must reckon with the possibility that the wares you buy in Ispahan will not find a market in Hindustan,[44] and you

---

[42] *Kulliyāt*, pp. 111–113. *Kalām*, pp. 108–113.

[43] One of the greatest medieval authorities on medicine, known in Europe as Avicenna (d. 1037).

[44] The term here means northern India only.

will have to take them as far afield as the Deccan. You never know in
the morning whether you will ever reach your destination for the
day,[45] and your evenings will be passed in anxious reckonings of gain
and loss. When you take your wares to some great man, you will be
astonished at the way he speaks to you, and an observer, noting the
price you are compelled to accept, would conclude that you are sus-
pected of selling stolen property. Moreover, you will not get your
money right away, but must go to the great man's agent for it, and
though you show him authorisation to pay, he will tell you that he has
not got the money to do so. So back you must go to his master, only
to be told, "Take your goods back; my steward says they are too dear."
But when you go for them, they are not to be found. So you lose both
the goods and their price, and you must stand outside the great man's
fortress hoping to waylay him as he comes out in his palanquin and lay
your petition for redress before him. And do not think you can make
a living from the land, for only if the rains are good can you survive,
and you pass your days in dread of drought or floods . . . But perhaps
you have thought of becoming a poet, for are not poets said to enjoy
freedom from all care? You will find it is not so. No one is such a prey
to worry as he. He cannot even concentrate on his Īd prayer,[46] for he
is trying all the time to compose an ode to his patron. No sooner is it
rumoured that the noble lord has fertilised his lady's womb than he
must rack his brains for a chronogram,[47] ready for the birth of the
child, and if she should miscarry, he must write such an elegy on the
abortion that no one ever after will want to read those on Imām
Husain.[48] If you think of becoming a teacher, bear this in mind, that
men able to teach the greatest works of Persian literature today get

[45] An allusion to the robber-infested roads.

[46] 'Īd is the day which marks the end of the month-long fast of Ramẓān. It is a day of great
rejoicing. Congregational prayers are said on a big open space, since the mosques cannot contain the huge crowds.

[47] In the Arabic alphabet, adopted by Urdū speakers—as by most other peoples who embraced Islām—for the writing of their own language, every letter stands for a particular
number. The dates of important events were marked by chronograms, or verses in which
would be included a word or phrase made up of letters whose numerical value when totalled
would give the date required.

[48] The grandson of the Prophet, who, with a band of his companions, was martyred at
Karbala, in Iraq. The *marsiya*, or elegy, is one of the major forms of Urdū verse, and early
became associated with the theme of Ḥusain's martyrdom; it developed to its highest point
after the close of our period.

paid no more than what will give them a cup of cheap lentils and two rounds of coarse bread to dine on. Calligraphers could once command great honours. But nobody appreciates their art these days, and even the greatest masters of the art must sit in the open street, soliciting work and selling their talents for a song. . . . Perhaps, then, in the end you will forsake all wordly professions and, taking no thought for the morrow, repose your trust in God. But do you know what will happen then? Your wife will think you a lazy good-for-nothing; your son will despise you; your daughter will think you have gone mad. And when your children begin to die of hunger, you must run after every great man's carriage and ask for the charity that your holiness deserves. And perhaps you may get a few coppers and a little chit saying, "This man merits your charity; he is a truly religious man and is learned in religious lore." In short, you will not find in Hindustan any means of earning a decent living. Peace and plenty have become empty words in this world. Some say that we shall know them in the next, but who can persuade himself that it is so? For my part, I think it only wishful thinking. Here, there is nothing but the struggle to live; there, nothing but the tumult of Judgement Day. Peace and plenty is an empty recollection: you will not find it either on earth or in heaven.

The second satire[49] tells how Sauda was approached by a person who asked him, "Why do you spend your days roaming aimlessly about? Why don't you buy a horse and ask for employment in some noble's army?" "Employment?" Sauda replied.

And can you tell me how it is sold these days? By the bushel or by the pound? Don't you know that only the wealthy and great can offer—or rather, *could* offer—employment? But how can they do so today? They can no longer realise the revenue from their estates. For years now the land has been a prey to lawless and rebellious men. Even the person supposed to be lord and master of twenty-two provinces no longer controls even the district of Aligarh.[50] All the real power belongs to lawless men. The great lords are helpless and impoverished. Their

---

[49] *Kulliyāt*, pp. 361–363. *Kalām*, pp. 114–120.
[50] A direct reference to the Emperor Shāh 'Ālam. The statement was literally true. Aligarh is only 80 miles south of Delhi.

peasants raise two crops a year, but their lords see nothing of either, and their agents on the spot are virtual prisoners in the peasants' hands, like a peasant kept in his creditor's house until he can pay his debt. So complete is the collapse of all order and administration that though the peasant reaps a harvest of gold, his lord does not see so much as a wisp of straw. How then can the lord keep the armed force he should? How can he pay the soldiers who should go before him when he goes out, or the horsemen who should ride behind him? They have fallen so low now that but for the beating of the drums to announce their coming, no one would know them for nobles. All their thought is of how to reduce their expenses, and if they do so much further, then even the drummers will be dismissed, and the palanquin-bearers who carry him —nay, the Navvāb himself sitting inside—will have to beat the drums themselves. But still they cling to their hollow greatness, though they have long forgotten how a noble should conduct himself, whether in peace or war. All their concern is to cling to their two peacock-feather fans and their robe of fur. Those who know the responsibilities of a noble and could discharge them have long since tested out the way things are run here and have withdrawn to their own dominions, leaving the Empire to its fate.[51] And now our all-wise nobles who are left have seen the conditions of the age and washed their hands of everything. They sit in their mansions surrounded by a little group of courtier-companions, with a man to fan them, and betel and spittoon before them, and if anyone should come to visit them, it all depends upon their mood whether they will see him or not. If the noble lord deigns to admit him and converse with him, let not his visitor be so rash as to speak of public affairs. "Brother!" he will be told, "for God's sake speak of other things!"

The ministers of the Empire have been summoned for consultation. See how they consult for the welfare of the state. The Imperial Paymaster is thinking up some scheme to stay at home doing nothing and still draw his pay, while the Chief Minister has his eyes on the silver knobs on the poles of the royal tent, and is calculating how much they will fetch in the market. They are all of them strangers to any sense of

[51] A reference to such men as the governors of the Deccan and of Oudh, who established their provinces as virtually independent states. Saudā blames the hopeless incompetence of the Emperor and of those who rule by his favour for this state of affairs.

shame. They spend their time in gambling and only come when summoned. A lifetime of their counsel has resulted only in this, that men who once lived in well-built houses now inhabit mud huts. Yet each of them is in his own estimation a veritable paragon. If war comes they creep out of their fortresses just long enough to draw up an army which, you may depend on it, will turn and run from every battle, soldiers who quake with fear even when they see the barber take out his razor to shave them, horsemen who fall out of their beds at night even at the dream of a horse rearing under them.

The royal treasury is empty: nothing comes in from the crown lands; the state of the Office of Salaries defies description. Soldiers, clerks, all alike are without employment. Documents authorising payment to the bearer are so much waste paper: the pharmacist tears them up to wrap his medicines in. Men who once held jāgīrs or posts paid from the royal treasury are looking for jobs as village watchmen. Their sword and shield have long since gone to the pawnshop, and when they next come out, it will be with a beggar's staff and bowl. Words cannot describe how some of these once great ones live. Their wardrobe has ended up at the rag merchant's. If the cow's tongue which comes out of their oven could speak, it would say, "Before my master could buy me, he had to do without three meals and sell his sable robe for next to nothing." Ask the steward who has charge of his beasts and cattle; he will tell you that there is neither grain nor fodder for them to eat and their condition is pitiable. The noble lord boasts of his elephants, but go to look at them and you will find an old blind she and a one-eyed bull, both without any hope of being fed and resigned to the prospect of death. The servants' hunger has made them bold and insolent. The doorkeeper, who should protect his master's privacy, cares nothing for his duties, and all and sundry get access to him. The cooks are told to prepare *pulāo*, but send up broth instead.[52] If the servant is told to straighten out the carpet on which his master is sitting, he will not wait for his master to rise, but will give a tug at the carpet there and then. But the truth is that servants and courtiers alike are weak from hunger and are not fit to perform even the lightest duties.

---

[52] The implication is that they use the ingredients of the ordered *pulāo*, or the money given them to buy these ingredients, to fill their own bellies. Pulāo is a rich dish prepared from rice, meat, and other ingredients.

The *salātīn*[53] are in such desperate straits that their clothes are all threadbare. They are ashamed to admit visitors to their homes and will slam the door in their faces rather than do so. Some are saying that if they are such a burden to maintain, it would be better to give them poison to take. In short, poverty has overtaken all, and a man may try his utmost for employment and still find none, unless he is prepared to emigrate as far afield as Ispahan or Istambul[54] . . .

How can I describe the desolation of Delhi? There is no house from where the jackal's cry cannot be heard. The mosques at evening are unlit and deserted, and only in one house in a hundred will you see a light burning. Its citizens do not possess even the essential cooking pots, and vermin crawl in the places where in former days men used to welcome the coming of spring with music and rejoicing. The lovely buildings which once made the famished man forget his hunger are in ruins now. In the once-beautiful gardens where the nightingale sang his love songs to the rose, the grass grows waist-high around the fallen pillars and ruined arches. In the villages round about, the young women no longer come to draw water at the wells and stand talking in the leafy shade of the trees. The villages are deserted, the trees themselves are gone, and the wells are full of corpses.[55] Jahānābād,[56] you never deserved this terrible fate, you who were once vibrant with life and love and hope, like the heart of a young lover, you for whom men afloat upon the ocean of the world once set their course as to the promised shore, you from whose dust men came to gather pearls. Not even a lamp of clay now burns where once the chandelier blazed with light. Those who once lived in great mansions now eke out their lives among the ruins. Thousands of hearts once full of hope are sunk in despair. Women of noble birth, veiled from head to foot, stand in the streets carrying in their arms their little children, lovely as fresh

---

[53] The *salāṭīn*, or princes, were the relatives and descendants of the imperial family, who, as may be imagined when the size of the imperial harems is borne in mind, were numerous. In 1836 there were no less than 795 receiving stipends of some sort. Cf. Spear, *Twilight of the Mughuls*, p. 39.

[54] Whereas formerly people flocked to India from the whole Islamic world and made their fortunes there.

[55] Of women who, in the days when armies were looting and raping, threw themselves into the wells to escape dishonour.

[56] Delhi.

flowers; they are ashamed to beg outright, and offer for sale rosaries made from the holy clay of Karbala.[57]

But Sauda, still your voice, for your strength fails you now. Every heart is aflame with grief, every eye brimming with tears. There is nothing to be said but this: We are living in a special kind of age. So say no more.

These two satires alone would be enough to show that the vehemence of Sauda's attack springs from a grievous awareness of all the evils of his day—in fact, that the mainspring of his satire, as of all good satire, is a deep compassion for humanity and a savage indignation against the conditions of an age in which humanity is degraded. And it is this that still gives his satires, two hundred years after they were written, a relevance and an interest for today.

[57] Cf. note 48 above.

CHAPTER THREE

Mir Hasan's "Enchanting Story"

MIR HASAN, the son of that Mir Zāhik to whom Sauda's verse brought so unenviable a fame, was born in Delhi probably in 1727 or 1728, and passed his early life there.[1] We do not know exactly when he left with his father to settle at Faizābād, in Oudh, but his own account tells us that it was "early in the days of my youth," and also that he did not want to go because it meant parting from a girl with whom he had fallen in love. From this we can infer that he probably witnessed the occupation, massacre, and looting of Delhi by Nādir Shāh in 1739. By comparison with

[1] The main source for the significant facts of Mīr Ḥasan's life is his own works. Two of these —the maṣnavī Gulzār i Iram and his taẕkira—contain brief autobiographical details. As indicated earlier, the date of his birth is disputed. Earlier authorities give it as A.H. 1140 (A.D. 1727–1728), but the most recent work on the subject, Maḥmūd Fārūqī's Mīr Ḥasan aur Khāndān ke dūsre shuʿarā, states that the correct date is A.H. 1151 (A.D. 1738–1739). However, he gives no adequate evidence for preferring this later date. It is known, he says, that Mīr Zāhik left Delhi and reached Faizābād while Ṣafdar Jang was still ruler of Oudh—i.e., before 1754—and therefore favours a date around A.H. 1163–1164 (A.D. 1750–1751) for this event. Then, taking this as the basis of his calculations, and noting that Mīr Ḥasan says that it was "early in his youth" that he left Delhi, he rejects 1140 as the date of his birth on the grounds that an age of 23–24 cannot be described as "early youth." However, if 23–24 is too old, 12–13 is surely too young. Mīr Ḥasan says that he left Delhi with a heavy heart because he had fallen in love there— an important statement which the authorities, with their customary sense of decorum, pass over in discreet silence. Further, Mīr Ḥasan figures in Mīr's taẕkira, and this is know to have been written in A.H. 1165 (A.D. 1750–1751); and it is hardly likely that he would already have made his name as a poet at the age of 14. Lastly, the mere knowledge that it was during Ṣafdar Jang's governorship of Oudh that Mīr Ḥasan and his father left Delhi does not warrant fixing this event in A.D. 1750–1751, for Ṣafdar Jang had been governor since 1739. For these reasons we incline to think that A.D. 1727–1728, or soon after, is the likely date of his birth.

The text of the masnavi Siḥr ul Bayān which we have used is that edited by ʿAbdul Bārī Āsī (Lucknow, 1941).

Mir and Sauda, his subsequent life seems to have been uneventful, for the province of Oudh in which he lived enjoyed relative peace during this period. All the same, his life was not an easy one. His patrons, unlike Sauda's, seem to have been none too generous. Mir Hasan himself hints at this, writing that he "received enough to live on," while a contemporary writer says bluntly that he "lived in penury."[2]

Although several manuscripts are extant, his collected verse has never been published. It contains poems in all the classical forms, but like his great contemporaries, he excelled in one form in particular, and devoted his main attention to it. As Sauda is the master of the qasīda and of satirical verse, and as Mir is the master of the ghazal, so Mir Hasan is the master of the masnavi. He wrote eleven in all, and some of them are of considerable length. But his fame is based on one of them alone, so much so that it is regularly called "Mir Hasan's masnavi," as though it were the only one he had written. This is the masnavi *Sihr ul Bayān* (The Enchanting Story),[3] a long poem of over 2,000 couplets. Completed in 1785, only two years before his death, it won immediate acclaim, and its popularity remains undiminished to this day. If one can only deplore the neglect of his other works, it nevertheless underlines the extraordinary popularity of this one, which has been published and republished innumerable times. This is the story it tells:

In a splendid city there once ruled a great and powerful king. His dominion extended far and wide, and kings as far away as Central Asia and China acknowledged themselves his vassals. Words cannot describe the beauty and prosperity of the capital. The streets were all paved, the buildings all solidly constructed and of dazzling whiteness; tanks and wells, fountains and watercourses, abounded in the city, which was made beautiful with parks and gardens in every quarter; and over all towered the great fort where the king held his court. The extent of the city was vast, and such was the prosperity and good order which reigned there that men flocked to it from near and far, and those who arrived penniless, quickly became rich and prosperous. In its bazaars one might see the finest craftsmen of every land and clime, and the splendour of the main market was such that to enter it was to linger on,

---

[2] Both statements are quoted by Maḥmūd Fārūqī, p. 41.
[3] *Sihr ul Bayān* literally means "the enchantment of story."

unwilling to depart. In the fort all was luxury and enjoyment, and beautiful slave girls stood constantly ready to satisfy every need.

Yet amid all this prosperity and happiness the king was not happy. For though he was now advanced in years, he had no son to bring joy to his heart and to succeed to the throne when he was gone. One day he called his ministers to him and said, "It is time for me to leave the world. What use is all this wealth and magnificence when I have no son to succeed me? In my concern for the affairs of state I have neglected my duties towards God. It is better now that I should forsake my kingdom and give myself up to religious contemplation." His ministers replied, "Such a course is not good, your majesty. You are a king, and you cannot fulfil your religious duty by neglecting that which your position lays upon you. Devote yourself to the service of God, but do so by ruling as a great and good king should, so that on the Day of Judgement you can stand before your Judge with a clear conscience and a good heart. And do not commit the sin of despairing of God's mercy. Who knows but that you may yet have a son? Call the Brahmins, the astrologers and geomancers, and ask them what the future holds in store for you." The king accepted their advice, and on an appointed day the astrologers and others waited upon him to determine by their studies what would be the future course of events. Every method of divination was used, and all foretold that in due course a son would be born to the king. Finally the king called upon the Brahmins to speak. They replied, "Your Majesty will have a son as beautiful as the moon, and your grief is now destined to be turned into joy; if it is not so, then we are not Brahmins. But there is something else prescribed by fate. For twelve years your son is threatened by danger. He must never be allowed to go up onto the roof of the palace; nor during all those years must he venture outside the palace walls. His life is not in danger, but it seems that he is fated to dwell some time in the wilderness. Some jinn or fairy will fall in love with him, and he will fall in love with some lady." The king heard their words with mingled joy and grief, but resigned himself with a trusting heart to the will of God and spent much time in earnest prayer. And before the year was out, one of his queens was with child.

Eventually a beautiful boy was born, to whom the name of Benazīr was given. At the good news great crowds assembled outside the palace.

The king distributed his bounty generously as a mark of his rejoicing, and by his decree the occasion was celebrated with music and dancing, and with feasting and festivity which lasted for six whole days. Celebrations no less magnificent marked the boy's first birthday; when he learned to walk, slaves were set free in his name as a token of rejoicing; and his weaning, as he entered his fourth year, was again the occasion of public rejoicings.

The king now built for the boy a beautiful garden, and equipped it with buildings and furnishings of indescribable magnificence. There were canopies and curtains of cloth of gold, cords of gold and silver thread, screens adorned with fine paintings, carpets of velvet, lamps which as they burned spread fragrant perfume throughout the rooms, furniture studded with jewels, and mirrors on all sides to enhance the beauty still further. The garden was laid out with walks and watercourses of marble, lined with cypresses and other graceful trees and beautiful flowers. Sweetly singing birds lived in the garden, and lovely maids were always at hand to serve the prince and keep him company. In this atmosphere of beauty the prince began his education; from the beginning he showed great promise, and within a few years he had mastered all the traditional and scientific branches of learning. Rhetoric, logic, literature, medicine, astronomy, geometry, astrology, calligraphy, archery, cudgel fighting, music, painting, the use of firearms—he was well-versed in all; and, above all, he learned the human kindness and consideration which is the hallmark of a real man, loving the company of good and talented men and despising that of the mean and worthless.

So the years passed by, and Benazīr reached his twelfth birthday. On this long-awaited day the king gave orders to prepare a state drive through the streets of the capital, and sent word that his son should be taken to the baths and then dressed in princely array ready to go out in procession. All that the king commanded was joyfully carried out. Lovely maidservants massaged his body and bathed him, joining happily in his involuntary laughter as the pumice stone tickled the soles of his feet; then they dressed him in clothes of the finest cloth and adorned him with jewels and pearls, and so made him ready.

Great was the enthusiasm of the people as the procession started out, amid a scene of breath-taking magnificence. As the prince came out, trays of pearls were scattered over his head and left where they fell on the ground for the bystanders to gather up. The city was a wonderful sight. The walls of all the buildings, the shops, and the houses were draped with decorations made of the finest silks and brocades, and big mirrors set up on all sides heightened the gaiety and colourfulness of the scene. There were horsemen riding two by two, lines of hundreds of elephants bearing their riders in gold and silver howdahs, palanquin-bearers dressed in resplendent livery hurrying here and there, and the flat roofs thronged with people dressed in their finest clothes, as the procession, to the sounds of drums and trumpets, and with standards and banners waving, made its way from the palace to the farthest bounds of the city. There the king and the prince refreshed themselves a while in a garden before returning as night fell to the palace. In the palace, revelry continued until late into the night.

It was the night of the full moon, and when the prince began to feel sleepy he thought how pleasant it would be to sleep, for the first time, on the palace roof. The maidservants conveyed his wish to the king, who gave his consent, stipulating only that watch should be kept over him as he slept.

But there had been a miscalculation. Unknown to the king and his servants, the twelve years of danger were not yet past, and one night still remained.

So the prince's bed was made on the palace roof, and he lay down to sleep in the quiet of the moonlit night and amid the scent of the flowers. Soon a cool breeze sprang up, and those who had been appointed to watch over him fell fast asleep. Only the full moon kept her watch above.

It so happened that a fairy,[4] travelling through the air on her flying throne, chanced to pass that way, and as she looked down, her glance fell upon the sleeping prince. Entranced by his great beauty, she brought her throne down onto the roof and advanced to where he was sleeping in a moonlight so brilliant that it seemed as though the whole earth and sky were radiant with it. She drew back the coverlet and

---

[4] "Fairy" is not really a satisfactory translation of the Urdu (and Persian) *parī*, for the English word suggests a tiny creature with gossamer wings, whereas a *parī* was a supernatural being in the form of a lovely woman. *Parī* has been naturalized in English as *peri*, but we have used the more familiar word despite its inadequacy.

pressed her cheek to his, and then carried him off, still sleeping in his bed, to the fairy kingdom.

When the maidservants awoke and found that the prince had vanished, they were overcome with grief. The bad news was quickly carried to the king and queen; the king himself came in tears to the spot from where the prince had vanished, but no trace of him could be found. As day broke, the news spread throughout the city, which was plunged into mourning. Even the trees and flowers, the birds and streams, seemed to join in the general sorrow, for though search was made far and wide and no expense was spared, there was no news of the prince to be brought back to the palace.

Meanwhile Benazīr was a prisoner in fairyland. The years passed by, and though he was treated with every consideration and surrounded with every luxury, he pined for the happy life he had led in his father's palace, surrounded by those who loved him. The fairy, who was named Māhrukh, tried all she could to dispel his grief, but without effect. One day she came to him and said, "Benazīr, you are my prisoner; but it makes me sad to see you pining like this. So listen to what I propose. Every evening I leave you here alone and go to visit my father, and in solitude you grow more and more dejected. So I will give you a magic horse, and for three hours every evening you may ride out on it and amuse yourself. It will carry you through the air wherever you want to go. But in return you must give me your written undertaking that if you give your heart to anyone else, then you will acknowledge your fault and accept my punishment." Benazīr accepted this condition, and Māhrukh gave him the magic horse[5] and showed him how to control it. After that he would go out every evening, but would always take care to return when the striking of the hour told him that his time was up.

He rode out one night at the beginning of the cold season. A cool breeze was blowing and the stars and the moon shone brightly in the sky, and as he rode on, he saw below him a lovely garden, and in it a building shining dazzling white in the moonlight. Attracted by the scene he came down onto the roof, and leaning over, tried to discover whether anyone were there. So charming was the scene that he made

---

[5] The words of the original make it clear that the "magic horse" was a kind of machine, and not a living creature.

up his mind to go down into the garden. He tiptoed down the stair and out of the door, and keeping in the shadows, made for a cluster of trees where he could see without being seen. As he looked around, he could see all the signs of people living there, and it was not long before he caught sight of a group of women sitting by a watercourse. In the centre sat a fifteen-year-old princess,[6] a girl of great beauty, reclining with her elbow on a cushion, and surrounded by her lovely hand-maidens as the shining moon is surrounded by stars. She was dressed in fine and delicate fabrics through which her fair body gleamed as the candle gleams in the chandelier, and was adorned with pearls and jewels of great price. Benazīr stood entranced in his hiding place, lost in admiration of her great beauty—the beauty of her form, and of her dress, and of her whole bearing—and as he stood there, one of the maidservants caught sight of him. Amid much excitement the word passed from one to another that someone was hiding behind the trees, until the princess herself heard it. In great agitation she called her maids to help her to rise and take her to the trees so that she might see for herself what was there. Though she summoned up all her courage, it was in fear and trembling that she went. In front of her walked some of her trusted maids repeating prayers for heavenly protection. When they reached the trees, they saw that a handsome young man was standing there motionless, either because there was no way of with-drawing from where he stood, or because love and amazement rooted him to the spot. He seemed to be about fifteen or sixteen years old, in the bloom of youth, finely dressed and adorned with jewellery. The girls were entranced at the sight of him, and quickly turning back, told their mistress, in the indirect way which delicacy demanded, of what they had seen, and assuring her that there was nothing to fear, urged her to come forward. Badr i Munīr (for that was the name of the princess) came forward, and as her eyes met those of Benazīr, both were smitten with love and fell down in a swoon.

With Badr i Munīr was her closest friend, the Vazīr's daughter Najm un Nisa, a girl of great beauty and full of the spirit of mischief. She now ran and fetched rose water, and by sprinkling it over her friend, succeeded in reviving her and helping her to rise. Benazīr too

[6] A year older than Shakespeare's Juliet.

had now come to his senses and was standing there lost in love and admiration. But Badr i Munīr averted her face from him and then turned and walked away, leaving him faint with love as he gazed at the nape of her neck and her shoulders and her slender waist and her long plait of black hair swinging across her hips. She knew very well the effect of her beauty upon him and was secretly glad. She wished to appear angry, but love was in her heart, and with her face hidden from him, she smiled as she said, "Who is this wretch who intrudes upon the privacy of my garden?" And so saying, she went quickly into the house, letting fall the curtain behind her.

Najm un Nisa came to her laughing and said, "Badr i Munīr, such deceitful airs are not good. Do not leave the young man to die of love for you. And you too should enjoy the pleasures of life and love while you are young: do as your heart tells you, and forget the heavy burdens which religion and society lay upon you. Your youth and beauty will pass away and never return, and missed opportunities do not come again. This handsome youth has come to you unbidden; so quickly make preparations to receive him and for the wine to flow." Badr i Munīr smiled and answered her, "Yes, Yes! I see! The young man has taken your fancy and I am to be the excuse for entertaining him." "I admit it," returned Najm un Nisa smiling. "It was I who fainted at the sight of him and you who revived me with rose water. Very well then, for my sake do as I tell you and send for him to come." With these words she quickly went and brought Benazīr and seated him in a room; and then taking Badr i Munīr by the hand, she brought her in and made her sit at Benazīr's side. Badr i Munīr came unwillingly, and took care as she seated herself that no part of her body should touch his. For a long time the two lovers sat side by side in embarrassed silence, each too shy to speak to the other, until Najm un Nisa lost patience and said to Badr i Munīr, "Why do you sit there without speaking a word? Here, take this cup and give it to your guest, and, if only for my sake, smile and talk a little." Badr i Munīr did not reply, but smiled and took up the cup, and then averting her face held out the cup to Benazīr and in indirect language invited him to take it. Benazīr laughed and drank first one cup and then another; then he in turn filled the cup and offered it to Badr i Munīr. With the wine their conversation began to flow more freely, and Benazīr told his whole story to the princess.

When he came to speak of the fairy, Badr i Munīr frowned and drew away from him and said, "You are welcome to your fairy and she is welcome to you. I am not one to share a lover with anyone else. You don't care for me, so why should I break my heart for you? Be off now, and do not come again." At these words Benazīr fell at her feet and cried, "Ah, Badr i Munīr! What am I to do if you turn me away? It makes no difference how much she loves me; what do I care for her? Body and soul I am yours and yours alone." "Take your head off my feet," she replied, "How am I to know what is in your heart?" But all the same she was pleased by his answer and no longer pressed him to go. And so as they sat talking together, the hour struck when Benazīr must leave. He started up and said, "Badr i Munīr, I must go. If I can escape again, I will come tomorrow at the same time. Do not think that there is any pleasure for me there, but what am I to do? I am completely within her power. God knows I do not want to leave you. I go leaving my heart here with you. Be kind to me and understand my plight." And so he went, leaving her as agitated as himself.

Somehow he passed the night with Māhrukh, and set himself to endure the heavy hours which must pass before evening came round again and he could fly to Badr i Munīr. She on her side awaited his coming with the same feelings in her heart. As she sat sadly alone, Najm un Nisa came to her, trying to drive away her sorrow and take her mind off her grief. "Tonight," she said, "I should like to see you dressed and adorned so that your beauty is seen in all its perfection"— and though Badr i Munīr scolded her, Najm un Nisa had only spoken what was already in her own mind. That day she bathed and performed her toilet with such care that she looked like a newly-wedded bride. Meanwhile, maidservants prepared the palace for the evening's meeting. They laid costly carpets on the floor, draped the rooms with hangings of silk and laid upon the bed coverlets worked with jewels. They made the rooms fragrant with flowers and with precious perfumes and brought in sweetly-smelling rare fruits. At the head of the bed they placed a richly bound volume of the selected verse of the great Persian poets Zuhūri and Nazīri, and another of the great Urdu poets, Sauda and Mir and Mir Hasan. Wine was made ready and detailed instructions given for the preparation of the food. In short, nothing was left undone, and when everything was ready Badr i Munīr went out to walk in the garden until evening.

Benazīr too prepared himself with special care for the meeting with his beloved, and when at last he was free to go, flew with all speed to the garden where she was walking.

She saw him coming and quickly hid herself behind some trees where she could stand unobserved and admire her lover's appearance. One of the maidservants came surreptitiously to her and asked her where they were to conduct the prince; and when they had seated him in the room which had been made ready for him, Badr i Munīr herself made her appearance in all her breath-taking beauty. Benazīr was fired with passion, and seizing her hand, led her resisting to sit by him. She struggled to free her hand, telling him scathingly to keep this warmth for the one he really loved; but he passionately rebuked her, telling her to torture him no more by such words but to sit at his side and give herself freely and unashamedly to his embrace. At length she was persuaded to sit down beside him, and as the wine cup passed from one to the other, they began to talk in a fashion which made the maidservants lower their eyes for shame and find pretexts one after another to withdraw from the room. Then Benazīr led Badr i Munīr to the bed, where they lay in one another's arms and drank the wine of union together, enjoying their love to the full. At length they came out from the bedchamber, the one radiant, the other pale, and sat silently together, still drunk with the wine of passion, until at the sounding of the hour, Benazīr rose with a start to take his leave. Badr i Munīr's face was the picture of distress: she neither looked at him nor spoke. "Darling, do not be angry with me; I shall come again," he said. "As you wish," she replied, and he left her, heavy at heart because she was displeased with him, and with the tears running down his cheeks.

But the following night he came again, and after that he would come every day; and in each other's company they would forget the grief which oppressed them during the hours of separation.

But fate never allows lasting happiness to anyone. One day a giant came to Māhrukh and told her that her captive had given his heart to someone else, and that as he flew over the garden, he had seen the two lovers standing hand in hand. Māhrukh was furious, and the moment

Benazīr returned, she poured out all her wrath upon him. "Did you not give me your written undertaking?" she cried. "Then prepare to honour your word, and take the punishment which I shall inflict upon you." At once she summoned a huge jinn and commanded him to drag Benazīr away to the desert and throw him down a dried-up well; there he was to be held imprisoned, and the mouth of the well closed by an enormous rock. The jinn was to feed him only once a day at evening, and no one was to pay any attention to his cries. So Benazīr was thrown into the dark well, from which there was no way of escape.

The next evening Badr i Munīr waited in vain for Benazīr to come, and the evening after that and the one after that. When several days had passed and she grew sick with love and sorrow and disappointment, she spoke to Najm un Nisa. "What can have happened to him?" she asked. Najm un Nisa, hoping to shock her out of her dejection, replied harshly, "Lady, are you mad? Do you think these handsome young men think twice about anyone? God alone knows where he is now or what he is doing. I have no patience with people who simply surrender themselves to love. Could you not control yourself? In love you must act as your lover acts. If he seems cool, you too be cool; if he inclines towards you, only then incline towards him." Badr i Munīr made no reply.

As the days passed she became immersed more and more in her sorrow, increasingly indifferent to all that went on around her. She would roam about the garden like someone distracted, lingering among the trees. She slept uneasily at night, and had bad dreams; and during the day she was always looking for some excuse to go to her bed, where she could be alone and weep. All appetite left her, and often when people spoke to her, she did not hear or could not bring her attention to bear on what they said, so that her answers had nothing to do with their questions. If others had not brought her food and drink, she would never have thought of it. Day and night Benazīr's image was before her eyes, and in her heart she talked to him alone. Sometimes she would sing poems of the sorrow of love, but generally even poetry had no charm for her. One day she rallied herself sufficiently to go into the garden and send for her dancing girl Aish Bāi to come and entertain her with song and dance. But though all the listeners were held spellbound by the grace and beauty of her performance, to Badr i Munīr the words and music only revived poignant memories, and bursting into tears she left the garden and went to her bed to weep.

A whole month passed in this way, and still Benazīr did not come. Badr i Munīr was on the verge of madness, unable to eat or sleep, completely heedless of her dress and appearance and even of the need to preserve a decent discretion about her love. Najm un Nisa made one more attempt to rally her. "Why do you grieve yourself so?" she said. "You who could once have given wise advice to others are today yourself behaving like a fool. What madness is this, to give your heart to a passing stranger? These travellers never stay in one place for long, and wherever they go, there they declare their love. You should know better, dear, than to give your love until your wooer has given unmistakable proof of his; and if he shows no concern for you, then you too should banish him from your thoughts. He has his fairy and is content with her. Otherwise would he have stayed away so long?" Badr i Munīr, gently but with deep emotion replied, "Listen to me, my dear. It is not good to speak ill of people, for only God knows everything about them. As for me, I know he is true at heart, and I am afraid only for what may have happened to him, that for all these days he has not come. Perhaps the fairy has heard of what happened here and has imprisoned him or given him over to some ogre to devour. I only know that for him I have borne all the sorrow of separation, and I would give my own life that he might live." Then bursting into tears she huddled herself up in the corner of her bed and covered her head with the coverlet.

When at last she fell asleep, she had a dream. She thought she saw, in the middle of a vast desert, a well closed by an enormous stone from which came the voice of Benazīr speaking of his love for her, and telling her of his plight. She tried to call to him, but no sound would come, and at this point she awoke. Though driven nearly to distraction, she at first told no one of her dream. But at last she could contain herself no longer, and calling her closest friends to her (and Najm un Nisa amongst them), she revealed her dream to them. Najm un Nisa at once made up her mind. "Do not weep any more," she said. "From now on lay all your sorrows upon me. I am going to the desert to find Benazīr and bring him back to you. If I live, I will return to throw myself at your feet again. And if I die, why then, I die, and I will gladly die for your sake." Badr i Munīr implored her not to risk her life in so dangerous an undertaking, saying that her company was the one thing that gave her some consolation and that without her she would die. But Najm un Nisa replied, weeping, "I cannot bear to see you like this, for the grief it brings me is more than I can endure." And weeping all the time, she tore her fine clothes and threw them aside. Then, putting on the dress of a wandering Hindu ascetic, and taking a lute with her, she got ready to go. Badr i Munīr and her companions gathered around her weeping, telling her not to forget them and praying that God's protection might go with her and bring her safely back.

So Najm un Nisa set out to wander in the desert, in the hope that sooner or later she might find out where Benazīr was. Wherever she sat down for a while, she would play on the lute, and all living creatures would listen, enthralled by the music and by the great beauty of the player, which her simple disguise enhanced rather than concealed.

One bright moonlight night in the desert she sat down to play. It was the night of the full moon, which shone so brilliantly that it seemed as though a dazzling white sheet had been laid down over the earth. Every thorn and blade of grass shone bright and clear; the leaves of the trees glistened with light and beneath them light and shade mingled as though the moonlight had passed through a net. As she began to play, the birds and beasts forgot their sleep, the breeze began to dance in the treetops in ecstasy, and the very moonlight lay still as though entranced. And at this moment there happened to pass that way on his magic throne Fīroz Shāh, the son of the king of the jinns, a handsome youth of some twenty or twenty-one years. Hearing the sound of the lute, he brought his throne to earth and drew near to listen, and his eyes fell upon Najm un Nisa. One glance was enough to make him captive to her beauty, and sensing that her dress was some disguise he approached and spoke to her, asking what misfortune had impelled her to wander forth in her present style and where she had come from and where she wished to go. Najm un Nisa was quick to realise the effect of her beauty upon him, and smilingly rebuked him saying, "Turn your thoughts only to God or else return whence you came." Fīroz Shāh protested at her severity, promising to go if she wished, but asking first to be allowed to stay and listen to her playing. "Then sit there quietly," said Najm un Nisa, and she again began to play. Fīroz Shāh sat down on the sand in front of her and was soon lost in contemplation of her beauty and of the sweetness of the music. Najm un Nisa played on until dawn, and he sat there before her weeping unrestrainedly. She stopped, yawned, and placing the lute on her shoulder, rose to go, when Fīroz Shāh, quickly seizing her by the hand, brought her to his magic throne and carried her off protesting to his father's court. There he brought her before his father, praising her perfect mastery of the art of music, and urging him to persuade her to play for them. The king received her with great deference and placed a house at her disposal for as long as she wished to stay at his court. The whole day was passed in entertaining her, and when night fell Najm un Nisa was asked to sing and play on her lute before those assembled there. She expressed some displeasure at this request. "Ascetics are not concerned with singing and music, but only with God, and these repeated requests are not pleasing to me. But so long as I am in your house, I am under constraint to carry out your wishes." The king replied, "No, No! What are you saying? Your very presence here is a favour to us. If it is your own wish we will ask you to play, but God forbid that you should do so against your will." She replied, "You have spoken well; for not in commands but in submission will you attain your desires."

With this she began to play. The sweetness of the music moved every hearer to tears, but on none was its effect so profound as on Fīroz Shāh, who every moment fell more and more hopelessly in love with her. Gazing upon her, now from in front, now from other angles, sometimes watching her from behind one of the pillars of the great hall, sometimes in his imagination kissing her face, he moved restlessly among the audience, weeping all the time. She on her side stole occasional glances at him, noting with satisfaction the effect which she was having upon him, but quickly averting her gaze if ever their eyes met.

At length she stopped playing, though all those present felt as though they could have gone on gazing upon her and listening to her forever. The king praised her performance highly and asked her to favour them every evening by playing to them and to stay as long as she wished, regarding the palace as her own and taking without ceremony whatever

she wanted. Najm un Nisa replied disclaiming any interest in material
things, but agreeing to his request. Secretly she was well pleased with
the king's invitation, and saw already the possibility that through
Fīroz Shāh she might yet achieve the purpose for which she had set out.
After that she would go for a few hours every evening to the court, and
when she had passed the time in pleasant conversation and in playing
the lute, would return to her house.

Meanwhile the plight of the unhappy Fīroz Shāh grew ever more
desperate, and Najm un Nisa took a delight in making it so. His
simplicity was no match for her art. She showed herself now kind to
him, now cold, until he was helplessly in her toils. One day in desperation he determined to speak out at the next opportunity, and finding her alone, threw himself at her feet. But before he could speak Najm
un Nisa forestalled him. Smilingly she said, "What are you doing?
Why are you so agitated? Has my long stay here become a burden to
you? If so, I am ready to go, with my blessings upon you; there is no
need to fall at my feet to implore me." Fīroz Shāh replied weeping,
"Enough! I cannot bear to hear such words! Why do you still go on
torturing me? Do you not know what has happened to me? I am devoted to you body and soul. But you are cold and unkind towards me:
what is there that I can say to you?" Najm un Nisa replied, "Now tell
me clearly what you mean and why you have fallen at my feet." Fīroz
Shāh said, "My love, how can I conceal any longer the inmost desire
of my heart? I cannot bear to go on living apart from you: marry me
and make me your slave." At this Najm un Nisa laughed and said,
"Then listen attentively to what I have to tell you; perhaps if you can
do what I want, you too may be the gainer." "Tell me quickly," he
replied. "I will do whatever is in my power." Najm un Nisa now told
him her whole story, revealing who she was and why she had set out
in her present disguise. She concluded, "You too are a fairy; if you
search for him, you may find where Māhrukh has imprisoned Benazīr;
then by your help we may be reunited and all our desires fulfilled; and
perhaps you too may get what you want." "Give me your hand on it,"
he said, but Najm un Nisa scolded him, telling him not to presume.
Fīroz Shāh then called his people together, and after explaining the
situation to them, promised a rich reward to him who should discover
where Benazīr lay confined. The fairies went out in search of him, and

before many days had passed, one of them returned to claim his reward.

Fīroz Shāh now sent a letter to Māhrukh rebuking her in the strongest terms and demanding that on pain of severe punishment she must give up Benazīr and swear never again to form any attachment to a human. Māhrukh was forced to agree, and she replied acknowledging her fault and asking only that the affair should not be made known to her father. And so at long last Benazīr, haggard and emaciated, was freed from his imprisonment and brought on Fīroz Shāh's magic throne to fairyland. When he arrived there, Fīroz Shāh left Benazīr at a little distance and went to Najm un Nisa. "Come," he said, "I have brought Benazīr." Najm un Nisa started up in agitation, and demanding to know where he was, would have gone straight to him had not Fīroz Shāh restrained her for fear that her uncontrolled joy might bring her to grief. Then taking her hand in his, he led her to where Benazīr was sitting. "Look at him well," he said. "Is he the one whom you are seeking or not?" "Yes! Yes!" she said. "It is! It is!" Then going near to the magic throne, she said, "Stand aside, fairy, and let me take his misfortunes upon me."[7] Fīroz Shāh replied smiling, "Very well, but mind you do the same for me afterwards." But she brushed him aside with an impatient gesture and started to walk round the prince, taking his misfortunes upon her. Then, falling on his neck, she wept without restraint. Benazīr, to his surprise, saw that it was Najm un Nisa, and asked in bewilderment how she came to be there and what had led to his release. Then as they embraced one another she told him the whole story; and from that day his grief left him and happiness was his once more.

One day soon after it was decided that all three of them—Fīroz Shāh, Najm un Nisa, and Benazīr—should fly on the magic throne to Badr i Munīr. They brought the throne down behind the clump of trees where Benazīr had concealed himself on his first visit to the garden, and Najm un Nisa told them to keep themselves hidden there while she went alone to Badr i Munīr to prepare her for the good news. When she came to where Badr i Munīr was, she fell at her feet, and for a moment Badr i Munīr did not recognise her. When she did, she

---

[7] A literal translation of the Urdū phrase. In former times a woman would signify her love and devotion to a person by drawing her hands over his head and then cracking her fingers over her own temples in token of taking all his impending misfortunes upon herself.

welcomed her with the utmost joy and affection, saying that she had never expected to live until her return. She tried her best to rise, but had become so weak that she fell to the ground in the attempt to do so, apologising for the weakness which made it impossible for her to stand. Najm un Nisa walked round her, taking her misfortunes upon her. She well remembered how pitiable had been Badr i Munīr's condition at the time when they had parted; but now the ravages of grief had reduced her to a still more pitiable plight, and the appearance of the house, the garden, and the maidservants all was such as could result only from prolonged neglect. The talk and happy laughter had long been stilled and the singers and musicians long silent; and as she surveyed the desolate scene, Najm un Nisa wept. Yet as the rumour of her coming spread, everything stirred to life; the maidservants thronged around her, expressing their joy at her return and wanting to know all about her adventures, until Najm un Nisa in desperation had to plead the fatigue of her long journeyings and ask them to leave her in peace, promising however that she would relate the whole story next day.

When they had dispersed Najm un Nisa looked around to see that no one was within hearing and then said to Badr i Munīr, "Princess, won't you take a stroll with me? There is something I have to tell you." Then when they were quite alone, she said to Badr i Munīr, "I have brought your Benazīr." At these words, Badr i Munīr fainted. When she had come to herself, she asked, "Is he really here? Or are you trying to tease me?" Najm un Nisa replied solemnly, "I swear to you by my life; if I am speaking falsely, may I die!" Then in answer to Badr i Munīr's questions, she told how she had found out where Benazīr was, and had brought about his release, and how, along with another, she had brought him here. "But see what misfortune this has involved me in; in order to bring your Benazīr, I have had to bring another captive too. Still, now let me bring Benazīr to you; the other I will find some means of sending away." At this the princess laughed aloud. "Why do you try to deceive me?" she said. "No more of such deceitful tricks! Go and bring them both quickly." "Will you appear unveiled before the jinn then," asked Najm un Nisa, "without first asking Benazīr?"[8] "Surely you do not think he will say no?" she

---

[8] A husband may allow (or command) his wife not to observe *parda* with his intimate friends.

replied. "But if you have any doubt, go first and I will wait. Go and ask him what his wishes are." Najm un Nisa went quickly, and calling out to them, summoned them to the house. Then she asked Benazīr if she should bring Badr i Munīr. He replied in astonishment, "What is the matter with you, beautiful one? Is there *parda* between brother and sister? Fīroz Shāh is a brother to me. Do I not owe my life to him? What then have I to keep from his eyes?" Badr i Munīr heard his words from behind the screen, and came out of her own accord. Going shyly to where he was sitting, she sat down by his side, and he felt as though for the first time he had begun to live again. Tears came into his eyes, and as they sat together, it was a scene to excite compassion. There they sat, their eyes red with weeping, a feverish flush on their pale cheeks, their whole form weakened and emaciated from the sorrow of their long separation, each weeping for the other's plight, until Najm un Nisa grew worried and spoke up. "Do you hear me, Badr i Munīr? Has not Benazīr wept enough tears already because of you, that you by your own weeping give him further cause for grief? Enough now! Where has he the strength to bear more sorrow? I brought him to you so that your love might make him whole. Talk to him now of happier things, and may God never give you cause to weep again." At this they all laughed, and the succeeding hours passed pleasantly in happy conversation. The night was already long spent when they had the food brought in, and after satisfying their hunger, the two couples each went to their beds to spend the rest of the night in loving converse and in sleep. Badr i Munīr and Benazīr long lay together, each recalling the misfortunes now so happily past. Benazīr told her of the hardships of his imprisonment, and of how only his love for her and the slender hope of reunion with her at last had kept him alive. She told him of the strange dream she had had, and of how this had led Najm un Nisa to go out in search of him. Meanwhile Fīroz Shāh and Najm un Nisa lay talking together, and for all four of them morning dawned all too soon. They rose, and turn by turn went to take their bath; and now Najm un Nisa showed that she had still not used the full extent of her power over Fīroz Shāh. When she returned from the bath, she was clothed from head to foot in garments of the finest red silk, edged with a border of gold thread. Her fair body gleamed through them as the flame gleams through glowing coals, and on her firm young bosom, brought into prominence by the tightness of her bodice, the dark nipples stood out in contrast to the fairness of her breasts. Fīroz Shāh was as though stunned as he gazed on her beauty, but shame and modesty would not let him speak.

And so the four lovers began to pass their days happily together. But at the back of their minds they were haunted by the fear that their happy life together might again be broken by enforced separation. They determined, therefore, to take steps so that they could be married and there would no longer be any need for concealment. While Badr i Munīr and Najm un Nisa visited their parents, professing their desire to be with them again for a while after being parted for so long, Benazīr and Fīroz Shāh retired to a city where they could make all the necessary preparations, and then got ready to act.

A letter in royal style was sent to Badr i Munīr's father, the king Masūd Shāh. "O kings of kings, pride of Jamshed,[9] peer of Farīdūn, scion of Sikandar's line, in whom are realised the hopes of the world: Rustam in valour, Hātim in generosity—I come as a poor guest to your dominions, brought hither by my fate, seeking your kindness with the request that you make me your slave.[10] Such has ever been the custom of mankind, for by such alliances the work of the world prospers. Men well know me and the line from which I am sprung. I am a prince, the son of king Malik Shāh, and young and old have heard my fame, for my name is prince Benazīr." He then went on to vaunt his noble ancestry, the formidable power of his army, and the vast extent of his wealth, and in the end, after every show of modesty and humility, wrote these words: "He who works against the Law of Islam is my mortal enemy; if you accept my proposal, it is well. If not, consider me already at your gates." Masūd Shāh read and reread the letter, and considered carefully what he should reply. He noted the strength of Benazīr's forces, and reflected that if it came to war, the struggle would be a

---

9 Jamshed, the legendary Iranian king, is traditionally thought to be the inventor both of the wine and the cup; the "goblet of Jam" (*jām-e Jam*) is the marvellous glass which shows the whole world. Farīdūn is the Iranian king of yore who excelled by his justice; Sikandar is Alexander the Great, one of the leading heroes even in Muslim and Persian tradition; Rustam the great warrior of old Iran, is the hero of Iranian folklore and the central figure in Firdausi's epic *Shāhnāmeh*; Hātim was considered by the pre-Islamic Arabs as the model of generosity among the Bedouins, and his name has, for this reason, become proverbial in the Islamic East. (A.S.)

10 I.e., give me your daughter in marriage.

heavy one and its outcome uncertain. Besides, what harm could there be in the proposed marriage? There was nothing unusual in the proposal: such marriages were made every day. There and then he sent the following reply: ''After praise to God and his Prophet be it known that your letter has reached me. Were I not constrained by the Law of Islam, you should have seen what my answer would have been, and were I to demonstrate my power you should know that kings before whom you are nothing can lay no claim upon my consideration. Such vaunting as yours does not become a mere lad fresh from his mother's home and without the knowledge to discern what is good and what is bad. But what can I do? I am constrained by the ways of the world and by my regard for the Law of Islam, for he who departs from the road marked out by God and his Prophet shall assuredly not attain his ends. Let, then, a suitable date be decided. I have commanded you. Come!''

When the news of the betrothal became known, there was great rejoicing in the city, and in this atmosphere the preparations for the wedding were put in hand.

Eventually the longed for day arrived, and as the bridegroom's procession left the palace to make its way to the bride's house, people thronged to see it, some mounted on horses, some on elephants, some in carriages or palanquins, and some on foot. On all sides could be heard the clash of sword-hilt on shield as people moved about. Everywhere the drums were booming and the trumpets sounding. On platforms raised above the level of the streets, courtesans were dancing and singing as the wedding procession moved through the gorgeously decorated city. Thousands of lighted lamps lined the route and burned brightly on the top of the ceremonial arches. On all sides were raised platforms made beautiful with flowers and coloured lights and displays of fireworks. The bridegroom, his face veiled by the strings of pearls hanging from his brow, mounted on a fine, slow-stepping horse, fanned by fans of peacock feathers, surrounded by a transparent screen, and preceded by drums and music, came to the bride's house. There too festivities were in full swing as all the traditional wedding rites were duly performed.

After the marriage ceremony the bridegroom was led to the bride who was seated inside the palace, resplendent in her wedding dress, and there too the traditional rites were performed—the bridegroom was made to sit close to the bride facing her, she, however, remaining veiled. Then the Holy Quran was placed between them, and on it a small mirror into which the bridegroom looked, and as she removed her veil, he saw her face for the first time, reflected in the mirror. Then the bride was made to sit and sugar was sprinkled all over her, and the bridegroom ordered, with jesting and laughter, to take up the sugar with his mouth, now from her eyes, now from her lips, from her waist, from her feet. At length the time came for the bridal pair to leave for the prince's home, and the procession moved off amid scenes of undiminished merriment and rejoicing. Thus Benazīr and Badr i Munīr were united in marriage.

Only a few days later, at Benazīr's request, Najm un Nisa's father consented to give her in marriage to Fīroz Shāh, and with pomp and ceremony no less spectacular than that which had accompanied the wedding of the prince and princess, their wedding too was celebrated. And thus the heart's desire of all four lovers was accomplished.

Now came the time for them to part. Fīroz Shāh and his bride, promising often to visit their friends, departed on their magic throne to fairyland, while Benazīr prepared to bring his bride home to his parents' house. Returning with his army, he came to the outskirts of the city and pitched camp on the banks of a river. It quickly became known who he was, and the news spread like wildfire throughout the city that the vanished prince had returned. The news was carried to the king and queen too, but they could not believe that such good fortune could be theirs, and the king was only with difficulty persuaded to come and see for himself that it was none other than his son Benazīr. Benazīr saw him coming, and ran and fell at his feet crying, "Praise be to God that I am restored to your service once more!" The king, weeping copiously, raised him up and clasped him to his bosom and then fainted away from the excess of his joy.

The prince's return was greeted with universal rejoicing, and in token of their joy the people high and low brought gifts to the palace. Meanwhile Benazīr presented his bride to his parents. As they entered the palace, Benazīr's mother came forward to greet them, and embraced them both weeping tears of happiness. By the wish of his parents, Benazīr's wedding was again celebrated in his own city, and life and happiness soon returned in full measure to the capital and its people.

"And thus may you and I, "concludes Mir Hasan, "see our fortunes change. Thus may God reunite all dear ones who are parted; may we live, like them, in a thriving and prosperous city like theirs; may God rain his blessings upon my patron, the Navvāb Āsaf ud Daula, and may I, Mir Hasan, attain the happiness I seek."

In a prose summary a good deal is inevitably lost, for in the original a strongly rhythmical metre carries the story forward. Its basic unit is a foot of one short syllable followed by two longs, and the line consists of four feet, in the last of which the final long is dropped, so that the line runs ◡ — — | ◡ — — | ◡ — — | ◡ — .[11] English has the long-short-short of the dactyl and the short-short-long of the anapaest, but it cannot effectively match this metre, in which the regularity of the rhythm contributes a sense of continuous flow, while the preponderance of long syllables prevents the verse breaking into a gallop. Nor can an English summary easily convey the effectiveness of Mir Hasan's diction. He seems to write with effortless simplicity, yet he tells us at the end of the poem that the labour he had spent upon it had changed him into an old man, and we realise how much care lies behind the apparently spontaneous expression. All Urdu critics have been struck by the freshness and, so to speak, the timelessness of his language. One, writing a century after Mir Hasan's death, said, "His language is that which you and I speak today. Turn to the verse of his contemporaries, and you will find on every page words and constructions which today are obsolete . . . Turn to his, and, apart from a few words, what you find is as current now as it was then." [12] And after the lapse of another hundred years the words are still valid today.

The same apparent simplicity conceals the skill with which he uses the devices of rhetoric. Some of these—the vivid similes, for example—come across in English, but there are others that defy translation. Many depend upon verbal conceit of the kind one finds in the earlier plays of Shakespeare, and their use—in both poets—sometimes seems, to modern taste, to detract from the charm of the poetry rather than add to it. Aptly used, however, they do make an appeal—as where, early in the

---

[11] This metre is called *mutaqārib*, and was also used in the greatest epic poem of Persian literature, Firdausī's *Shāhnāmeh*. (A.S.)

[12] Āzād, *Āb i Ḥayāt*, p. 250.

poem, the king's earnest prayers for the gift of a son are described, and Mir Hasan continues: "Udhar lau lagāya to pāya cirāgh." The words *lau lagāya* and *cirāgh* bear both a literal and a metaphorical meaning. "Lau lagāna" means literally to light a flame and metaphorically to concentrate one's whole thought on something. "Cirāgh" means literally a lamp, but is also the regular metaphor for a son, who brings radiance to his parents' home. Here the metaphorical meaning is the primary one: the king concentrated all his thought on prayer, and obtained a son. But Mir Hasan has just told us that as part of his devotions the king set a lamp in the mosque and kept it constantly burning; so the literal meanings are also relevant and help to heighten the atmosphere.

The poem shows an equally firm grasp of the larger aspects of craftsmanship. It has the steady flow, the sense of proportion between the constituent parts, and the timely variation of theme which the art of narrative demands. The descriptive passages are, in general, long enough to add colour to the story, but not long enough to pall. There is an eye for vivid and significant details which evoke a whole atmosphere. Thus Mir Hasan, describing how Najm un Nisa ceases playing her lute as dawn breaks, says, "She stopped, yawned, and placing the lute on her shoulder, rose to go"—and the one word "yawned" conveys all the pretended indifference by which she aims to captivate Fīroz Shāh. In every part of the poem there are vivid touches like these—the young prince in the bath, laughing as the pumice stone tickles his feet; Badr i Munīr's long black plait swinging across her hips as she turns to go back to the palace; Benazīr at his marriage being compelled by the laughing womenfolk to take up with his mouth the sugar sprinkled over his bride; and many more.

The Enchanting Story belongs to what may be described as the Arabian Nights class of literature, and one does not therefore look for complex analysis of character in it; it is a tale, not a novel. But the portrayal of the characters is convincing, if not deep, and they are presented not through static descriptions but through their actions and their speech. When Najm un Nisa is first introduced, Mir Hasan's own comment on her is confined to just half a line, in which we are told that she is "a girl of great beauty and full of the spirit of mischief." After that her dialogue and her actions are allowed to speak for themselves. Once again, English can only partially convey the excellence of the dialogue. The whole tone—even the turns of phrase—of each speaker is in character. That of the Brahmin astrologers is proud and self-assured, and contains more Hindi [13] words than the other characters employ (except Najm un Nisa in her role of Hindu ascetic); Māhrukh's is shrill and coarse; Najm un Nisa's, mischievous, self-possessed, and full of humour; Badr i Munīr's, simple and sincere.

The appeal of the poem owes much to the skill with which Mir Hasan has blended romanticism with realism—literary methods that are too often regarded as mutually exclusive. All critics have agreed that the masnavi is a romantic poem; but generally all they have meant by this is that it is a love story with a happy ending, or that the supernatural plays a part in it. Both these things are true, but neither contributes much to the understanding and appreciation of the poem. The fact that the characters include supernatural beings is of quite minor importance; like the fact that the other characters are all royal personages or their close associates, it represents nothing more than Mir Hasan's use of a convention which had been established for this kind of romantic masnavi long before his day. The characters, both supernatural and human, are universal in their significance; their emotional experience is universal human experience; and it is with the treatment of this experience that Mir Hasan is concerned. *The Enchanting Story* is a romantic poem in a deeper sense. The poet does not place his story in a setting drawn from the real world which he sees around him, or from that of an earlier historical period; the world he portrays is largely an idealised world, in which the aspirations of the poet and of his audience are shown as being realised, and in which men live happily in a community where true love ultimately triumphs over all difficulties. Yet this world is depicted with all the power of the realistic method.

Mir Hasan's portrayal of love illustrates this method. The description of love and of the emotions to which the lovers' experiences give rise is absolutely real. But the setting is largely unreal. Neither in Mir Hasan's own day nor in the earlier period of the glory of the Mughal Empire, which he consciously recalls, did the course of true love run so smooth as it does in *The Enchanting Story*. As we shall see later, true love stories in the social conditions of Mughal India were nearly all tragedies. Of course,

---

[13] Hindī is the other literary form of the dialect on which Urdū is based. Its literature has a Hindu background in the same sense as Urdū literature has a Muslim background.

there are in the poem allusions to the need for secrecy and to the lovers' fears that discovery may dash all their hopes and doom them to enforced and permanent separation; but these things are touched on in the lightest possible way and are given no prominence. In real life the tragedy of separation is due to the conditions of social life; in *The Enchanting Story* it is due to the power of Māhrukh over Benazīr, a power achieved and maintained by supernatural means.

Much the same is true for Mir Hasan's picture of the society in which his story is set. He depicts a society in which the atmosphere is one of general happiness, a society abounding in wealth, where kings rule justly, where the leaders of society conform to the highest ideals that popular opinion prescribes for them, and where the subjects live in peace and prosperity. But here too the element of realistic description is strong. No city ever existed like that described in the opening pages of the narrative, but imperial Delhi had once resembled Mir Hasan's imaginary city in many ways, and it is the recollection of that Delhi which provides the basis of his picture. No prince ever existed so perfect in all accomplishments as the youthful Benazīr, but those familiar with the lives of such men as Bābur, the founder of the Mughal dynasty, and Akbar, its greatest representative, know that these men at an equally early age had accomplishments hardly less remarkable. The pomp and magnificence of the great royal processions are painted, so to speak, larger than life; but not so much larger that they do not bear a close resemblance to historical truth. Mir Hasan was still writing the masnavi when the British Governor-General visited Lucknow, and the fantastic magnificence of the welcome which Āsaf ud Daula gave him is well attested. Thus romance and reality are again fused into a single whole.

It may be because Mir Hasan wrote this, his greatest poem, so late in life, that his contemporaries did not rank him with Mir and Sauda. He himself ventured to differ from them. In the passage in the masnavi where he describes how in preparation for Benazīr's coming the maidservants placed "at the head of the bed . . . a richly bound volume of . . . the great Urdu poets, Sauda and Mir and Mir Hasan," he is, in a characteristically graceful way, asserting a claim to a place alongside them. One can only speculate as to the ways in which he felt he could compare with them. Perhaps he has in mind simply his mastery of the craft of poetry.

But the words could bear a deeper meaning: they could be a claim also that he upholds, with the same artistic power as they do, the values for which they both stand. And such a claim would be justified. His poetic method is distinct from theirs, but he does indeed share their essential outlook, and he fully deserves a place at their side.

CHAPTER FOUR

The Love Poetry of Mir

THE REPUTATION which Mir Hasan's *Enchanting Story* won him long over-shadowed that of other masnavi writers, and it was not until nearly a century later that the accomplishment of Mir in handling the same form began to be rediscovered.[1] His masnavis differ from Mir Hasan's in important respects, and we find for once that the textbook definition of masnavi suffers not from the usual fault of being overelaborate and over-precise but from the opposite defect. Masnavi means simply a poem in rhymed couplets. One has to add that, in Urdu at any rate, the largest single class of masnavis consists of love stories, and that these fall into two distinct classes. Some, like *The Enchanting Story*, are long romantic tales. Others are, in their essential story, directly realistic, and these are by convention much shorter poems. Mir's love masnavis are all of this second kind.

---

[1] The source for virtually the whole of this chapter is Mīr's own verse, collected in *Kulliyāt i Mīr*. At the time when the chapter was written, the best edition was that of 'Abdul Bārī Āsī (Lucknow, 1941). The slightly more comprehensive edition by Dr. 'Ibādat Barelavī, published from Karachi in 1958, is marred by numerous copyist's mistakes, and as this edition is now, like Āsī's, out of print, we have not thought it worth while to undertake the laborious task of collating the references to Āsī's edition with the paging of Dr. Barelavī's and giving references in terms of the latter. There are six dīvāns of Mīr's ghazals, and we have indicated in Roman numerals the dīvān from which each verse quoted has been taken. The references have been given as briefly as possible. Thus I.164.14 means that the verse comes from the first dīvān and will be found at line 14 on p. 164 of Āsī's edition of the *Kulliyāt*. Verses from poems not included in the dīvāns are referred to as (e.g.) *Kulliyāt*, p. 920, line 13.

Perhaps the best of them is *Mu'āmlāt i Ishq* (The Stages of Love),[2] in which he tells the tragic story of his own love affair with a frankness that has caused most critics to pass over the poem in discreet silence. Mir was perhaps eighteen years old when he fell in love with a girl who was already married to someone else.[3] She seems to have been related to him, perhaps quite closely; for the poem suggests that she was not expected to observe parda towards him with the same strictness as would be demanded outside the family circle. The poem, which was written long after the events it describes, does not tell the whole story, but recalls and describes in a series of pictures those episodes which remained especially vivid in Mir's memory.

It all began, he says, when he heard others in the family talking about the girl, praising her appearance and bearing, her good qualities and her kind nature. He became curious to see her, and when he did, he at once fell in love with her, and she with him, though she at first hid this from him. What followed may be told largely in Mir's own words:

> I would watch her whenever I was unobserved, but though my heart was full, I could not speak to her. Later we met discreetly when we could, and she was unfailingly kind and compassionate to me, though at times she would tease me too. For a long time things went no further than that, but in time we became more intimate, and she would let me hold her by the hand or touch her feet as I sat near her on the ground. I cannot describe her perfect beauty. She was as though cast in the mould of my desire, and her every limb was lovely. Her walk was incomparably graceful, and with all her beauty she was kind and loving too, and if she teased me, it was with such affection that it made me love her all the more. I would want to caress her, but she would only laugh, and would not let me. One day when she was eating betel leaf, I asked her to kiss me, and let me take the liquor of her mouth into my own; she laughed and refused at first, but later let me do as I wanted. Our love for each other increased, and I began to urge her to meet me where we should not have to fear any interruption. She too would speak of the same thing. But she kept delaying the day, and one day she said to me, "No good can come of our love; how long

---

[2] Literally, "Transactions of Love," but this sounds awkward in English, and "Stages" accurately conveys the structure of the poem. It occupies pp. 918–928 of the *Kulliyāt*.

[3] *Kulliyāt*, p. 920, line 13.

can we go on pining for each other like this ?'' I was too consumed by love to see the truth of her words, but today I think of them and weep.

How can I describe what I suffered in separation from her ? At nights I imagined her with me, but the days were unbearable. For years we did not see each other again. I was indifferent to the world, and to my wife and my children and my family. I would think with longing of the days when, in spite of all difficulties and dangers, I would sometimes come to her and sit silently by her. For her sake all my relatives and friends had set their faces against me and called me mad, and the meanest and most contemptible people had taunted me to my face. At last the grief of separation became more than either of us could bear. We met, and this time satisfied all the yearning of our hearts. We were together for several days, but there came a day when we again had to part. It was not her fault. Our fate was against us. She said, ''It is best that we should part for some time. In love there comes a stage when such things have to be faced. Do not think I am forsaking you, and do not grieve too much. As long as I live, you will be in my heart. I too grieve at this parting. But what can I do ? My honour must be my first concern.'' I could not speak in reply. I sat stunned and silent before her, trying to keep back the tears and speaking only if she spoke. After night fell, we parted, and I went from her lane as one who leaves behind him everything that is precious in the world.

I bear my sorrow alone. There is no one to whom I can tell my secret. Sometimes a message comes from her and I live again, but mostly nobody comes. How can I live parted from her like this ? The memory of her is always with me—her loveliness, her tender love for me, her gentle speech, her grief at my distress, her longing to see me happy—and every memory brings the tears to my eyes. I long to be with her again, and without her I shall die.

An affair of this kind involved the families of both sides in deep disgrace, for which they usually took their revenge on the lovers. In Mir's case they persecuted him so bitterly that they drove him mad, and this experience too he has described in another masnavi entitled *Khwāb o Khayāl i Mīr* (Mir's Vision).[4] He says he became afraid to look at the moon at night and yet felt an irresistible desire to look, and when he did

---

[4] *Kulliyāt*, pp. 968–974.

he fancied he saw there the form of a lovely woman. Her image began to be before his eyes night and day, and he could neither eat nor sleep because of her. Sometimes she would be kind to him; at other times she would seem to be angry. His preoccupation with her became more and more complete, and his madness more and more pronounced. His relatives and friends were deeply concerned for him and tried to get him cured. After trying amulets, spells, and incantations without success, they resorted to more drastic measures, and had bitter medicines administered to him; and when he showed an inclination to run away, they shut him in a small room—"narrower than the grave," says Mir—and half starved him, giving him only an occasional crust of bread and drink of water. They were afraid to come near him, and for hours together he was left alone in this cell. At length they decided to try the effect of bleeding him. Mir gives a vivid picture of the bloodletting. He lost so much blood that he became unconscious, and remained in a swoon until the next day. Violent noises were made to arouse him from it, and his eyes opened upon the same scene of the leech standing there with the lancet in his hand. More blood was let, until his clothes were all dripping wet and he again fell into a swoon. For days together after that he only occasionally recovered consciousness, and his life was despaired of. But as the days passed, his strength returned to him, and his madness gradually left him.

Mir's love story is a tragedy, and the realistic love masnavi in Urdu always is. This is not because the poets select only the tragic stories for their themes, but because in the society in which they lived, love *was* a tragedy. In their day love and marriage were two quite separate things, and were generally regarded not only as separate but also as mutually opposed. When a young man reached marriageable age, his parents would look for a bride for him, and she would have to be a Muslim of social status comparable to his own. When a suitable candidate was found, negotiations with her parents would follow, and if these succeeded, the marriage would be arranged. The boy and girl did not see each other until they were already man and wife. The main danger to this ordered course of life was love, and society exerted every effort to forestall the danger or to deal with it drastically if it arose. Its main preventive measures were parda and early marriage. Parda meant the most complete segregation of the sexes: no Muslim boy was allowed to see the face of any Muslim girl who had reached the age of eleven or twelve, except where close kinship precluded the possibility of their falling in love. In every house there were separate women's apartments—the *zanāna*—and a woman who went out of the house (which she rarely did) had to wear a *burqa*—a flowing garment which enveloped her completely from head to foot; a flap hanging down over the face, or a strip of material finer than the rest across the eyes, enabled her to see out without others seeing in. Early marriage was also a safeguard against love. Before marriage the boy was to have no chance to fall in love; after marriage, society hoped, he would have no occasion to.

In this way society did what it could to prevent love. When it could not prevent it, it punished it, and punished it drastically. A boy and girl who were unfortunate enough to fall in love brought great shame upon their families, who generally retaliated with savage persecution and even with murder, for the lovers were held to be violating laws upon which the very foundations of ordered social life were based. It is most important that the modern reader should realise that the lovers themselves did not quarrel with this view. They too believed that love was a force which threatened to disrupt the foundations of society, and that society was obliged to defend itself against it, even if they themselves were to be the victims. Stories of love were common, and if the average man felt sympathy for the lovers, he reacted also with the fervent hope that he himself would never fall in love. The love poets themselves often express this feeling. Thus Mir writes:

زنداں میں پھنسے طوق پڑے قید میں مر جائے

پر دامِ محبّت میں گرفتار نہ ہووے

Live in the chains of slavery, and die in jail
But do not fall into the snare of love. (I.165.16)

ان صحبتوں میں آخر جانیں ہی جاتیاں ہیں

بے عشق کو ہے صرف بے حسن کو محابا

To enter love's dominion is to throw your life away
For love makes no allowances, and beauty does not spare.

(I.24.24)

اگ تھے ابتدائے عشق میں ہم

اب جو ہیں خاک انتہا ہے یہ

I was all fire when first I fell in love:
Now at the last nothing but ash remains.   (I.136.10)

قیامت ہی یہاں چشم و دل سے رہی

چلے بس تو وہاں جا کے کرئے قیام

نہ دیکھے جہاں کوئی آنکھوں کی اور

نہ لیوے کوئی جس جگہ دل کا نام

Man's eyes and heart have plunged him in disaster—
If only he could go and make his home
Where no one ever looks into another's eyes,
And what is meant by "heart" is still unknown!

(I.90.13–14)

One verse pictures him on his deathbed, using his dying breath to impart
to a young friend the essence of his life's experience, and thinking how,
when he is dead, the boy will say:

وصیّت میرے نے مجھ کو یہی کی

کہ سب کچھ ہونا تو عاشق نہ ہونا

Mir's last behest to me was only this:
"Do what you will, my son, but do not love!" (II.236.17)

In his masnavis the same ideas are reiterated. Love is a fire in which the
lovers burn to death, or a raging sea in which they drown.⁵ One masnavi
concludes with the words:

⁵ *Kulliyāt*, p. 917, line 23; p. 901, line 10.

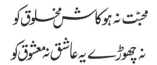

Would that mankind were immune to love,
For it spares neither lover nor beloved.
(*Kulliyāt*, p. 899, lines 19–20)

A boy growing towards maturity would feel this fear of love more than most, because he could not help feeling also the intensely strong desires which come with adolescence. The parda system intensified these desires by denying him an outlet for them, and also by the very view of love on which it was based; for its underlying assumption was that love is so powerful a force that only the most stringent measures could hope to combat it; and this very assumption helped to make it so. Thus the young man desired love as strongly as he feared it, and the modern reader can only with difficulty visualise something of the intense emotional stress to which this subjected him. It is this all-pervading fear which in Urdu poetry distinguishes the young lover from his counterpart in English literature, where the young man "in love with love," the passionate would-be lover who has no one to whom he can give his devotion, is a slightly comic, though not unsympathetic, figure. In Urdu poetry the comic aspect is overshadowed by the tragic.

Mir's masnavi *Darya i Ishq* (The River of Love)[6] shows what is likely to happen to one in his position. The story begins with a description of the boy and of his state of mind—"a handsome boy, tall and graceful as the cypress, his heart within him softer than wax, and with love in every fibre of his being"[7]—and goes on to tell how one day as he was passing down the street he saw a girl looking at him from the window of one of the houses. As soon as their eyes met, he fell in love with her, but she cared nothing for him, and rising from her seat, she shook out the folds of her dress and disappeared into the house. But he was in love with her, body and soul, and from that day onwards he spent every moment he could near her house, looking up again and again at the window at which he had first

---

[6] *Kulliyāt*, pp. 900–910.
[7] *Kulliyāt*, p. 901, lines 15ff.

seen her in the hope of catching sight of her again. People began to stare at him as they passed by, and some who thought he must have suffered some great mental shock showed sympathy for him. But it was not long before everyone realised what was wrong, and then he was blamed on all sides. His family and the girl's were near neighbours, and her parents soon came to suspect him. At first they planned to have him murdered, and so get rid of him once and for all, but then they reflected that responsibility might be traced to them and they would be disgraced. So they spread it about that the boy was mad, and egged people on to stone him and tor-ment him. He was quite unaffected by all this, and the vehemence of his love continued as before.

At length the girl's family thought it best to send her away to stay with relatives who lived in another city on the other side of the river. She set out, seated in a closed palanquin and escorted by her old nurse. Her lover, who was at his usual place in the lane where she lived, guessed that it was she who was being taken away, and ran beside the palanquin, calling out to the girl inside to have pity on him and relent towards him. She did not answer, but the old nurse saw her opportunity and spoke to him en-couragingly, holding out the hope that the girl would soon come to return his love and that one day they would be united. They reached the river, and went aboard the boat which was to ferry them across. When the boat was in mid-stream, the nurse took the girl's slipper and threw it into the water, and then challenged the boy, if he really loved her, to jump in and bring it back. He at once jumped in, but he could not swim and was drowned. The girl, who had until then been completely indifferent to him, was greatly moved by his devotion to her; but for the moment she said nothing.

Now that the young man was dead, there was no longer any reason why the girl should not be brought back home again, and escorted by her nurse as before, she set out on the return journey. As they made the return crossing, she told her nurse that she would like to see the river; for she had lived all her life in seclusion and had never seen a big river before. The nurse opened the palanquin so that she could see, and she asked a great many questions about all she saw, and in the end wanted to know where it was that the young man had jumped into the water and been drowned. When the boat reached the place, the nurse pointed it out, and the girl at once threw herself in and was drowned in the same

spot. When the nurse reached home and told her parents what had happened, they ran lamenting to the riverside. The river was dragged, and
the bodies of the two lovers, who in life had never been able to come together, were recovered clasped tightly in each other's arms.

Another masnavi tells the story of a young Afghan settled in Gujarat.[8]
He was a strikingly handsome young man, and yet he enjoyed no less a
reputation for the purity of his life, his modesty, and his devotion to his
religion. So shy was he, says Mir, that if one of the houris of Paradise had
advanced to meet him, he would have done his best to avoid her. Yet the
day came when he too fell in love, with a young Hindu woman who he
saw passing by in the street, and who looked at him as he glanced shyly
at her. In the same moment she fell in love with him. But neither spoke
to the other; they would see each other as she came up the road carrying
water from the well, and that was all. In short, they behaved as true
lovers should, and neither did anything which could bring the other into
bad repute. A long time passed, and the woman's husband fell ill and
died; and she, as the Hindu custom of *sati* (suttee) demanded, went to be
burned on her husband's funeral pyre. When her lover heard of it, he
ran to the place and threw himself into the flames, determined that if she
must die, he too would burn to death with her; but bystanders rushed in
and dragged him away, badly burnt, but still alive. They set out to take
him home, where his injuries could be treated; but after they had gone
some way, he asked them to lay him down for a while in the shade of a
tree at the roadside, until he had recovered enough strength to continue
the journey. He lay there the whole day until evening. For most of the
time his eyes were closed, but whenever they did open, they turned to
look back along the way they had come. As evening fell a woman was seen
coming down the road, and as she drew near, she was recognised as the
widow who had been burnt on the pyre that morning, looking now just
as she had done in life. Everyone was too amazed to move as she went up
to the boy and held out her hand to help him rise. Then hand in hand
they walked away together down the road and were never seen again.

In *Sho'la i Shauq* (The Flame of Love) the story portrays a situation unusual in eighteenth-century life and literature alike, where the lovers are
husband and wife. The central character is a young Hindu named

[8] *Kulliyāt*, pp. 911–917.

Parasrām.[9] He was a very good-looking boy, and was loved and admired by many of his friends. Among these was one whose love Parasrām returned, and the two would spend much of their time in each other's company. But there came a day when Parasrām stopped visiting his friend, and for days together nothing was seen of him. When at length they did meet, his lover taxed Parasrām with his sudden indifference towards him and wanted to know the cause. Parasrām replied that he had recently married; he loved his wife dearly and could not bear to be parted from her a moment longer than was necessary; and she loved him with the same passionate devotion, so much so that he was convinced that she could not live without him. His lover replied: "I cannot believe it is so. This is only woman's deceit. Do not be taken in by it. What woman was ever constant in love? And what woman ever failed to survive her husband's death? Outwardly they are all fair, but within is deadly venom. God himself has spoken of their deceit:[10] no living being is more treacherous. The whole world knows of their treachery, and their deceit is on all men's tongues." He went on to say that if Parasrām doubted his words, he should put his wife to the test; then he would see that he spoke the truth. Parasrām agreed to do so, and a man was sent to his house to tell his wife that Parasrām had been drowned while bathing in the river. When she heard the news, she gave one despairing look towards the door through which Parasrām used to come, and then fell down in a faint and died.

When the messenger returned with the news of what had happened, Parasrām went nearly mad with grief, and his friend was overwhelmed with shame and regret. One day as he was wandering aimlessly about, Parasrām found himself at the riverside. A fisherman and his wife were talking together, and the wife was scolding her husband, because for the

[9] *Kulliyāt*, pp. 890–899. An inevitable consequence of the parda system was the prevalence of homosexual love, and here as elsewhere Mīr portrays it without comment as one of the common manifestations of love. Some modern Urdū critics, especially those who pride themselves on having studied Western literature and assimilated its standards of taste, condemn classical Urdū poetry for the prevalence of this attitude, which, they claim, debars it from consideration as good literature. Such critics have either not noticed or have forgotten that, for example, 126 of Shakespeare's sonnets out of a total of 154 are about his love for a beautiful young man. (Cf. G. B. Harrison's Introduction to the Penguin edition [1938], pp. 10–11.) One commonly finds with this school of critics that the application of their canons would condemn a great deal of the literature from the study of which these canons are allegedly derived.

[10] The speaker means that God has spoken thus in the Qur'ān. (In fact, however, there is no verse in the Qur'ān declaring deceit to be an attribute of women in general.—A.S.)

past few days he had caught so little that his family had had to go hungry. He replied that just lately he had been afraid to fish at night, because every night a flame appeared on the river bank and a voice called out, "Parasrām! Where are you?" Parasrām that day seemed to become his old self again. He went to his friend and said that what was past, was past, and that there was nothing to be gained by grieving over it. Why should not they and a few friends go for an outing on the river that evening? His friend was delighted to see him so calm again, and readily agreed. When evening came they got into the boat, taking with them the fisherman whom Parasrām had heard speaking to his wife, for they needed someone who knew the river well and could make sure that they did not run into difficulties after darkness fell. Parasrām sat by him in the boat, and while the others were talking together, questioned him more closely about the flame he had seen and the exact spot where he had seen it. As they were talking, the flame appeared, and a voice was heard calling, "Parasrām, where are you?" Parasrām, in great agitation, got out of the boat unnoticed by the other passengers. The fisherman saw him standing as though in conversation with the flame, which seemed to stay still for a moment, then flare up and envelop him, after which it disappeared and was never seen again.

In spite of obvious differences, Mir's masnavis remind one of the English ballad. Both tell in a simple verse form a straightforward narrative, in which the situations and characters are of a kind thoroughly familiar to their audience, so that a few strokes are often enough to convey the whole picture and a few words of dialogue establish a full character. In both, the essential story is realistic, and though the supernatural element is also prominent, it blends in complete harmony with the rest and heightens the whole atmosphere. Above all, the atmosphere of both is at once tragic and heroic, for the themes of both are the stories of men and women who face with simple courage and dignity what they know to be an inevitable fate.

The similarities extend also to style. Indeed, the masnavi, the ballad, and the Homeric epic all have one striking feature in common: all use in a completely naive and undisguised way the conventions which are considered appropriate to the form, involving, for instance, a constant repetition of stock phrases, epithets, and similes, which nonetheless never seem to lose their freshness—perhaps because one finds alongside them an ability to rise to the very height of poetic power, where a bare statement in the simplest words makes an unforgettably vivid impact. Just as in Homer the sea is always "the wine-dark sea," the dawn "rosy-fingered," and the cattle "shambling," so in the ballads words like "fair," "red," "silver," or the numbers "three," "seven," "nine," and so on, are often employed with similar effect, an effect in which welcome familiarity blends with a seemingly inexhaustible freshness. With the masnavi it is the same, and one savours the descriptions of the "moon-faced" beauties, "tall and graceful as the cypress," whose hair is "long and black as the night of separation," whose eyebrows are "curved like the scimitar" and equally dangerous, and whose long eye-lashes are like sharp arrows that pierce their lovers to the heart. These are the comparisons which convention prescribes for Urdu love poetry and which the poet employs simply and naturally.

It seems also—as the textbooks recognise—that certain metres were also considered peculiarly appropriate to the masnavi. Of the five masnavis described above, three are in the same eleven-syllable metre as Mir Hasan's *Enchanting Story*: ˇ — — | ˇ — — | ˇ — — | ˇ — (mutaqārib). The other two are in another metre, commonly used for the masnavi, and evidently a favourite with Mir. Its unit is basically a ten-syllable line, with a less regular, but still strongly marked, rhythm: — ˇ — — | ˇ — ˇ — | — — (khafīf). More variations are permitted in this metre than in most, and once its rather complex pattern has been grasped, it makes a great appeal. Mir's own love story, *The Stages of Love*, is in this metre.

The masnavis cover only a relatively small part of Mir's love poetry. The rest is expressed in his ghazals, which make up not only the largest but also the best part of his poetry. They are much more difficult than the masnavis for the modern reader to understand and appreciate. In the first place, the ghazal form is completely strange to him. It has a closely knit, formal unity, and to our way of thinking, unity of form demands a cor-responding unity of theme, or at the very least, a unity of mood. And this the ghazal does not usually possess. Secondly, many of the experiences of love with which it deals are of a kind almost incomprehensible to one who has lived only in a modern society. Thirdly, the conciseness of the ghazal form, which requires the expression of an independent experience within a single couplet, has made it allusive in the extreme. The poet

assumes in his reader precisely what the modern reader does not possess—
a full knowledge of all the situations of love to which the social conditions of Mughal India gave rise. In the masnavi the poet can describe
these situations at some length; in the ghazal he has no room to do more
than hint at them, leaving it to the reader's imagination (as he safely
could) to supply the full picture. This same requirement of conciseness
produced also the characteristic diction of the ghazal; there was no room
to waste words, and every word was made to bear all the connotations of
which it was capable and which successive generations of ghazal writers
had given to it. Finally, there is an extravagance and exaggeration in the
emotional tone and language of the ghazal which the modern reader finds
it hard to accept.

A good many of these difficulties are resolved once their background is
understood. But it is as well to say at once that not all of them are. Some
of the unfamiliar features of the ghazal have simply to be accepted as
conventions to which the reader must accustom himself. Like most conventions in literary taste, they are not easy to accept when one first en-
counters them, but it is often easier and more profitable to accept them
than to attempt to reason about them. Nowadays the pun is regarded as
the lowest form of humour; yet Shakespeare and his audiences felt that
it heightened the expression of tragic emotion. They could probably not
have explained why it ought to be regarded in this way, but the modern
would not find it any easier to prove that his attitude is a more proper
one. Similarly, in approaching the Urdu ghazal he has to accept its lack of
all but formal unity, and to realise that whereas with us a unity of form
demands a unity of context, in eighteenth-century Mughal India it was
not so; the poet and his audience felt no dissatisfaction with a poem of
which every couplet, though linked by rhyme with every other, was a
separate entity.[11]

The intense, extravagant emotion of the ghazal is another matter.
This is not simply a convention of literature but also a true expression of
life, as the masnavi stories help to show. Brought up in isolation from
women, taught by society and by his own emotions to believe in the over-
mastering power of love, fearful of the drastic reprisals he must face if he

---

[11] The fact that Urdū poetry was, and still is, composed in the first place to be recited before
others, and not to be read in private, undoubtedly has a bearing on this feature of the ghazal
form. This point is elaborated in the Appendix, p. 273.

falls in love, himself believing that love is a danger to society, the lover is submitted to a strain which often proves literally unbearable and drives him mad. All such desperately intense emotions are expressed without restraint in the ghazal, and this unrestrained and frequently self-pitying expression is another stumbling block to the modern reader, who has been brought up to regard such things as unmanly. Dorothy Sayers, in explaining a similar feature of medieval French poetry, has put the point very well. "There are fashions in sensibility as in everything else," she writes. "The idea that a strong man should react to great personal and national calamities by a slight compression of the lips and by silently throwing his cigarette into the fireplace is of very recent origin." [12] One does not have to go outside English literature to see that this is true. Shakespeare's *Romeo and Juliet* is full of the same intense, extravagant emotion as the Urdu ghazal; and the fact that Romeo is a spirited, courageous, and resolute man does not prevent him from responding to the news of his banishment in a speech which equals in its passionate self-pity anything the Urdu ghazal can produce.

In short, to appreciate the ghazal one has to bear two things constantly in mind: first, the ghazal has its own conventions, and if some of these are strange to us, that does not necessarily make them absurd. Secondly, many features which may appear at first sight to be purely conventional are in fact a direct, natural expression of emotions that seem foreign to us only because we are no longer familiar with the situations that produce them.

One meets this sort of situation at the very starting point of Urdu love poetry. Love in the Urdu ghazal is always love at first sight. The modern tends to regard this as a romantic absurdity, quite remote from real life. From the real life which he knows perhaps it is remote, because he lives in a society where boys and girls mix freely, where a marriage is made by the mutual free choice of the two parties to it, and where love is seen as the prelude to marriage. He knows that the immediate strong attraction which even in his experience is sometimes felt between a boy and a girl is rarely an adequate basis for marriage, and because he knows this, and because there are plenty more fish in the sea, he plays down its importance. But his counterpart in Mughal India was in quite a different situation. He might go through life without ever experiencing passionate

---

[12] In the Introduction to her translation of *The Song of Roland* (Harmondsworth, 1957), p. 15.

love, without even seeing in his own community a beautiful girl whom he could love; and if some sudden accident of fate enabled him to do so, the impact upon him could be overwhelming. Considerations of a possible marriage did not affect his attitude towards her, for in any case he could only love her: he could never marry her. For him, therefore, love at first sight was not some rare, romantic absurdity, but the normal inception of love in the real-life conditions of his day.

Thus it is a real experience, and a common one, that Mir describes[13] when he writes to his mistress:

زلفیں کھولے تو تو تک آیا نظر

عمر بھر یہاں کام دل برہم رہا

I caught a glimpse of you with hair dishevelled
And my distracted heart was yours for life. (I.40.25)

Or when he says:

ہوش و صبر و خرد و دین و حواس و دل و تاب

اُس کے اک آنے میں کیا کیا نہ گیا مت پوچھو

She came but once, but do not ask what left me as she went—
My strength, and faith, and fortitude, and will and heart and soul.
(I.133.19)

---

[13] We have throughout this chapter written on the assumption that the beloved of Mīr's ghazals is, like his mistress in *The Stages of Love*, the typical woman of parda society. *The Stages of Love* is itself substantial evidence for the view that for Mīr's ghazals this assumption is probably justified. But in parda society, like every other in which there is drastic segregation of the sexes and a marked difference between the cultural level of men and that of women, love also found outlets in homosexual love and in resort to a class of cultured courtesans. Thus boys and courtesans, as well as respectable parda women, appear in the Urdū ghazal in the role of the beloved. In most verses the expression is too generalised for the class or sex of the beloved to be identifiable. In any case, in the philosophy of Urdu love poetry (which will be described in the next chapter), *all* beauty engenders love as its natural and proper human response, and there is no abhorrence either of pederasty or of love for courtesans. Nor is the concept of constancy a, so to speak, monogamous one. Constancy to one's beloved meant complete submission to her or his will: it did not necessarily imply that a man might not have more than one beloved. Mīr, like most of the cultivated men of his day, must have mixed freely and intimately with courtesans. In the passage quoted on p. 35 above, the "beautiful women . . . whose long tresses held me their captive" can surely only have been courtesans.

Or in a line that expresses in a single image not only the compelling beauty of a woman but also the terrible danger which her lover must be prepared to face:

میرؔ تلوار چلتی ہے تو چلے

خوش خراموں کی چال ہے کچھ اور

> Mir, *let* the bright sword flash—in dreadful beauty
> A lovely woman's walk is something more.   (I.71.15)

Or in a line like:

آنکھیں جنھوں کی زلف و رخِ یار سے لگیں

وے دیکھتے نہیں سحر و شام کی طرف

> Morning and night mean nothing any more
> To him whose eyes have seen her hair and face.
>
> (II.278.8)

The apparent simplicity of the line is deceptive, and it well exemplifies the extreme allusiveness of the ghazal technique. The first and obvious meaning is that one glimpse of her face and her hair is enough to captivate the young lover forever. But the words used suggest much more than this. In the ghazal the black night and the black hair of the beloved are regularly compared; so are the dazzling radiance of her face and the sun or the bright day. Thus one meaning of the couplet is that the beauty of the night and the beauty of the day recede into insignificance before the beauty of her hair and face. But the words also mean that for the lover the passage of time is unimportant: his love engrosses him wholly all his life through, and its intensity does not vary. Thirdly, the line may also suggest that true love continues unaltered not only by time but also by joy and sorrow alike. Where all love is clandestine, and where the lovers have to contend with a system organised for the very purpose of making impossible all contacts between boys and girls of marriageable age, such secret meetings as can be arranged frequently take place by day. The day symbolises therefore the joy of union, and the long nights (their length affords another comparison with the beloved's hair), the grief of enforced separation. All these shades of meaning are relevant to the understanding of the line. And if the modern reader should object that this is to read into the line more than is written in it, the ghazal poet and his audience could reply in Olive Schreiner's words, "Certainly, the whole of the story is not written here, but it is suggested. And the attribute of all true art . . . is this, that it says more than it says, and takes you away from itself. It is a little door that opens into an infinite hall where you may find what you please." Olive Schreiner elaborates her point with another comparison: "If we pick up the finger and nail of a real man, we can decipher a whole story—could almost reconstruct the creature again, from head to foot."[14] The image can be very aptly applied to the ghazal, many of whose best lines are indeed in just this sense like "the finger and nail of a real man."

Not all lines, of course, demand for their appreciation the degree of background knowledge that this one does. There are many in which the poet expresses his delight in the beauty of his mistress, and of beautiful women generally, in tones that would be intelligible in any country and any age:

جمع خوباں میں مرا محبوب اس مانند ہے
جوں مہِ تابندہ آتا ہے کبھو تاروں کے بیچ

Where lovely women gather my beloved shines among them
As when the shining moon appears among the twinkling stars.

(VI.640.16)

سرگرمِ جلوہ اس کو دیکھے کوئی سوجانے
طرزِ خرام کیا ہے، حسن و جمال کیا ہے

Until you see her walk you will not know
What grace and poise and matchless beauty are.

(II.357.12)

---

14 Ralph Iron (Olive Schreiner), *The Story of an African Farm* (London, 1896), pp. 171–172.

آ نکلتا ہے کبھو ہنستا تو ہے باغ و بہار
اس کی آمد میں ہے ساری فصل گل آنے کی طرح

Now and then she passes smiling, and for me the roses bloom
All the advent of the spring is in the grace of her approach.

(II.260.11)

ان گُل رُخوں کی قامت ہلکے ہے یوں ہوا میں
جس رنگ سے لچکتی پھولوں کی ڈالیاں ہیں

Their cheeks are fresh as roses, their swaying walk as lovely
As flower-laden branches moved by the morning breezes.

(III.412.24)

اتنی سڈول دیہی دیکھی نہ ہم سنی ہے
ترکیب اس کی گویا سانچے میں گئی ہو ڈھالی

A body beautiful as hers I never saw or knew of
As flawless is her form, as if cast in a perfect mould.

(VI.674.8)

ساتھ اس حسن کے دیتا تھا دکھائی وہ بدن
جیسے جھمکے ہے پڑا گوہر تر پانی میں

As the pure pearl shines through the limpid water
So does the beauty of her body shine. (II.294.1)

گوندھ کے گویا پتّی گل کی وہ ترکیب بنائی ہے
رنگ بدن کا تب دیکھو جب چولی بھیگے پسینے میں

In the hot season, when the sweat soaks through her bodice then I think
God gathered roses for His task and made her out of them entire.

(IV.503.24)

تنگیِ جامہ ظلم ہے اے باعثِ حیات
پاتے ہیں لطف جان کا ہم تیرے تن کے بیچ

For you I live—whose tightly-clad, firm body
Teaches my soul what joy it is to live. (III.392.12)

لطف اس کے بدن کا کچھ نہ پوچھو
کیا جانیے جان ہے کہ تن ہے

Her body yields such joy, I know no longer
Whether it is her body or my soul. (II.360.12)

چشمِ مشتاق اس لب و رخ سے لحظہ لحظہ اٹھتی نہیں
کیا ہی لگے ہے اچھا اس کا مکھڑا پیارا پیارا آج

Her lips and cheeks hold fast in thrall my yearning eyes,
How good her lovely face appears to me today! (V.553.5)

میر اُن نیم باز آنکھوں میں
ساری مستی شراب کی سی ہے

Her wakening eyes, half-opened, seem to hold
All the intoxicating power of wine. (I.159.4)

ناز کی اُس کے لب کی کیا کہیے
پنکھڑی اِک گلاب کی سی ہے

What words can tell the soft and tender beauty
Of the red rose's petal, or her lips? (I.158.21)

گُلبرگ کا یہ رنگ ہے مرجاں کا ایسا ڈھنگ ہے

دیکھو نہ جھکے ہے پڑا وہ ہونٹھ لعلِ ناب سا

When did the petal of the rose, or the red coral match with theirs?
See how the colour of her lips glows with the purest ruby's fire.

(I.9.8)

یاقوت کوئی ان کو کہے ہے کوئی گُل برگ

ٹک ہونٹھ ہلا تو بھی کہ اک بات ٹھہر جائے

Some call them rubies, others rose petals
Just part your lips, and say the final word!   (I.181.20)

On the one hand Mir tries to convey his mistress' beauty by comparisons such as these. On the other, he feels that none of these things is adequate to convey its overwhelming power. He tells her:

اے گُل نو دمیدہ کے ماند

ہے تو کس آفریدہ کے ماند

Perhaps the flower in spring compares with you—
Yet what created thing compares with you?   (I.63.19)

جس گھر میں تیرے جلوہ سے ہو چاندنی کا فرش

وہاں چادرِ مہتاب ہے مکڑی کا سا جالا

In that house where the moonlight of your radiance lies spread
The moonlight seems as lustreless as does the spider's web.

(I.39.16)

And he tries to explain to others:

مشک و سنبل کہاں وہ زلف کہاں
شاعروں کے یہ شاخسانے ہیں

Let poets chatter on of musk and hyacinth:
When did such things match with *her* fragrant locks?

(II.297.7)

سرو و گل اچّھے ہیں دونوں رونق ہیں گلزار کی لیک
چاہئے رۆ اس کا سارۆ ہو، قامت ویسا قامت ہو

The cypress and the rose are fine, and both adorn the garden—yet
Would that the rose had *her* cheek's beauty, would that the cypress had
her poise.

(I.129.15)

Often, by a convention common in Urdu poetry, he represents things
which are proverbial for their beauty as overcome with shame when confronted with hers: the proud rose, the beloved of the nightingale; the
tall, slender, perfectly proportioned cypress, which, conscious of its
beauty, stands proudly aloof from the rest of the garden; the candle,
whose bright flame lures her lover, the moth, irresistibly to her, even at
the cost of his life:

قدِ یار کے آگے سرو چمن
کھڑا دُور جیسے گنہ گار تھا

Seeing her poise, the cypress in the garden
Stood afar off, as though it had done wrong. (II.247.13)

بلبل خموش ولالہ وگل دونوں سرخ و زرد

شمشاد محو بے کلی اک نسترن کے بیچ

کل ہم بھی سیرِ باغ میں تھے ساتھ یار کے

دیکھا تو اور رنگ ہے سارے چمن کے بیچ

The nightingale fell quiet, the tulip blushed, the rose turned pale
The cypress stood like one amazed, the eglantine distraught.
I too walked with my mistress in the garden yesterday
And all around I saw the changes that her beauty wrought.

(II.258.19–20)

آگے جب اس آتشیں رخسار کے آتی ہے شمع

پانی پانی شرمِ مفرط سے ہوئی جاتی ہے شمع

Her glowing, radiant face confronts the candle
And overwhelmed with shame, it melts away.   (III.401.17)

Alternatively, if nature possesses any charm which can be compared with hers, that is because that charm is derived from her:

چشمکِ انجم میں اتنی دلکشی آگے نہ تھی

سیکھی تاروں نے اس کی آنکھ جھپکانے کی طرح

I never saw the stars so bright before:
It was her eyes that taught them how to shine.   (II.260.12)

کھلنا کم کم کلی نے سیکھا ہے

اُس کی آنکھوں کی نیم خوابی سے

It was her eyes, just wakening from sleep
That taught the rosebud its half-opened grace.   (I.207.23)

اب جو نسیم معطّر آئی شاید بال کھلے اس کے
شہر کی ساری گلیاں ہو گئیں گویا عنبر سارا آج

Perhaps when it passed by that way my love was combing out her hair:
The scented breeze of morning brings a fragrance into every lane.

(V.553.7)

A boy who falls passionately in love for the first time in his life does not
find it easy to conceal the fact, and he had to prepare himself to pay the
penalties that society imposed, mounting progressively from the cold
hostility that the first suspicions produced to physical violence that might
even put his life in danger. But in many ways these were the least of the
possibilities he had to dread, for here he did know what was in store for
him. Much worse in his eyes was the uncertainty as to how the girl he
loved would behave towards him. Quite often, in the conditions of parda
society, she would not even have seen him, for she would not be without
her burqa except in circumstances where she thought no man could see
her, and she might continue quite unaware that she had been seen. But
even if she had seen him too, and sensed his love for her, she might well
feel indifferent or even hostile to him; for love at first sight is not
necessarily mutual. Whether indifferent to him or not, she reacted usually
with a new-found consciousness of and pride in her beauty, and realising
the power over her lover which this gave her, took a keen pleasure in
exercising it. All this is understandable; but it becomes doubly so when
one realises how rarely in Mughal society a woman could exercise such
power. She lived in a society in which man was her master in every
sphere and at every stage of her life. In childhood she was subject to her
father's authority, after marriage, to her husband's, and in old age, to her
son's; and this was not all. Under the joint-family system of Indian
society she would go immediately after marriage to live in the house of her
husband's parents, where she would be expected to subordinate herself
to a whole hierarchy of superiors—above all to her mother-in-law but
also to her husband's elder sisters and his elder brothers' wives. They,
whose life-experience was, like hers, one of subjection to male domi-
nance, often felt a compensating pleasure in dominating her, even in the

most trivial matters, and the young bride expected as a matter of course that at least the early stages of her life in her new home would be a trying experience. As late as the 1860s an Urdu novelist describes her situation:

> The freedom she had enjoyed in her parents' home was no longer hers. As soon as she arrived in her mother-in-law's house, everyone was intent on watching her and scrutinising her every action. One scans her features; another notes the length of her hair; another guesses her height; another examines her jewels; and another takes stock of her clothes. When she eats, they watch her all the time. How much did she put in her mouth? How wide did she open it? How many times did she chew it? And how much at a time did she swallow? If she gets up from her seat, they look to see how she robes herself in her mantle, how she holds up her skirts. And if she sleeps, they count the hours; what time did she go to bed? When did she get up? In short, every aspect of her conduct was under observation.[15]

The Muslim woman in Mughal India knew of no other kind of life and did not question its rightness, though this is not to say that she did not feel the hardness of her lot. But she in her turn would one day tyrannise over her juniors, when seniority eventually gave her the right to do so, and she might derive a similar pleasure from tyrannising over one—and that too, a man—whom the accident of fate had put at her mercy. The Urdu ghazal is full of the anguish which the lover felt when she did, an anguish that mingles, however, with an involuntary admiration for her proud self-possession and for the majesty with which she exercises her tyranny over him. These very qualities, which are the source of so much pain to him, make her even more attractive in his eyes. He looks at her and thinks:

مر جاؤ کوئی پروا نہیں ہے

کتنا ہے مغرور اللہ اللہ

A man may die, and she will never care.
Oh God! Oh God! just see how proud she is!   (I.137.23)

---

[15] Nazīr Aḥmad, *Mir'āt ul 'Arūs* (Delhi, 1898 ed.), p. 88. The translation is adapted from that of G. E. Ward, *The Bride's Mirror* (London, 1903), p. 63.

جی گیا یہاں بے دماغی سے انھوں کی اور وہاں
نے جبیں سے چیں گئی ، نے ابروؤں سے خم گئے

Her cruel pride has robbed me of my life—yet as she looks on me
Her eyebrows' curve, her furrowed brow tell of her high displeasure
    still. (II.350.2)

فلک نے بہت کھینچے آزار لیک
نہ پہنچا بہم اس دل آزار سا

Fate has struck many blows, but none like that
Which destined her to be my torturer. (II.240.8)

And for all this, in the last resort, he blames himself. He should not
have let her see how he loves her, for it was her knowledge of his love
which made her for the first time conscious of her beauty and of the
power it put into her hands.

میرا اظہارِ محبّت میں گیا جی تیرا
ہائے نادان بہت تو نے چھپایا ہوتا

You told your love, and that was your undoing.
    Fool! You should have concealed it all you could. (II.233.8)

Her complete absorption in her own new-found beauty is the theme of
many lines. Sometimes the tone is bitter:

وہ محوِ جمال اپنے ہے پروا نہیں اس کو
خواہاں رہو تم اب کہ طلب گار رہو تم

The study of her beauty occupies her. What are you?
Though you desire her and petition her day in, day out.
                                                        (III.407.7)

She is beautiful, and beautiful women are a law unto themselves:

کرتے ہیں جو کہ جی میں ٹھانے ہیں

خوب رُوکس کی بات مانے ہیں

> They do as *they* think fit: no beauty yet
> Took notice of what other people say.   (II.296.25)

Sometimes, along with the involuntary admiration and the bitterness, there is a hint of sarcasm and mockery too:

تناسب پہ اعضا کے اتنا تبختر

بگاڑا تجھے خوب صورت بنا کر

> *Such* pride in your fair symmetry, my love?
> God marred you when He made you beautiful.   (III.396.20)

And sometimes the poet speaks in terms which, perhaps deliberately, leave one in some doubt as to how they should be interpreted:

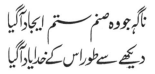

> My idol, my fair torturer stood before me:
> Stricken with awe, God came into my mind. (II.228.15)

Several interpretations are possible. The verse *may* be a direct tribute to his mistress. So awe-inspiring is her presence that he turns to God to sustain him, as one does in moments of great stress. Or, so majestic is she that she brings to mind the majesty of God himself. Or, Mir may be saying sarcastically, "The airs she gives herself! Who does she think she is? God Almighty?" In addition to which, the contrast between the "idol" of the first line and the "God" of the second suggests other trains of thought. All of which is entirely characteristic of the ghazal idiom.

The experience of his mistress' calculated cruelty towards him was one which every lover had to undergo. But it might be motivated by things other than a real indifference. Even a girl who responded to him with a love as spontaneous and complete as his own was likely to treat him in the same way. For her both the penalties and the prizes of love were greater than they were for him. A man might have a love affair in his youth, and once the scandal had died down, still be able to take his place in the normal life of society. That was not possible for a woman, and if once her love was discovered, things commonly ended with her suicide. Yet the prospect of being truly loved by a man contrasted so markedly with the normal course of her life that it seemed infinitely attractive to her, despite the almost certain penalty she must some day pay. For one in her position the whole problem was to know whether her lover did love her truly, and whether he had the devotion and the courage to remain true to her in the face of every trial, and so sustain her in all she would have to undergo. And so, if she could, she would conceal her love from him and put him to the test, offering him every discouragement until she could feel that his steadfastness was proved. Which is not to say that she didn't at the same time exult in her beauty and take pleasure in her power to make him miserable.

Her lover understood all this very well. He accepted that it was for him to prove his devotion to her, and he would try all he could to do so, hoping that her indifference would prove to be only feigned, or that even if it were real, his constant devotion might one day change it into love. He did not conceal the emotional stress to which this subjected him. The modern Englishman is naturally reticent about such things, but the ghazal poet, equally naturally, pours out with all the extravagance that he feels, the violence of his love and pain, self-pity and humiliation, anger and bitterness. He tries to explain what he, and all true lovers, feel:

عشق و محبّت کیا جانوں میں لیکن اتنا جانوں ہوں

اندر ہی اندر سینے میں میرے دل کو کوئی کھاتا ہے

I do not know what love and passion are.
How can I tell? But this alone I know
Within the inmost chamber of my breast
Something is tearing at my heart always.   (V.609.22)

گھبرا کے یوں لگے ہے سینے میں دل تڑپنے

جیسے اسیرِ تازہ بیتاب ہو قفس میں

As the new-captured songbird beats his wings against the cage
So beats my agitated heart, imprisoned in my breast.   (III.420.10)

دل جلتے کچھ بن نہیں آتی حال بگڑتے جاتے ہیں

جیسے چراغِ آخری شب ہم لوگ نِبھرتے جاتے ہیں

A slow fire burns our hearts away, and slowly
We sink and sink in helpless agonies
As when the lamp of night, as dawn approaches,
Drinks up the last few drops of oil, and dies.   (V.588.16)

Not only is the violence of his own feeling destroying him. He has also
to contend with the persecution from society which a lover had to face:

اس کی طرف جو لی ہم نے ہے اپنی طرف سے پھرا عالم

یعنی دوستی سے اس بت کی دشمن ساری خدائی ہوئی

I take my stand for her—the world turns and assails me:
I am her friend—and all creation is my enemy.   (V.602.8)

کہے ہے جس کو ملامت جہاں میں ہی ہوں

اجل رسیدہ، جفا دیدہ، اضطراب زدہ

Whom all the world reviles and persecutes, that man am I—
Struck down by fate, and by her cruelty, and my distress.

(I.138.14)

But worst of all is her callousness and cruelty:

کیا جانے ہوتے ہیں سخن لطف کے کیسے
پوچھا نہیں ان نے تو ہمیں پاسراب تک

How should I know the meaning of fair words?
She never yet asked kindly after me. (I.82.21)

دوستی یاری الفت باہم عہد میں اس کے رسم نہیں
یہ جانیں ہیں مہر و فا اک بات ہے گویا مدّت کی

Friendship, devotion, mutual regard—
All are outmoded fashions in her eyes.
She thinks that love and loyalty are things
One reads about in tales of days gone by. (III.437.14)

لطف و مہر و وفا وہ کیا جانے
ناز ہے خشم ہے عتاب ہے میاں

مہر و فا و لطف و عنایت ایک سے ان میں نہیں
اور تو سب کچھ طنز و کنایہ رمز و اشارا جانے ہے

To taunt and sneer and wound and speak unkindly—
She has all these accomplishments, my friend;
Friendship and love and graciousness and kindness
Are things that she could never comprehend.
(V.607.5; III.417.12)

How complete is the contrast between her attitude and his:

میں جی سنبھالتا ہوں وہ ہنس کے ٹالتا ہے
یہاں مشکلیں ہیں ایسی وہاں یہ مساہلے ہیں

I nurse a wounded heart; she laughs and turns away.
Such is my heavy grief: so light she makes of it.   (II.305.5)

وہاں سے جز ناز و تنجتر نہیں کچھ یہاں سے میرؔ
عجز ہے دوستی ہے عشق ہے غمخواری ہے

From her, pride and disdain and nothing else—from me
Honour, devotion, love, strength to sustain her.   (V.617.21)

And with all this it is he whom she and society alike hold guilty:

یہاں مہر تھی وفا تھی وہاں جور تھے ستم تھے
پھر نکلے بھی تو میرے یہ ہی گناہ نکلے

On my side, love and loyalty: on hers, vindictive cruelty.
And this they know; yet it is I must bear the brand of infamy.
     (II.342.9)

In some lines he addresses her direct, reproaching her, appealing to her pity or to her sense of justice, suggesting even that if she rejects his love, it will be her loss as well as his.

بن کچھ کہے سنا ہے عالم سے میں نے کیا کیا
پر تو نے یہ نہ جانا اے بے وفا کہ کیا تھا

My lips returned no answer to all the world's revilings;
But what was that to you, love? You did not even notice.
     (I.47.4)

کرتا ہے کون منع کہ سچ اپنی تو نہ دیکھ

لیکن کبھی تو میرے کر حال پر نظر

See your own beauty and rejoice: I never said ''Do not do so.''
But sometimes spare a glance for me, and see what it has brought me to.

(I.65.14)

دشمن ہیں اپنے جی کے تھارے لیے ہوئے

تم بھی حقوق دوستی کے کچھ ادا کرو

For love of you I count my life as nothing.
Is nothing in return then due from you?   (II.316.22)

پامال کرکے ہم کو پچھتاؤ گے بہت تم

کمیاب ہیں جہاں میں سر دینے والے ہم سے

Trample me in the dust then—and rue the day you did so;
You may not find another to lay his life down for you.

(I.155.10)

Sometimes he imagines her companions pleading his cause for him:

تم کبھو میر کو چاہو سو کہ چاہیں ہیں تمھیں

اور ہم لوگ تو سب اُن کا ادب کرتے ہیں

You should love Mir the way that he loves you.
The rest of us all hold him in regard.   (III.423.11)

Along with verses in which all his intense emotions are expressed, one
finds others in which a certain wry humour is evident, an awareness that

there is something in his position, and in hers, and in the whole situation which some might feel to be a little ludicrous. This note appears in many instances. He sees how all his devotion seems to go for nothing; it cannot stimulate even her sympathy, let alone her love; and he thinks to himself:

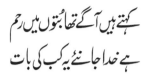

People have told me beauty once was kind—
That must have been God knows how long ago.　(I.59.10)

He imagines people telling his fair, cruel beloved:

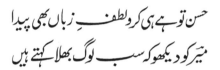

Beauty you have—now find fair words to match it.
This is what makes men speak so well of Mir.　(II.290.8)

—not knowing that of all the examples they could hold up to her, none could be more inappropriate than his, for it is he above all others who provokes her cruelty.

Sometimes he jokes even at his mistress' expense. Like every true lover, he knows that she is sensitive in the extreme and quick to take offence at the slightest cause; and he accepts this as her rightful prerogative. But he is impudent enough to suggest that she is not the only one: he too may feel as she does, and she should bear this in mind. He tells her:

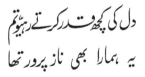

Have *some* consideration for my feelings:
My heart was delicately-nurtured too.　(I.42.20)

And:

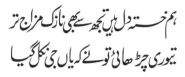

I am more sensitive, my love, than even you can be;
For you have but to knit your brow, and I am like to die.

(I.17.10)

This rather wry humour is especially characteristic of Mir. It derives in
the last resort from a sureness of himself, a complete confidence that he
has the strength to stand all the tests of love without breaking, and can
therefore see them and love, and his mistress and himself, without il-
lusion, and even laugh at what he sees. In some verses he speaks ruefully
of his fame as a poet, and smiles at its pitiful irrelevance to his standing as
a lover:

کچھ وسیلہ نہیں جو اس سے ملوں
شعر ہو یار کا شعار اے کاش

We have no common ground on which to meet.
If only *you* had been a poet too!   (IV.485.13)

دکھّن پورب پچّھم سے لوگ آ کر مجھ کو دیکھیں ہیں
حیف کہ پروا تم کو نہیں ہے مطلق میری صحبت کی

Men come from south and east and west in hopes to get a glimpse of me
Sad, that it should be you alone care nothing for my company.

(III.437.12)

This calm, humorous acceptance of his position is well-expressed in a
short ghazal devoted wholly to the theme. In this stage of love, Mir says,
complete devotion on his side and complete indifference on hers are part

of the natural order of things, and if people suggest anything to the contrary, they are lying:

هم اور تیری گلی سے سفر دروغ دروغ

کہاں دماغ ہیں اس قدر دروغ دروغ

تم اور ہم سے محبت تھیں خلاف خلاف

ہم اور الفت خوب دگر دروغ دروغ

غلط غلط کہ رہیں تم سے ہم تنگ غافل

تم اور پوچھو ہماری خبر دروغ دروغ

کسو کے کہنے سے مت بدگماں ہو میرے سے تو

وہ اور اُس کو کسو پر نظر دروغ دروغ

I would be fancy-free? They lie! They lie!
Can such presumption be? They lie! They lie!
You are in love with *me*? Absurd! Absurd!
I love another she? They lie! They lie!
No! No! I *never* cease to think of you.
You asking anxiously? They lie! They lie!
They have their doubts of Mir? Pay them no heed.
He is not false, not he! They lie! They lie!

(I.80.4, 5, 6, 8, 9)

The humorous note persists when he puts to one side the distress
which her cruelty is inflicting on him, and calmly avows his love for her,
asserting that this is no crime and that she has no right to punish him:

کچھ تمھیں ملنے سے بیزار ہو میرے ورنہ

دوستی ننگ نہیں، عیب نہیں، عار نہیں

You do not want my love, but all the same
To love you is no slur, no fault, no shame.   (III.415.20)

Or if it is a crime, then not he but she should be called to account; for if
he loves her, it is because her loveliness compels him to:

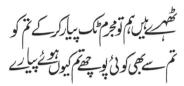

The guilt is mine alone, then—simply because I love you?
But why are you so lovely? *You* should be called to answer.

(V.615.7)

Despite all this, in loving her, he makes no demands of her; he may ask
for everything, but he demands nothing as of right. He comes not to demand her love, but to offer her his own, and he tells her that while she
is free to reject him, she should consider that in doing so, she may be
throwing away something that is precious. This point too is sometimes
made in quite a flippant tone. Speaking to all mistresses, and in the name of
all lovers, he says,

دلبراں دل جنس ہے گنجائش
اس میں کچھ نقصاں نہیں سرکار کا

Fair mistresses, accept the hearts we bring you.
You can't lose—and perhaps you'll even gain.   (VI.631.22)

He means what he says, and what is here put almost jokingly is elsewhere
expressed in real earnest:

آئینے کو بھی دیکھو پر ٹک ادھر بھی دیکھو
حیران چشم عاشق دکھے ہے جیسے ہیرا

Yes, gaze into your mirror too; but for a moment glance this way:
Intent on you, your lover's eyes shine brilliant as diamonds.

(II.229.21)

All the allusive power of the ghazal form is here brought into play, so that it "says more than it says, and takes you away from itself." It says, like the verse quoted earlier, that the lover thinks his mistress' preoccupation with her own beauty fully justified, and asks only that she should spare an occasional glance for him. But the second line carries the clear implication that if only she will look his way, she will see something more arresting and more valuable to her than what she sees in the mirror; and this implication is reinforced by the use of words which carry a wide range of allusion. "Mirror" itself is one such word. "Mirror" is regularly used as a symbol of beauty; it is often used metaphorically of the beauty of the universe, for the universe itself is conceived of by the poets as a great mirror created by God in order that His divine beauty might be reflected. And on a more mundane level, as we have seen in *The Enchanting Story*, mirrors were set up as part of the preparations for great occasions of public rejoicing. Thus the mirror itself is a thing of great beauty for the beloved to gaze upon, in addition to which it shows her her own perfect beauty reflected in it. Yet even so, she is asked to look into her lover's eyes, and the very first word suggests that they can compare with the mirror. The root meaning of the word *hairān*, here translated as "intent," means at a loss—at a loss because overwhelmed by some emotion—in this case, by the emotional impact of the beauty that it sees; and it is a regular epithet of the mirror, which is pictured as staring intently, as though hypnotised, at the face reflected in it. Once the comparison with the mirror is established, the poet goes further and compares the lover's eye with a shining diamond, which is at once more bright, more beautiful, and more valuable than a mirror is. It is so not only because it holds the promise of all that her lover's complete devotion can give to her, but also because it can even fulfil, and more than fulfil, the function of a real, tangible mirror. If she looks into her mirror, it shows her only what she herself has put into it—namely, her own beauty and her own estimate of it. If she looks into her lover's eyes, she will find her beauty more accurately portrayed, for she will see reflected there something of what her beauty means to him, and that, for all her own pride in it, is much more than what it means to her. If the modern reader should feel once again that all this is too fanciful, it can only be repeated that to one steeped in the traditions of the ghazal all such overtones readily suggest themselves.

This proud assertion of the lover, in words and in deeds, that his love makes no demands of her, and that it is for her own sake that she should accept it, is his most effective plea; and if he is patient and bears steadfastly all the tests to which his mistress puts him, the day may come when she shows signs of returning his love. She still likes to use her beauty to inflame him, while yet denying him access to her; but now there is an occasional hint that she not only recognises his devotion, but likes him for it. His first reaction is surprise:

پوچھا تھا راہ جاتے کہیں ان نے میرے کو

آتا ہے اس کی بات کا اب تک عجب مجھے

> As she went on her way she asked about me
> And I am lost in wonder at it still. (I.196.3)

He begins to realise how infinite are her attractions:

چشمک غمزہ عشوہ کرشمہ آن انداز و نازو ادا

حسن سوائے حسن ظاہر میرے بہت ہیں یار کے بیچ

> Her sidelong glance, imperious airs, her charm and grace and poise and pride—
> Not just the beauty of her form, but how much beauty more beside! (V.556.16)

خندۂ و چشمک و حرف و سخن زیر لبی

کہے جو ایک دو افسوں ہوں لدار کے پاس

> Her smile, her glance, the way she talks, the murmur barely heard—
> Not one or two the spells she casts, but past all reckoning. (II.273.8)

She asks him what he wants of her. He thinks to himself:

دل میرا دلبروں سے چاہا کرے ہر کیا کیا

کچھ انتہا نہیں ہے عاشق کی آرزو کو

What does my heart *not* want of my beloved?
For, Mir, a lover's longings have no end.   (IV.507.11)

And he answers her frankly:

کیا کہیئے کیا رکھیں ہیں ہم تجھ سے یار خواہش

یک جان و صد تمنّا ایک دل ہزار خواہش

My love, I cannot tell the tale of all the things I want of you.
A hundred longings fill my soul, a thousand yearnings throng my heart.
    (II.275.3)

But to desire is not to ask, still less to demand; and he is anxious to re-
assure her that the smallest sign of her regard would be precious to him.
And so he says:

صبر کہاں جو تم کو کہیئے لگ کے گلے سے سو جاؤ

بولو نہ بولو بیٹھو نہ بیٹھو کھڑے کھڑے ٹک ہو جاؤ

"Sleep in my arms!"—no, these are words I cannot find the strength to
say.
You need not speak; you need not stop; just pause as you pass by this way.
    (IV.511.7)

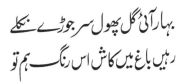

بہار آئی گل پھول سر جوڑے نکلے

رہیں باغ میں کاش اس رنگ ہم تو

The spring has come, the flowers bloom cheek by cheek—
Would you and I might stand thus in the garden!   (VI.659.5)

یک نگہ ایک چشمک ایک سخن

اس میں بھی تم کو ہے تاّمل سا

One glance, one kindly look, one word I ask—
But even so I see you hesitant.   (II.227.2)

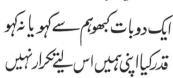

ایک دو بات کبھو ہم سے کہو یا نہ کہو

قدر کیا اپنی ہمیں اس لیے تکرار نہیں

Speak to me now and then—or do not speak.
I know my worth. How can I press you to?   (III.415.21)

گرچہ کب دیکھتے ہو پر دیکھو

آرزو ہے کہ تم ادھر دیکھو

I cannot think that you could look at me
Yet I will wish that you would look at me.   (I.124.22)

He does not even ask her to be kind to him alone:

کون کہتا ہے نہ غیروں پہ تم امداد کرد

ہم فراموش ہوؤں کو بھی کبھو یاد کرو

I do not ask you not to favour others
But only to remember me sometimes.   (I.130.14)

If she is moved by these appeals, there now comes a stage when, for
her, the emotional stress is at its most unbearable. She wants his love, and
wants to give him hers in return; but she cannot feel the complete certainty which she so desperately needs: she cannot *know* whether it will be
worth the price she must pay, whether she can trust him to be true to the
very end, or whether she can herself find the strength which the trials of
love will demand of her; and the closer she comes to committing herself,
the more likely she is to draw back in sudden panic before it is too late.
In such a state of mind every spontaneous impulse tends for the time
being to govern her, so that at one moment she will surrender to love,
and at the next draw back in fear; at one moment swear to be true forever, and at the next go back on her promise and determine to have
nothing more to do with her lover. These violent alternations of feeling
may persist over a long period, for as long, in fact, as the slightest

possibility of retreat remains to her. Thomas Hardy, in his novel *Under the Greenwood Tree*, set in rural England about a century ago, has portrayed in the character of Fancy Day a girl who resembles in many ways the heroine of the Urdu ghazal. He shows at the climax of the story how in her impulsiveness and uncertainty Fancy takes a step which amounts to complete betrayal of her lover, and which could mar her own happiness for life. But so well has Hardy portrayed her that the reader understands why she does it, and does not withdraw his sympathy from her.[16] With the heroine of the ghazal most of the background is left to the reader's imagination, but if he can understand Fancy Day, he can understand also how the girl in Mughal India, faced with alternatives so much more complex and so much more drastic than Fancy was, could act as she did.

The effort to attain to imaginative sympathy with her is all the more necessary, because in the ghazal we see her not directly but through the eyes of her lover. To him her conduct necessarily appears more perverse and her cruelties more capricious than ever, and even though he understands something of the state of mind which causes it, he cannot help expressing the misery it makes him feel, and protesting against it:

ملنا نہ ملنا ٹھہرے تو دل بھی اپنا ٹھہرے

اقرار ہے ہمیشہ انکار ہے ہمیشہ

> Make up your mind to one thing;
>   my heart is restless always.
> Always you say you love me;
>   always you keep me from you.   (VI.661.15)

But very often there is an implicit sympathy for her position and a note of humour to relax the tension:

ہے عشق میں صحبت مرے خوباں کی عجب کچھ

اقرار سے بے زار ہیں انکار سے ناخوش

> Strange is the loving converse which my mistress holds with me.
> My pledge of love earns her disgust—denial her displeasure!
>   (IV.486.8)

---

[16] *Under the Greenwood Tree*, Pt. IV, Chap. 6.

کیاکریں نیچی نظر کرنے سے غصّہ کھائے وہ

اور مجلس میں جو رہیئے دیکھ تو شرمائے وہ

What must I do? I lower my gaze from her and she is angry
And if I gaze only on her, she blushes and feels shy.   (III.435.5)

جو چپکے ہوں کہے چپکے ہو کیوں تم

کہو جو کچھ تھارا مدّعا ہے

سخن کریئے تو ہو وے حرف زن یوں

بس اب منھ موند لے میں نے سنا ہے

If I am quiet she aks me, "Why so quiet?
Speak up if you have anything to say!"
And if I speak she quickly interrupts me,
"Now hold your tongue! I'll hear no more today!"

(II.355.23–24)

When she deliberately ignores him, he tells her with mock naivete:

وجہ بیگانگی نہیں معلوم

تم جہاں کے ہو واں کے ہم بھی ہیں

I cannot see why you should act the stranger,
For you and I sprang from a common source. (III.413.11)

They sit together, not knowing what to say to each other, until at last she asks him why he does not say something. He answers with a straight face:

ہم تو تھارے حسن کی حیرت سے ہیں خموش

تم ہم سے کوئی کرتے نہیں بات کیا سبب

I sit in silent wonder at your beauty.
And you? What is it that has struck *you* dumb? (V.549.4)

As they grow more intimate and his occasional boldness provokes her
anger, this playing the simpleton is often his way of disarming her:

بوسہ لبوں کا مانگتے ہی منھ بگڑ گیا

کیا اتنی میری بات کا تم کو بُرا لگا

I ask you for a kiss and you get angry.
Why should a little thing like this upset you?   (II.216.4)

بوسہ لبوں کا مانگتے ہی تم بگڑ گئے

بہتیری باتیں ہوتی ہیں اخلاص پیار میں

Such anger? Just because I want to kiss you on the lips?
But things like this keep happening all the time when you're in love.
                                                    (III.420.1)

آنکھیں غصّے میں ہو گئیں ہیں لال

سر کو چھاتی پہ رکھ کے خواب کرو

Your wrath has made your eyes all tired and bloodshot
Come, lay your head upon my breast and sleep.   (VI.658.18)

But whether he can placate her or not, whether he understands her or
not, no matter how irrational and unpredictable in her ways she is at this
stage, he simply cannot help loving her:

دیر بد عہد وہ جو یار آیا

دُور سے دیکھتے ہی پیار آیا

Time after time she broke her word, but when she came at last
I saw her from afar and knew: to see her was to love her.
                                                    (VI.632.8)

As she inclines more and more towards him, he can hope that she will surrender herself completely to love and that all the barriers which for so long she has raised against him will be gone:

لطف سے لبریز ہے اس کام جاں کا سب بدن

مختلط ہو جائے ہم سے جو کبھو تو ہائے وہ

Joy of my life, her body overflows with all delights.
Ah for the day when she will come and sleep in my embrace!

(III.435.8)

چاہتا ہے جی کہ ہم تو ایک جا تنہا ملیں

نازِ بے جا بھی نہ ہووے کم نگاہی بھی نہ ہو

I want to be alone with you—just you and I together
Where haughty airs and distant looks no longer come between us.

(I.135.6)

گرمیاں متصل رہیں باہم

نے تساہل ہوئے نے تغافل ہو

Let us love one another all the time—
No feigned reluctance, no indifference.   (II.311.8)

And that stage is reached—but not without a long conflict between shame and love. At first her shyness makes him desire her all the more:

ہوتا ہے شوق وصل کا انکار سے زیاد

کب تجھ سے دل اٹھاتے ہیں تیری نہیں سے ہم

You think your "No!" can ever cool my love for you? Not so.
My longing to possess you burns more strong because of it.

(II.289.21)

اقرار میں کہاں ہے انکار کی سی خوبی

ہوتا ہے شوق غالب اس کی نہیں پر

Her sweet reluctance fires me with a keener love for her,
And her resistance gives a joy compliance cannot give.

(VI.644.5)

Yet as it continues, it puzzles him:

راتوں پاس گلے لگ سوتے ننگے ہو کر ہے یہ عجب

دن کو بے پردہ نہیں ملتے ہم سے شرماتے ہیں ہنوز

We pass the long nights naked in each other's arms. How strange
That in the daytime still she shyly veils her face from me.

(V.566.17)

At last she no longer feels any shyness when she is with him; and in her
simplicity and lack of all affectation, he finds her more irresistibly attractive than ever before:

ایک فقط ہے سادگی ترا سب بلائے جاں ہے تو

عشوہ کرشمہ کچھ نہیں آن نہیں ادا نہیں

You use no charms, no sidelong glance, no wayward airs to win me now—
Nothing but your simplicity—and this has won me heart and soul.

(I.110.3)

And though he has lost everything in loving her, he knows now that she
will respond to him fully when he says:

آج ہمارے گھر آیا تو کیا ہے یہاں جو نثار کریں

اِلّا کھینچ بغل میں تجھ کو دیر تلک ہم پیار کریں

Now you have come I've nothing left to offer you but this:
I'll draw you into my embrace and love you all day long.

(II.298.22)

   Lines like these depict a stage where love has at length triumphed over
every difficulty. But such lines are comparatively rare in ghazal poetry,
for, unlike the masnavi, the ghazal is, in the main, the poetry of un-
requited love. Both kinds of experience were abundant enough in real
life, and at first sight it seems that both the masnavi and the ghazal
present a false picture; for in all the masnavi stories, the girl, having once
given her love, is constant to the end, while in the ghazal this never
happens. The truth seems to be that here, once again, we are faced with
a convention which we must simply accept, and that one poetic form alone
was considered appropriate for the portrayal of each type of experience.
   Be that as it may, the ghazal portrays in countless verses the picture of
a girl cooling towards her lover and trying to break the ties that have
bound them. As always, it expresses only what the lover feels when this
happens; the motives of the girl's conduct are left to the imagination.
They no doubt included everything which in universal human experience
causes love to grow cold; but one must add to the picture all the strains
imposed by the Mughal social setting. The need to maintain complete
secrecy, and the ever-present fear of discovery and of the punishment
that discovery would bring, put the whole relationship between them
under tremendous stress. In general their meetings could only be in-
frequent, brief, and dangerous, and the atmosphere of strain would make
for misunderstandings and quarrels which caused them both the most
acute misery. Finally there was the feeling, especially on the woman's
part, that her conduct was shameful and dishonourable. If, faced with all
this, she felt that she could not go on, that is understandable. No doubt
in real life the same situation led as often—perhaps more often—to a
similar conclusion on his side, but the ghazal portrays only the constant
lover. He sees her love for him dying out, until the days when she responded fully and freely to his love survive only as memories:

هر آن تھی سرگوشی یا بات نہیں گا ہے
اوقات ہے اک یہ بھی اک وہ بھی زمانہ تھا

We whispered to each other then; now you don't speak to me.
Well, those were other times, and now another age has dawned.

(III.375.13)

وصل میں اس کے روز و شب کیا خوب گزرتی تھی اپنی

ہجراں کا کچھ اور ہے ساماں اب وہ لیل و نہار نہیں

How happily the days would pass when she was with me day and night.
It is a different picture now: the nights and days are not the same.

(VI.653.21)

اب وہ سماں نہیں ہے کہ وہ کام جانِ خلق

مغموم ہم کو دیکھ کے دوڑا لپٹ گیا

When I was sad she used to run and throw her arms about me—
She whom the whole world worshipped—but, alas, those days are gone.

(II.242.9)

But his memories are vivid, and they sustain him in his sorrow:

یہ بھی سماں خوش ترکیبوں کا میرے نہ اپنے دل سے گیا

سوتے سے اٹھ کر آنکھیں ملی ہیں لی انگڑائی جمائیں ہیں

I loved to see her wake from sleep, and rub her eyes, and stretch and
   yawn.
The beauty of this scene lives on unfading in my memory. (V.587.21)[17]

رہتے ہو تم آنکھوں میں بھرتے ہو تمھیں دل میں

مدّت سے اگر چہ یہاں آتے ہو نہ جاتے ہو

---

[17] The original has not "her" but "them."

My eyes still see you; *you* live in my heart
Though years have passed since you would come and go.

(II.312.8)

روز آنے پہ نہیں نسبتِ عشقی موقوف

عمر بھر ایک ملاقات چلی جاتی ۔ ہے

The bond of love does not depend on seeing you each day;
You came but once, but you are with me still my whole life through.

(I.197.15)

As the days pass, he sees that the openness and confidence which once
existed between them is dwindling, and that reserve is taking its place.
Now when he speaks to her of what he feels for her, she does not want to
hear him out:

سُن سُن کے درد دل کو بولا کہ جاتے ہیں ہم

تو اپنی یہ کہانی بیٹھا ہوا کہا کر

I told the story of my heart: she listened for a while, and said
"I have to go. But you can stay; sit there, and go on with your tale."

(IV.482.13)

He tries to tell his story as though it were someone else's, hoping that
perhaps her sympathies may be engaged before she realises that it is
really of himself that he is speaking, and that then it will be too late for
her to retreat; but this too fails:

اک شخص مجھی سا تھا کہ تھا تجھ سے یہ عاشق

وہ اُس کی وفا پیشگی وہ اُس کی جوانی

یہ کہہ کے جو رو یا تو لگا کہنے نہ کہہ میرؔ

سنتا نہیں میں ظلم رسیدوں کی کہانی

"There was a man like me loved one like you—[18]
Loyal and true and young and brave was he."
Tears came into my eyes. "Enough!" she said,
"I cannot bear these tales of cruelty."   (I.151.20–21)

Both verses describe an ambiguous situation, and express the uncertainty which the lover himself feels. Why will she not hear him out?
Perhaps because she is no longer interested in him; or perhaps because her
resolution to break with him is one which does violence to her own
feelings, and she cannot trust herself to uphold it if she thinks of the unhappiness it would cause him. In the situation described in the second
verse, it is her own conscience, as much as the tears in his eyes, which
tells her that the story is going to be a tragic one; and the reason *why* she
"cannot bear these tales of cruelty" is again left in doubt. Her lover is
again in the same uncertainty as when he first wooed her; he sees that
she wants him to believe she no longer loves him, but whether she really
has stopped loving him or whether it is fear impelling her, against her own
impulses and desires, to try and drive out love, he does not know.

While his hopes and his fears struggle with each other, he makes every
kind of approach that might move her. He complains jealously,

یا ساتھ غیر کے ہے تمھیں ویسی بات چیت
سو سو طرح کے لطف ہیں اک اک سخن کے بیچ

یا پاس میرے لگتی ہے چپ ایسی آن کر
گویا زباں نہیں ہے تھارے دہن کے بیچ

You sit with *him*, and talk flows freely from you—
Kindness unending as the day is long
And when *I* come to you, you fall so silent,
That one would think that you had lost your tongue.
                                        (II.258.21–22)

[18] In the first line we follow a different reading from that of Āsi's text.

Or he appeals to her pity:

جب نام ترا لیجئے تب چشم بھر آوے

اِس زندگی کرنے کو کہاں سے جگر آوے

Your name is spoken: tears come to my eyes.
Where shall I find the strength to live like this? (I.166.12)

گئی عمر میری ساری جیسے شمع باد کے بیچ

یہی رونا جلنا گلنا یہی اضطراب تجھ بن

The candle gutters in the draught, and my life too must waste away.
Like it I weep, and burn, and melt, and pine away parted from you.

(I.117.24)

Or he is gentle and persuasive:

دیر سے ہم کو بھول گئے ہو یاد کرو تو بہتر ہے

غم حرماں کا کب تک کھینچیں شاد کرو تو بہتر ہے

For many days you have not thought of me:
Recall me to your mind; that would be well.
How long must I bear separation from you?
Show me that you are kind; that would be well.

(IV.518.9)

Or he warns her that to spurn him will bring her unhappiness in days to come:

اب کر کے فراموش تو نا شاد کرو گے

پر ہم جو نہ ہوں گے تو بہت یاد کرو گے

Forget me now; and do not think how I shall bear the sorrow.
Today I die; it will be you who grieves for me tomorrow.

(I.169.11)

But more and more he finds that when he sees her, there is nothing he can say. He tries to persuade himself that it is because their meetings are too short:

دیر پچھ کھچتی تو ـکہتے بھی ملاقات کی بات

ملنا اپنا جو ہوا اُس سے سو وہ بات کی بات

Had there been time I would have told her what was in my heart
But when we met time was so short we could but meet to part.
(II.254.13)

Or that it is because he cannot catch her in the right mood:

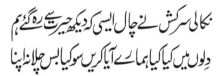

She walks in pride—so dread a sight I can but stand and stare.
Thoughts throng my mind—What of it, when I lack the strength to
     speak? (VI.633.16)

کچھ کہنے کا مقام نہ تھا وہ دا ہوتا تو کہتے کچھ

آنا نہ آنا یکساں تھا واں ہوتے اِدھر ہم گو آۓ

I get no chance to plead my case to her;
Her mood is such it does not let me speak.
I go there, but what does it signify?
To go or not to go is all the same. (V.603.24)

But he knows very well what the real reason is. Now that he fears he is going to lose her, his longing for her is so great that he cannot trust himself to speak:

جی میں تھا اُس سے ملئے تو کیا کیا نہ کہے میر

پر جب ملے تو رہ گئے نا چار دیکھ کر

I told myself, ''If we could meet I'd talk and talk to her.''
But when I did, all I could do was gaze in silence at her.

(I.70.7)

He tells himself:

كہتے تو ہو میں لوں کہتے یوں کہتے جو وہ آتا

یہ کہنے کی باتیں ہیں کچھ بھی نہ کہا جاتا

You tell yourself ''I'd tell her this, and this, and this if she would come.''
Yes, so you *tell* yourself, and yet when she is present you are dumb.

(II.237.2)

He sends word to her, and she does not even reply:

نہ کہا کچھ نہ آ پھرا نہ ملا

کیا جواب ان مرے سوالوں کا

She sent no word, nor passed my way, nor let me come to her.
Why then do I petition her? She will not answer me.   (III.384.4)

But still he does not give up hope. Her indifference—apparent or real—
changes to anger; and for that very reason he feels that all is not yet lost,
for as he tells her:

ہوتے ہو بے دماغ تو دیکھو ہو تم کو ادھر

غصّہ ہی ہم پہ کاش کے اکثر رہا کرو

I rouse your wrath,—and when I do at least you glance this way.
If only I could make you angry with me all the time!   (II.316.18)

In other words, while he is still significant enough to her to be noticed,
no matter in what emotional context, there is still a basis on which he

may build some hope. So he still comes to her lane, not in the high hopes that others do, but hoping silently for some crumb of her attention:

میر صاحب بھی ترے کوچے میں شب آتے ہیں لیک

جیسے دریوزہ گری کرنے گدا جاتے ہیں

Mir Sahib too comes to your lane each night
But as a beggar goes to beg for bread. (I.94.11)

He no longer even hopes for more than a minimum of human kindness from her; yet even that hope is vain:

اتنا کہا نہ ہم سے تم نے کبھو کہ آؤ

کاہے کو یوں کھڑے ہو وحشی سے بیٹھ جاؤ

"Don't stand there all alone. Come and sit down."
These words you could have said, but never did. (II.308.19)

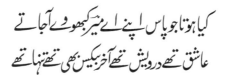

کیا ہوتا جو پاس اپنے اے میرے کبھو وہ آجاتے

عاشق تھے درویش تھے آخر بیکس بھی تھے تنہا تھے

Once in a while if she had come, what harm would it have done her?
I loved her, and was poor, and weak, and helpless and alone.

(IV.528.7)

And since even so modest a hope is not to be fulfilled, he consoles himself with the thought that even if it had been, it would not have amounted to evidence of any vestige of love on her side:

ہم تو عشق میں ناکس ٹھہرے کوئی نہ ایدھر دیکھے گا

آنکھ اٹھا کر وہ دیکھے تو یہ بھی اس کی مروّت ہے

In love you are a failure, Mir—she will not look your way.
And if she does, that is not love but common courtesy.

(V.608.14)

And if he has failed, he is in good company, for Farhād and Qais, the great lovers of Persian and Arabic legend, had fared no better:

فرہاد وقیس ومیر یہ آوارگانِ عشق

یوں ہی گئے ہیں سب کی ہی من کی من کے بیچ

Outcasts of love, Farhād and Qais and Mir roamed through the world;
And when they died their heart's desire died with them unfulfilled. [19]

(II.258.23)

Love has taught him the courage even to smile at his defeat:

دیکھا کروں تجھی کو منظور ہے تو یہ ہے

آنکھیں نہ کھولوں تجھ بن مقدر ہے تو یہ ہے

To keep my eyes on you, and you alone:
        my one and only heart's desire is this.
To open them only if you are there:
        the height to which I can aspire is this.   (I.190.7)

And after all what real difference does it make? Nothing can change the fact that he has learned to love. Nothing can stop him going on loving to the end, loving with undiminished intensity, no matter whether he can be with his beloved or is fated to live out his life parted from her, welcoming every trial, every hardship, every cruelty, in that it enables him to perfect his capacity to love, until his love is stronger than death and he is ready at any time to prove it so. Love has become a way of life for him, has developed all the potentialities which lay dormant in him, and

[19] Farhād, also called Kohkan "the mountain-digger," was, according to the Persian legend, in love with Shīrīn, the wife of Chosroes Parvez (d. 628), and the king promised her to him if he could dig a channel through solid rock. Contrary to the king's expectations, love gave him the power to complete the task, but the king sent him false news that Shīrīn was dead, and he died of a broken heart. As for Qais, he belongs to the stock of early Arabic legend. Qais was in love with Laila, but since he was unable to win her, he lost his senses and wandered through deserts and mountains, and hence was known as Majnūn, the madman. Both Farhād and Majnūn have become symbols of "absolute love," and their fate has been immortalized by the great Persian poet Niẓāmī and by many other Persian and Indo-Muslim poets, from Amīr Khosrau Dihlawī on. (A.S.)

has made him a real man. And for this no suffering is too great a price to pay. The man who has never loved is to be not envied but pitied. He tells his mistress:

ظلم و جور و جفا ستم بیداد

عشق میں تیرے ہم پہ کیا نہ ہوا

ہم تو ناکام ہی جہاں میں رہے

یہاں کبھو اپنا مدّعا نہ ہوا

میرا افسوس وہ کہ جو کوئی

اُس کے دروازے کا گدا نہ ہوا

> Much have I suffered in my love for you—
> Cruelty, persecution, and much more
> And life-long deprivation of the joys
> I spent the years in endless yearning for.
> > Yet from my heart I pity any man
> > Who never stood a suppliant at your door.

(I.54.7–10)

The man who has not loved appears in the ghazal in the stock character of the *nāsih*, or counsellor. He is portrayed as a man who thinks he understands the lover's point of view, sympathises with him, and wants to help him, but who in the last resort no more understands what love is about than do the lover's persecutors. The only difference between them and him is that what they try to do by violence, he tries to do by sweet reasonableness. But he lacks even the capacity to love, let alone the experience of it, and his advice is ludicrously irrelevant and ineffective. The lover's tone towards him ranges between angry sarcasm and good-humoured tolerance. Sometimes his advice is quoted without comment:

قدم تک دیکھ کر رکھ میرے سر دل سے نکالے گا

پلک سے شوخ ترک کانٹا ہے صحرائے محبّت کا

O Mir, be careful where you tread; their points can thrust right through
   your heart.
For sharper than her eyelashes are thorns that strew the path of love
(I.48.16)

—as though the lover did not know this even better than he! The
counsellor enlists the help of a bystander:

اے وہ کہ تو بیٹھا ہے سرِ راہ پہ زنہار

کہیّو جو کبھو میرؔ بلا کش ادھر آوے

مت دشتِ محبّت میں قدم رکھ کہ خضر کو

ہر گام پہ اس رہ میں سفر سے حذر آوے

O you who sit and watch the people going by, take heed!
Tell Mir, if you should chance to see him passing in the street.
''Don't go into the desert-lands of love—Khizar himself,[20]
If he should wander off that way, turns back his straying feet.''
(I.167.4–5)

Elsewhere, the counsellor's solemn advice is quite fatuous:

چاہت روگ بُرا ہے جی کا میرؔ اس سے پرہیز بھلا

اگلے لوگ سنے ہیں ہم نے دل نہ کسوٗ سے لگاتے تھے

Love is a mortal sickness, Mir; keep clear of it if you would thrive.
Our ancestors, I understand, used not give their hearts away.
(V.613.15)

If the lover ignores this counsel, backed though it is by reference to such
excellent precedent, the counsellor puts it down to his youth and in-
experience, but thinks it his duty to warn him:

---

[20] Khizar is a legendary figure who appears to travellers who have lost their way and sets
them on the right path again.

اب تو جوانی کا نشہ ہے بے خود تجھ کو رکھے گا

ہوش گیا پھر آوے گا تو دیر تلک پچھتاوے گا

You're young, of course, and drunk with love; the future is not clear to
   you.
Your senses will return one day; *then* see what you will have to rue.

(IV.467.2)

And so it goes on, with the counsellor ready at every stage with warnings
and good advice:

چھوڑ واس اوباش کا ملنا اور نہ سر کٹواؤ گے

چاہ رہو گے بہتیروں کو سر جو میرے سلامت ہے

Mir, give her up before your life is forfeit—
That way you'll live to love another day.   (V.621.18)

ضعف بہت ہے میرے تمہیں کچھ اس کی گلی میں مت جاؤ

صبر کرو کچھ اور بھی صاحب طاقت جی میں آنے دو

Mir, stay at home awhile until you're stronger—
You've worn yourself quite out in serving her.   (III.425.2)

And at last:

میر سدا بے حال رہو ہو مہر و وفا سب کرتے ہیں

تم نے عشق کیا سو صاحب کیا یہ اپنا حال کیا

To be good friends is very right and proper:
   You *loved*—and see the state it brought you to! (IV.466.7)

Mir replies to him quite plainly, and sometimes impatiently, but without malice, preferring to make fun of him rather than rail at him:

طنز میں عبث کرو ہو غش رہنے پر ہمارے
دو چار دن کسو سے دل کو لگا تو دیکھو

You mock in vain to see me swoon under the stress of love.
Try loving for a day or two and you will understand! (II.310.16)

رفتہ عشق کسو کا یا رو راہ چلے ہے کس کے کہے
کون رہا ہے آپ میں یاں تم کس کے تئیں سمجھاتے ہو

Friend, do you never stop to ask yourself
If lovers ever heeded what you say?
You think they hear your words? Let me tell you
They and their thoughts are miles and miles away.

(IV.509.5)

After all, he tells himself,

کیا جاتا ہے اس میں ہمارا چپکے ہم تو بیٹھے ہیں
دل جو سمجھنا تھا سو سمجھا ناصح کو سمجھانے دو

It does not cost me anything to listen
So I sit quiet and let him lecture on.
All my heart had to learn is learned already:
Poor fellow, let him give his good advice. (III.425.1)

Occasional verses make fun of the nondescript, respectable man in the street, who is too lacking in imagination and too immersed in his own petty affairs to notice the lover, or, if he does notice him, to ascribe more than the most commonplace interpretation to what he sees. He

amuses himself by imagining what such a person might have said to him
had they both lived in the days of Farhād, or Kohkan, and Qais:

کوکہن ومجنوں یہ دونوں دشت وکوہ میں سرماریں

شوق نہیں ملنے کاہم کو میرا ایسے آواروں سے

Both Qais and Kohkan roam about the deserts and the mountainsides.
Mir, I have not the least desire to mix with vagabonds like these.

(IV.514.25)

Mir, too, like Farhād and Majnūn, is reputed in some quarters to be
a man possessed by a great love; but such down-to-earth, stand-no-
nonsense people know better. One says to another:

ہوگا کسؤ دیوار کے سایہ میں پڑا میؔر

کیا ربط محبت سے اس آرام طلب کو

You'll find Mir lying in the shade of someone's wall:
What have such idle fellows got to do with love?   (II.317.17)

The first line is an effective example of the idiom of the ghazal. At first
reading it conveys plainly enough the immediate impression that his
worldly-wise critics receive when they see him—that here is an idle
fellow who does not care where he lies so long as it is in the shade. But
to men of imagination and sympathy the words themselves suggest the
real situation. They know at once that the "someone" is his mistress,
and they know why he is there, for in the symbolism of the ghazal the
constancy of the lover is represented by the picture of him watching and
waiting constantly in her lane or outside her house. They begin to
realise, too, all the implications of the word "shade," for it has many in
addition to the obvious meaning. The cool shade is a pleasant concept in
English, but it is even more so in a country where the intensity of the
heat becomes almost unbearable in some seasons of the year, and in
Urdu a wide range of metaphorical use reflects this fact. For example,
when a child's father dies, leaving him helpless and unprotected, it is

said that he has been deprived of the "shadow" of his father, in which he could rest, protected from the heat and dust of life. In this verse it suggests two things: first, an ironical situation in which what appears to others to be a life of ease and comfort passed in the cool shade is in fact the life of the lover, with all its inevitable and never-ending suffering; but secondly, it suggests also a proud acceptance of all the pleasant connotations of shade as indeed applying to the life of the true lover, for with all its suffering, it is his unbreakable constancy in love which provides the whole meaning and content of his life and brings him a profound spiritual happiness.

The tone of the lover's rejoinder to his well-meaning critics is generally mild, but there are times when he loses all patience with them. He sees that in the long run there is nothing to choose between their attitude and that of those who are openly and uncompromisingly hostile to him; and he knows that if he were to live forever, he could never hope to change them. So he allows himself the pleasure of outraging them instead. To the counsellor's reproach that his love is a sin against religion, he replies:

مذہب سے میرے کیا تجھے تیرا دیار اور

میں اور یار اور مرا کارو بار اور

Is my religion your concern? No, yours are other realms.
I, and my love, and what I do is foreign ground to you.

(III.397.7)

—a reply that deliberately invites his critic to conclude that the lover's religion *is* love. He avows this quite openly, and indeed proudly, in other lines couched in terms which he knows will shock his adversaries. Thus he tells his mistress:

سجدہ اس آستاں کا نہ جس کو ہوا نصیب

وہ اپنے اعتقاد میں انسان ہی نہیں

The man who was not fated to bow down and worship you
In my belief has not attained the stature of a man.   (I.100.11)

The words imply, and are meant to imply, something which is anathema to the orthodox Muslim—namely, that to worship one's beloved is a better religion than to worship God; though as we shall see later, what the poet is in fact contrasting with true love is not true religion but the lifeless, formal worship of a falsely-conceived God, to which he believes that most of his fellow Muslims have fallen prey. The same contrast is made when he flouts the Muslim's intense abhorrence of idolatry to say of lovers like himself:

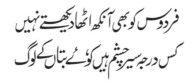

If Paradise itself were theirs they would not look at it—
Such bliss is the idolatry of gazing on her form.   (II.282.12)

The symbol of idolatry is only one of those commonly used in the ghazal to express the situation of the lover in his relationship with the ordinary, conventional man. Such a man looks upon love as a sort of madness, and the lover is proud to wear this "madness" as a badge of honour, distinguishing him from the much-prized sanity of the counsellor and the conventional citizen. His madness becomes the symbol of his complete possession by love, which so consumes him that material comforts, the social conventions, the cruelty of his beloved, and the bitter persecution of society are alike ineffective to turn him from his path. In his madness he loses all he has, lets his home fall into ruins, tears his clothes, and flees the cities and inhabited places to wander in the deserts, where the burning hot sands blister his feet and the great thorns tear at his body until it is all lacerated and bleeding, thus following the example of Qais, or Majnūn, who, in his madness, realized the reality of love. The desert becomes the symbol of the world in which he lives, his wounds the symbols of his sufferings at society's hands, and his deliberate choice of his lot and his rejoicing in it, the symbol of his deepest conviction that love is the highest ideal to which man can aspire.

But mostly the lover is less concerned with assailing the values of his adversaries than with proclaiming his own. He declares his faith that only the lover knows what it is really to live. The joy he finds in the anguish

of love's tortures, even though they reduce him to dust, is something
beyond the conception of the ordinary man. He speaks for all lovers
when he says:

اب بھی دماغ رفتہ ہمارا ہے عرش پر

گو آسماں نے خاک میں ہم کو ملا دیا

And still we dwell enraptured in the stars
After our stars have ground us in the dust.   (II.214.2)

A life of trial is the only life worth living. To suffer endlessly for one's
love, and to triumph endlessly over suffering, gives meaning to life:

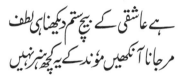

In love, to face the torture open-eyed is purest joy.
To close your eyes and die is something anyone can do.

(II.300.5)

The supreme joy, however, is to lay down one's life for one's love; to
die like this is better than to live forever. Mir uses Muslim legend to
bring this home more effectively. There is a legend that Khizar and
Sikandar (Alexander the Great) set out in search of a spring from which
flowed the water of eternal life. They found it only after facing many
dangers and difficulties, and Sikandar died before he could drink of it; but
Khizar drank, and so never dies. Mir says:

اب حیات وہی نا جس پر خضر و سکندر مرتے رہے

خاک سے ہم نے بھرا وہ چشمہ یہ بھی ہماری ہمت تھی

I found the water of eternal life
That Khizar and Sikandar strove to find.
I stopped it up until it ceased to flow.
In this you see the lover's high resolve.   (V.609.3)

The lover is of the same company as Īsa (the Muslim name for Jesus) whom Muslims revere as one of the great Prophets, for,

اب جو عیسیٰ فلک پہ ہے ہے وہ بھی

شوق میں برسوں خاک چھان گیا

If Īsa lives in heaven, it is because
For years he roamed the desert lands of love.   (II.241.6)

But he is even more fortunate than Īsa, who—since according to Muslim belief, Jesus did not die on the Cross, but was taken up, still living, into Paradise—never knew the joy of giving his life for love:

لذّت سے نہیں خالی جانوں کا کھپا جانا

کب خضر و مسیحا نے مرنے کا مزا جانا

To spend your strength unstinting till your life is forfeit too—
This is a joy that Khizar and Masīha never knew.   (II.211.15)

—Masīha meaning Christ, the Messiah. And he sums up in a striking metaphor the sustained, intense joy of the man who lives his life possessed by love. The tears of blood which, both in English and Urdu metaphor, one weeps when pain and suffering have reached their extreme, come, in the symbolism of Urdu poetry, from the heart, which constant anguish reduces to blood. And so, Mir says:

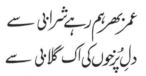

I passed my life in love's intoxication
Drunk with the rose-red wine of my heart's blood.

(I.207.21)

Verses like these express the spiritual exaltation of the man who has by constant self-discipline passed all the tests of love. He has a long road to travel before he can reach this goal. The path is the more difficult because his conception of love is not the ascetic one, which renounces love once and for all at every level except the spiritual. He wants to win his mistress physically too, to hold her in his arms and sleep with her, and hope for this outcome never wholly deserts him. But he must combine this hope with a clear understanding that it may never be fulfilled, and with an ability to make his love sufficient in itself, so that its intensity and sustaining power can bring him spiritual peace whatever may befall.

It is Mir's proud claim that he succeeded in this, and in *The Stages of Love* we have already seen him as a man whose delight in all the physical joys of love is frank and unashamed, and yet one who can also love, for as long as he lives, a woman whom he expects never to see again. As he puts it in one of his ghazals:

عشق میں وصل و جدائی سے ہیں کچھ گفتگو

قرب و بعد اس جا برابر ہے محبّت چاہیئے

> This is a realm where near and far are one;
> With her or parted from her, you must love.   (I.160.16)

To reach this ideal the lover needs a steady resolve to see things as they are, and to acquire an imaginative foreknowledge of all the possible situations of love so as to school himself beforehand to meet them. Mir reproves the young lover who feels too keenly the early trials of love:

شکوۂ آبلہ ابھی سے میّر

ہے پیارے ہنوز دلّی دور

> Already you bewail your blistered feet?
> "It's a long way to Delhi yet," my son   (I.71.21)

—as the proverb goes. He tells him that tears should not be shed too lightly:

ابتدائے عشق ہے روتا ہے کیا

آگے آگے دیکھیے ہوتا ہے کیا

Why do you weep ? Love's trials have just begun.
Keep back your tears; see what is yet to come.[21]   (I.29.11)

And he holds up his own example, stressing that one must see clearly
what the end will be and accept it without fear or equivocation even before one sets out on the long journey of love:

جب جی سے گزر گئے ہم اے میر

اس کوچے میں تب ہوا گزارا

I washed my hands of life, and only then
Could I set foot in my beloved's lane.   (III.382.16)

And he adds half-humorously:

درد سراب جو عشق کا ہے گور تک ہے ساتھ

کچھ یہ نشہ ہی اور ہے اس کا خمار اور

You are in love: your head splits, and the pain is there for life.
Love's is a different drunkenness, a different aftermath. (III.397.13)

He warns him:

عشق میں گام اوّل اپنے جی سے گزرنا پیش آیا

اس میداں میں رکھ کے قدم کیا مرنے سے ڈر جاویں ہم

At the first trial your life may be demanded.
If you're afraid, don't come into the field.   (IV.493.11)

But the first step, he tells him cheerfully, is the worst:

گزر جان سے اور ڈر کچھ نہیں

رہِ عشق میں پھر خطر کچھ نہیں

Just sacrifice your life, and fear is banished.
Go on your way; all danger will have vanished. (I.119.22)

[21] The verse quoted is one traditionally attributed to Mīr, though Āsī says that in the correct version the first words are different (cf. I.29.11 and Āsī's note).

He stresses too that readiness to give one's life is not enough. Love is a skill which must be learned like any other:

شرطِ سلیقہ ہے ہر اک امر میں
عیب بھی کرنے کو ہنر چاہیئے

In everything he does a man needs skill.
Even the art of sinning must be learned. (I.158.17)

The crises he will have to face are many and varied; he must learn how they may be overcome, and go on learning as long as he lives, and learning, above all, from his failures:

میرے سلیقے سے میری نبھی محبّت میں
تمام عمر میں ناکامیوں سے کام لیا

All my life through I learned the skills to pass the tests of love
And passed because my failures taught me how I must succeed.
(I.12.10)

Among the skills he must learn is that of perfect self-restraint, for nothing that he does must give any clue to the secret of his mistress' identity, and this means that while he may give vent to all the extravagance of his emotions when he is alone or with a trusted friend, in company where his mistress is present his conduct must be such that not even a shade of suspicion can arise. This is the severest test of his sense of honour and of his overriding regard for his mistress' good name:

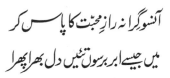

آنسو گرا نہ رازِ محبّت کا پاس کر
میں جیسے ابر برسوں تئیں دل بھرا پھرا

I keep love's secret in my heart: none ever sees me shed a tear;
Heavy as the rain-bearing cloud I wander on year after year.
(II.230.9)

تالوگ بدگماں نہ ہوں آۓ نہ اس کی اُور

ہم تو کیا ہے عشق میں دور از قیاس پاس

That no one might suspect her, I have never walked her way.
Such is the unimagined price I paid for loving her.　　　(II.274.4)

He imagines what people will say of him when he is dead:

مرتا تھا جس کی خاطر اس کی طرف نہ دیکھا

میرِ ستم رسیدہ ظالم غیور کیا تھا

Dying to see his mistress, he never glanced towards her.
Truly a man of honour was Mir, her hapless victim. (IV.462.2)

And, as so often, he expresses an essentially serious point with a touch of
humour when he says,

غیرت سے نام اس کا آیا نہیں زباں پر

آگے خدا کے جب ہم محوِ دعا ہوۓ ہیں

So jealous is my silent tongue to guard and keep her from all blame,
It calls on God to bless her, but will not tell even Him her name.
　　　　　　　　　　　　　　　　　　　　　(VI.658 n.)

The same self-restraint is needed so that the lover may accept without
hesitation and without complaint everything that his mistress may see fit
to do. He tells her,

لطف و مہر و خشم و غضب ہم ہر صورت میں راضی ہیں

حق میں ہمارے کر گزر و بھی جو کچھ جانو بہتر تم

Kindness and love and anger and disdain are all alike acceptable to me.
Whatever you think fit to do to me, make up your mind and do it out of
　　hand.　　　　　　　　　　　　　　　　　(IV.493.23)

And if her cruelty destroys him, there is no ground for complaint in that. It is in the nature of beauty to be cruel, and she can no more help it than the rose can help the nightingale dying of love of her, or than the lightning can help striking the nest:

آتشِ رنگِ گل سے کیا کہیئے

برق تھی آشیان پر آئی

Burn in the red fire of the rose in silence—
Lightning must strike, and it has struck your nest. (I.141.25)

He sustains his resolution by attributing to some fault in himself every bitter experience for which at first sight she would seem to be to blame:

مجھی کو ملنے کا ڈھب کچھ نہ آیا

نہیں تقصیر اس ناآشنا کی

I did not know the way to bring her to me.
She never came, but it was not *her* fault.   (VI.670.7)

میر صاحب ہی چوکے لے بہ عہد

ورنہ دینا تھا دل قسم لے کر

Mir was at fault in trusting to your promise:
He should have made you *swear* your love for him.   (I.73.9)

He even tells himself that it is better they should not meet, in case he should fail in his duty towards her:

ہے فرق ہی میں خیر نہ کر آرزوئے وصل

مل بیٹھیئے جو اس سے تو شکوہ دراز ہو

Better that we should stay apart; so do not yearn to see her.
Meeting would be one long complaint against her cruelty.

(I.127.3)

If death overtakes him, and she has still not fulfilled her promise to come to him, he reasons:

اس کے ایفائے عہد تک نہ جیے
عمر نے ہم سے بے وفائی کی

Life could not stay for her to keep her promise;
It was not she, but life that played me false.   (I.141.14)

If he sometimes allows himself, with a straight face, a mild joke at her expense, this is not because his attitude has changed, but because he hopes that his superficially unexceptionable statement may prompt some feelings of guilt in her heart which will incline her to relent towards him. So he replies indignantly to her suggestion that perhaps he has been complaining against her:

شکوہ کروں ہوں بخت کا اتنے غضب نہ ہو جاناں
مجھ کو خدا انخواستہ تم سے تو کچھ گلا نہیں

How *could* you, lovely one? 'Twas Fate that I complained against.
God grant I never see the day I murmur against you!   (I.109.23)

And he replies to hints from his friends that she has no intention of meeting him:

جھوٹ ہر چند نہیں یار کی گفتار کے بیچ
دیر لیکن ہے قیامت ابھی دیدار کے بیچ

My mistress promised I should see her; and she does not lie.
Though I must wait till Doomsday, I shall see her by and by
(II.258.25)

—an unanswerable argument, for every Muslim knows that on the last day the whole of mankind will meet together on the great plain to hear God's judgement.

He fully expects to die from the wounds her constant cruelty in-
flicts upon him—a situation portrayed in the conventional imagery of the
ghazal as the mistress striking off her lover's head with the sword of her
glance—and he accepts his fate with such calm composure that he can
joke even about this, telling himself:

تلوار کے تلے بھی ہیں آنکھیں تری اُدھر

تو اس تم کا میر سزاوار کیوں نہ ہو

> The sword falls, Mir, and still you stare at her.
> Is that not proof that you deserve to die?   (I.131.18)

Or he dies of love, and his friends debate whether or not this is tanta-
mount to murder at his mistress' hands. From beyond the grave he interrupts them impatiently:

خواہ مارا اُنھیں نے میرکو خواہ آپ موا

جانے دو یارو جو ہونا تھا ہوا مت پوچھو

> Natural death or murder—what's the difference?
> What had to be has been, friends. Let it pass.   (I.133.22)

He loved his mistress truly, and true love necessarily entailed unfailing
respect and reverence for her. He imagines the final proof: he has died in
her lane and turned to dust; yet when the dust is stirred by the passing
wind, it settles again at a respectful distance from his mistress' house.
His friends see it and reflect:

دُور بیٹھا غبارِ میر اس سے

عشق بن یہ ادب نہیں آتا

> Mir's dust has settled at a distance from her;
> Respect like this is only learned from love.   (I.31.21)

Superhuman restraint, absolute submission to his beloved's will, unfailing respect for her, and complete constancy—these are the qualities

which the lover must learn. Above all, constancy. Mir extols it in verse after verse, sometimes speaking directly of himself and sometimes quoting, so to speak, the testimony of others:

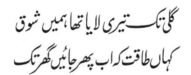

He went into her lane; then all was silent.
"Mir! Mir!" I shouted; but no answer came.   (I.26.23)

To those who warn him to come away before it is too late, he replies with grave humour:

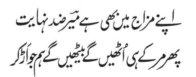

It was *love's* strength that brought me to her lane:
Where shall *I* find the strength to go back home? (I.84.5)[22]

Or he agrees pleasantly that it is sheer obstinacy that keeps him there:

اپنے مزاج میں بھی ہے میرؔ ضد نہایت
پھر مر کے ہی اُٹھیں گے بیٹھیں گے ہم جو اڑ کر

Obstinate? That indeed I am—and to the last degree.
Once I sit down nothing this side of death will get me up.
(I.70.19)

In short, so constant is he that he cannot be bothered even to reply seriously to advice to change his ways, however sympathetic and well-intentioned it may be. He has determined his course, and "though the

[22] Cf. I.181.13.

sword-blows rain upon his head,'' he will not turn aside. For him the only swords and daggers that matter are those which his mistress wields:

چھبیں تھیں جی میں وے پلکیں، لگیں تھیں دل کو وے بھوویں

یہی شمشیر چلتی تھی ، یہی خنجر جہاں میں تھا

Her eyelashes pierce to my soul, her eyebrows strike me to the heart.
These are the scimitars that cut; these are the daggers that can wound.

(III.379.5)

Yet she too has no weapon in her armoury which he cannot withstand:

تیرے تیر ناز کے جو یہ ہدف ہوئے ہیں ظالم

مگر آہنی تو سے ہیں جگر نیاز مند اں

The arrows of your pride fly fast against the target of our breasts,
But iron breastplates are the hearts of those that pledge their love to you.

(I.99.6)

He knows the treatment he must expect of her, even though she herself should promise him something else:

کہتے تو ہیں کہ ہم بھی تجھیں چاہتے ہیں میر

پر اعتماد کس کو ہے خوباں کی چاہ پر

True, you have said, ''And I love you too, Mir.''
But who would trust a lovely woman's love? (VI.643.9)

And so engrossed is he in his love that he simply does not feel anything else; pain and joy alike do not affect him:

خوش ہیں نہ گل تر سے نہ ہم خار سے ناخوش

The fresh-blown rose gives me no joy, its piercing thorn no pain.

(IV.486.6)

Whatever her treatment of him, his love is ever fresh, and he renews every day of his life his vows to serve her:

وہ سرکشی سے گو متوجّہ نہ ہو ادھر

ہم عاجزانہ کرتے ہیں اس کو سلام روز

> Each day she passes by, too proud even to glance my way:
> I in humility bow low to greet her every day.

منظور بندگی نہیں میری تو کیا کروں

حاضر ہے اپنی اُورسے یوں تو غلام روز

> My service is not pleasing to her; yet what can I do ?—
> Other than come and stand and wait to serve her every day.
>
> (II.272.15, 17)

And he must serve her with all his strength:

عشق میں کیا دخل ہے نازک مزاجی کے تئیں

کوہکن کے طور سے جی توڑ کر محنت کرو

> In love there is no room for the unduly delicate:
> Like Kohkan, toil with all your strength—yes, though your heart
>> should burst   (III.427.15)

—a line which itself implies that you may well toil only to meet with failure in the end, like Farhād Kohkan "the mountain-digger."

Love, and only love, gives him the courage and the strength to meet the dangers in which love's realm abounds. That is why, when he meets Khizar roaming in the deserts of love, he warns him that "this is a place where lions roam" (VI.632.19) and expresses concern for his safety—even though Khizar is immune to death.

مِلا جو عشق کے جنگل میں خضر میں نے کہا

کہ خوفِ شیر ہے مخدوم یاں کدھر آیا

He must be ready to face death itself at any time, and never to hesitate:

برسوں سے مری اس کی رہتی ہی ہی صحبت

تیغ اُس کو اٹھانا تو سر مجھ کو جھکا جانا

For years together this has been the converse that we hold:
She lifts the sword to strike: I bow my neck without ado.

(II.212.4)

Not only ready to die, he is eager to show that he can, eager to win the satisfaction of giving his all for love:

نظر میں آوے گا جب جی کا کھونا

ملے گا نیند بھر تب مجھ کو سونا

Let me once see my life is forfeit to you
And I shall sleep the sleep of peace at last. (II.236.15)

For

جی دیتے ہیں مرنے پر سب شہر محبّت میں

کچھ ساری خدائی سے یہ طور نیا دیکھا

Men of love's city give their lives to win the chance to die.
Search God's creation through and through: you will not find their like.

(II.228.12)

And though she is unrelenting to the last, this makes no difference.

وقتِ قتل آرزوئے دل جو لگے پوچھے لوگ

میں اشارت کی اُدھر ان نے کہا مت پوچھو

Led out to die, the people asked me what was my last wish.
I glanced towards her; she replied, "Say nothing. Do not ask."

(I.133.21)

زیرِ شمشیرِ ستم میرؔ تڑپنا کیسا

سر بھی تسلیم محبّت میں ہلایا نہ گیا

The sword of tyranny was falling, and I could not flinch.
I did not move my head—not even to avow my love.   (I.27.9)

And so the lover dies, reminding those who condole with him:

عشق جانا تھا مار رکھے گا

ابتدا میں تھی انتہا معلوم

I knew that love would take my life as forfeit.
When I began I knew how I would end.   (II.286.4)

مجھ سے کیا میرؔ جی صاحب ہم کو ہوش تھے کیا کرے

جی سے ہاتھ اٹھائے گئے پر اُس سے دل نہ اٹھائے گئے

I knew what I was doing when I chose to die; what could I do?
I washed my hands of life: I could not wash my heart of love for her.

(I.207.13)

For to die for love, to remain constantly in the beloved's lane until one
is reduced to dust, is the hallmark of the true lover:

آوارگانِ عشق کا پوچھا جو میں نشاں

مشتِ غبار لے کے صبا نے اُڑا دیا

I asked the breeze, "Where shall I find the vagabonds of love?"
It gathered up a little dust and raised it in the air.   (I.54.22)

CHAPTER FIVE

Mir and the Lover's Way of Life

IT IS NOT DIFFICULT to see that this conception of love as a way of life is one which lends itself to a wide range of symbolic application, with the beloved as the symbol of a man's ideals in life and his constancy to her as the symbol of his constancy to those ideals. As might be expected in a medieval society, it was to the sphere of religion that this transference of the experiences and the value of earthly love was first made. Long before the Urdu poets adopted the ghazal form from the Persian, ghazal poetry was moving simultaneously on two levels, so that almost any line might be interpreted as an expression either of a man's love for his mistress or, in the mystic sense, of the worshipper's love for his God. Love was divided into two categories—*ishq i majāzi*, or symbolic love, and *ishq i haqīqi*, or real love—and it is again characteristic of the medieval mind that contrary to what a modern would expect, it was earthly love which was characterised as symbolic, and mystic love which was called real.

The idea that a man's passionate love for a woman and his love for his God are two closely parallel experiences has long been unfamiliar to the modern world, and it is not easily reacquired. In the modern West in particular, people are inhibited by the strong Protestant tradition, which tends to regard sexual love as sinful, or if not sinful, at least not religious, and for this and other reasons feels very uncomfortable with the symbolic identification of God with an irresistibly beautiful woman. They would do well to remember that it did not occur to their ancestors—not even to some of their Protestant ancestors—that there anything objectionable in the parallelism between sexual and divine love. Thus in the Bible, in the Song of Solomon, one finds that the chapter headings take the most sensuous descriptions of the beloved—her feet, her thighs, her belly, her navel, her breasts—as Christ's description of the graces of the Church. This treatment is not exceptional. J. M. Cohen in his *History of Western Literature* speaks of love poetry "translated *a lo divino* for pious reading, according to the strange custom of the time, with a divine lover carefully substituted on all occasions for an earthly one."[1] True, the ghazal symbolism is here reversed, and God is not the beloved but the lover. However, the ghazal symbolism is also commonly found. The most notable instance is in Dante's *Divine Comedy*, where the figure of Beatrice appears both as Dante's earthly beloved and on other occasions as the symbol of Christ.[2] Even the *Romance of the Rose*—that most celebrated of all medieval love poems—was read by some in the divine sense, with the rose as the symbol of Jesus.[3]

Once this symbolic identification of God with the mistress is accepted, the recurring parallels between earthly and divine love are not difficult to grasp. For the starting point of mysticism is that true religion is inconceivable without a direct and intimate relationship between man and his God, and that this relationship comes into being, like earthly love, through a process which is experienced with overwhelming intensity, and which in the last resort cannot be reasoned about. In both loves there is the same yearning for union with the beloved, the same striving for perfect constancy, the same unhesitating submission to the beloved's will—even where that will seems to be cruel and capricious—the same readiness to sacrifice even life itself where love demands that price. In the Urdu ghazal the parallel goes further, for it is taken for granted that the true lover of God will face persecution and martyrdom at the hands of the world as certainly as the true lover of an earthly mistress does. A good deal of history lies behind this assumption and provides the logic on which it is based.

It is not difficult to see that mysticism is potentially a doctrine subversive of the medieval order, and therefore deeply suspect to it. For if

---

[1] *History of Western Literature* (Harmondsworth, 1956), p. 139.
[2] Cf. Dante, *The Divine Comedy*, trans. Dorothy Sayers (Harmondsworth, 1949), I. 67–68.
[3] Cf. J. Huizinga, *The Waning of the Middle Ages* (Harmondsworth, 1955), pp. 119–120.

a man's one overriding aim in life is to draw ever closer to his God, then the great ones of this world are unimportant in his eyes; and the great ones of this world do not like those who do not think them great. If he relies upon his love of God to guide him, he does not need the guidance of learned divines and does not accept their pretensions to be in some special sense the guardians of true religion; and these spiritual pillars of the medieval order do not like this attitude any more than their temporal counterparts. Islamic mysticism has a wide range of expression, and it should not be thought that this potentially subversive trend in it was everywhere made explicit, still less that it was the dominant trend in Islamic mysticism as a whole. But in the convention of the Urdu ghazal it does dominate, and is not only made explicit but, like almost everything else in the ghazal, is carried to an extreme; and piecing together the lines of Mir's ghazals, one can trace the logic of its development.

To the mystic the essence of religion is man's love of God, a love as all-consuming as love for a beautiful mistress. Rituals of worship are of no significance as compared with it, and at this point the clash with orthodoxy begins. The "Five Pillars" of orthodox Islam—that is, the five fundamental duties of a Muslim—are faith in God and his Prophet, prayer (saying the five daily prayers, the words and postures of which are minutely prescribed), almsgiving (a fortieth of one's income, in money or in kind), fasting (especially the month-long fast of Ramzān), and the pilgrimage to Mecca. To the mystic the last four are good only if they are an aid to the expression of the worshipper's love for God; they are meaningless if they are performed as a mere ritual, and positively harmful if they give rise in the worshipper's heart to the Pharisee's satisfaction that he is "not as other men are." So Mir says:

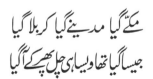

I went to Mecca, and Medina, and to Karbala 4—
And what I was, I still remain now that I have returned.

(IV.464.14)

4 Places of Muslim pilgrimage.

And:

جچ سے کوئی آدمی ہوتو سارا عالم جچ ہی کرے
مکّے سے آئے شیخ جی لیکن ہے تو وہی ہیں خرکے خر

> If pilgrimage could make a man a man
> Then all the world might make the pilgrimage.
> But *shaikh ji* [5] is just back, and look at him—
> An ass he went: an ass he has returned.   (V.560.22)

Mir is equally contemptuous of the man who serves God in order that at the last he may taste the delights of Paradise: the true lover of God would see Paradise turned into Hell sooner than have the purity of his love tainted with greed for reward:

حور و قصور و غلماں نہر و نعیم جنّت
یہ کلّہم جہنّم مشتاق یار ہیں ہم

> Houris and boys and palaces and streams of Paradise—
> Cast every one of them to Hell, and I will love my Love.
>   (III.407.24)

This is already an Islam different in kind from that of the orthodox, ritual worshipper. But the mystic takes a step beyond even this, and declares that God is known in many forms and worshipped under different names by men of different creeds. The community of his worshippers includes all men—Muslims, Jews, Christians, Zoroastrians, Hindus—whose hearts are filled with passionate love for Him, no matter in what form or under what name they conceive of Him, and who dedicate themselves wholly to doing His will. In this community differences of formal creed are of no account.

---

5 In the ghazal the shaikh is the type of the Pharisee. The root meaning of the word is "an old man," but it comes to mean "a venerable old man," "an elder," and in the context of the ghazal means the custodian of orthodox formalized Islam. Mir often sarcastically calls him "Shaikh ji"—the jī being the Indian suffix of respectful address. He is the frequent target of Mir's attacks, as we shall see.

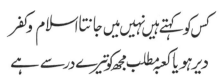

What does it mean to me? Call me "believer," call me "infidel."
I seek His threshold, be it in the temple or the mosque.   (II.366.3)

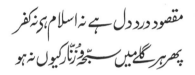

The bond of love is all—Islam and unbelief are nothing:
Take rosary *and* sacred cord and wear them on your neck.

(I.131.16)

The rosary is here the symbol of Islam, while the *zunnār*, the word here translated "sacred cord," is a very comprehensive symbol. In an Indian context it first suggests the sacred thread worn by the high caste Hindu, but it is used also for the cord worn by Eastern Christians and by Zoroastrians.

Just as the Muslim who truly loves his God is at one with the Hindu who truly loves his, so, for all their detestation of each other, is the Muslim shaikh at one with the Hindu Brahmin, for each sees himself as the jealous guardian of what he conceives of as the true religion, but what is in fact an empty ritual. In some verses the mosque and the temple are seen as their special preserve, in which the lover of God therefore has no place:

شرکتِ شیخ و برہمن سے میرؔ
کعبۂ و دیرسے بھی جائیے گا
اپنی ڈیڑھا اینٹ کی جُدی مسجد
کسی ویرانے میں بنائیے گا

Mir, quit the company of Shaikh and Brahmin
And mosque and temple too—leave them behind.
Lay one stone on another in the desert:
Worship your Love at your own humble shrine.

(I.39.8–10)

Desert, as we have seen, is an expressive word, and suggests all the connotations discussed in the previous chapter. Neither shaikh nor Brahmin is capable of seeing that

اس کے فروغِ حسن سے جھمکے ہر سب میں نور
شمعِ حرم ہو یا کہ دیا سومنات کا

It is the power of *His* beauty fills the world with light,
Be it the Ka'ba's candle or the lamp that lights Somnāth.[6]

(II.210.7)[7]

The idea of God's radiant beauty occurs again and again in Mir. God manifests himself in the universe as in a great mirror: He is immanent in all things, so that God *is* all things, and the true lover may adore Him in His handiwork:

لبریز جلوہ اس کا سارا جہاں ہے یعنی
ساری ہے وہ حقیقت جلوے نظر جہاں تک

The universe brims over with His radiance—
Nothing but He, look wheresoe'er you will.   (VI.645.22)

ہے ماسوا کیا جو میرے کہیئے
آگاہ سارے اُس سے ہیں آگاہ

---

[6] Site of one of the most famous of Hindu temples, which was destroyed in 1025 by Maḥmūd of Ghazna.
[7] The original has not "Ka'ba" but simply "mosque."

جلوے ہیں اُس کے شانیں ہیں اُس کی

کیا روز کیا خور کیا رات ۔ کیا ماہ

ظاہر کہ باطن اوّل کہ آخر

اللہ اللہ اللہ اللہ

Tell me, what else exists but He?
To him who has the eyes to see
The day, the sun, the night, the moon
Show forth His forms, His Majesty.
Manifest, hidden, first and last
Is He, is He, is He, is He!   (I.138.8–11)

And it follows that reverence for God's creation is as incumbent on the
true Muslim as is reverence for the Holy Quran, every verse of which is
His authentic word; for

آیات حق ہیں سارے یہ ذرّات کائنات

The atoms that compose the universe
Are verses written by the hand of God.   (I.131.6)

The example of the universe itself shows man the way, for it is inspired with unceasing love and adoration of the Divine Beloved, its
Creator. The stars shine like the bright eyes of the lover gazing ex-
pectantly in the direction from which he expects his beloved to come.

دیکھیں ہیں راہ کس کی یا رب کہ اختروں کی

رہتی ہیں باز آنکھیں چندیں ہزار ہر شب

Whose coming do they look for, O Lord? The stars, bright shining
Gaze on in all their thousands, wide-eyed, night after night.

                                                      (I.55.10)

The waves of the sea rise and fall like a lover repeatedly trying, and repeatedly failing, to draw his mistress into his embrace:

اُٹھتی ہے موج ہر اک آغوش ہی کی صورت

دریا کو ہے یہ کس کا بوس و کنار خواہش

Its every wave is rising up as though to clasp its love;
Who is it whom the ocean thus seeks ever to embrace?

(II.275.9)

To love and to worship the beauty of the universe is to worship God,
whose manifestation that beauty is:

عالَمِ حسن ہے عجب عالَم

چاہیے عشق اس بھی عالَم سے

The world of beauty is a wondrous world;
A man must fall in love with that world too.   (V.614.25)

گُل ہو، مہتاب ہو، آئینہ ہو، خورشید ہو میر

اپنا محبوب وہی ہے جو ادا رکھتا ہو

Whether it be the rose, the moon, the mirror, the bright sun—
Mir's love is for each thing in which the grace of beauty dwells.

(I.129.5)

The symbols of beauty are wine, the spring, youth, love—and the intensity of Mir's love for it is heightened by his ever-present consciousness
that all these things pass quickly away. The very beauty that you see
today springs from the soil of other beauties long since turned to dust:
the rose grows from the dust of some beautiful woman; the nightingale
in some way preserves the traces of some dead poet; and he who walks

in the garden today thinks of these things and feels his joy tinged with sadness: [8]

جمشید جس نے وضع کیا جام، کیا ہوا

وے صحبتیں کہاں گئیں کیدھروے ناؤنوش

جُز لالہ اُس کے جام سے پاتے نہیں نشاں

ہے کوناراس کی جگہ اسبو بدوش

جھومے ہے بیدجائے جوانان مے گسار

بالائے خم ہے خشت سرپیرِ مے فروش

The great Jamshed who made the wine cup, where is he today?
Where are the revellers whom wine and music used to thrill?
His cup is gone—save that the tulip still preserves its shape.
Only the poppy's shoulder now supports its wine bowl still.
A fragment of the tavern-keeper's skull closes the vat.
The willows sway where slender youths once came to drink their fill.

(I.78.9–79.1)

And present beauty in its turn will quickly fade. Beauty is like the running water of a fast-flowing river, in which you may just dip your hand before it is gone from you forever.[9] All beautiful things are short-lived, and life is like them:

بوئے گل یا نوائے بلبل تھی

عمر افسوس کیا شتاب گئی

The rose's scent, the nightingale's sweet song
And life—alas! how soon they fade away!　　(IV.529.5)

---

[8] Allusions to IV.503.14 and I.50.5–6.
[9] Allusion to II.288.21.

And youth, the springtime of life, passes yet more quickly, like the flash of light on a cup of wine.[10] The young lover tells his mistress:

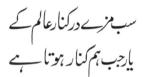

My darling, come to me tonight: the days move on:
Tomorrow you, and I, and youth will all be gone.   (V.608.1)

Enjoy beauty while you may and let all else go by the board:

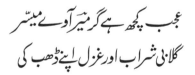

I spurn all other joys the world can offer
When my beloved lies in my embrace.   (V.619.24)

Rejoice in the coming of spring, when the rosebuds, red as wine, appear in the garden, and the green plants sway like drunkards. Soon the green leaves come out on every branch, and the plants bend under the weight of their flowers, and the breeze tugs, as it were, at your heart, as though to draw you towards the rose garden; and you must respond and take your flask of wine and go out.[11] And poetry crowns your enjoyment of it all:

What wonderful good fortune when you get
Both rose-red wine, and poetry like Mir's.   (I.143.25)

[10] Allusion to I.40.2.
[11] Allusions to II.334.23, IV.521.15, III.404.21.

The memories of these days last when they are gone beyond recall; and you remember how

مے گلگوں کی بوُ سے لبسکہ میخانہ مہکتا تھا

لبِ ساغر یہ منھ رکھ رکھ کے ہر شیشہ بہکتا تھا

The fragrance of the rosy wine pervaded all the tavern;
The bottle babbled to the cup, his mouth upon her lip.

(680.3)

کیا لطف تھا کہ میکدے کی پشتِ بام پر

سوتے تھے مست چادرِ مہتاب تان کر

What days those were!—when I would drink and climb up to the tavern roof
And fall asleep, the white sheet of the moonlight over me.   (II.270.13)

That these beauties are short-lived is a lesson you find it hard to learn, for you do not want to believe it. Each year you hope that the rose will bloom a little longer, but such hopes are foolish self-deception:

کہا میں نے کتنا ہے گل کا ثبات

کلی نے یہ سُن کر تبسُّم کیا

I asked how long the rose would bloom.
The rosebud heard my words and smiled.   (I.4.2)

The word "smiled," to repeat Olive Schreiner's words, "says more than it says." The rosebud smiles, first at the foolish hopes that lie behind so naive a question, and secondly because in smiling it answers the question. "To smile" is a regular metaphor for the blooming of a flower; the moment the bud blooms, it loses its existence as a bud; and its implication is that the rose itself will fade and pass out of existence as quickly and irrevocably. So learn the lesson while you are young; learn to treasure every moment of beauty that is given you; make the love of beauty your way of life, and it will not forsake you even in old age. In verses written quite late in his own life, Mir says:

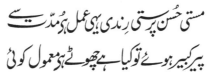

Drinking, worshipping beauty, revelry—
These three have occupied me all my days.
I am an old, old man, but what of that?
After so long, I cannot change my ways.   (V.606.14)

I cannot sit down quietly to die.
Yes, even now my heart will not be still.
While I have breath, with each returning spring
I must go out—my eyes must look their fill.   (IV.519.19)

The man who has learned this way of life will, to his last breath, be grateful for every crumb of beauty life still gives him. In the ghazal the lover's mistress is a falconer and he the hunted bird, who loves her the moment he sees her, and regrets only that he is dying and will never see her more. And yet

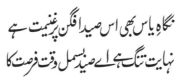

Even the last despairing glance you cast towards the fowler
Is treasure: for, O dying bird, your time is short indeed.
                                                    (I.48.13)

A man can and should cultivate a capacity for the worship of beauty, but in the last resort the full awareness of the beauty of the universe, which is the beauty of its Creator, comes to him as a revelation, and a revelation of such power that he can do no other than surrender to it. It becomes something so precious to him that he will give anything to make it his own. Mir pictures it being offered for sale in the market place: hermits leave their solitary life to come to bid for it; the shaikh offers for it his robes—the essential symbols of his shaikhhood. All men's eyes are on it: the rake comes from the tavern and the sober, pious worshipper from the mosque,[12] and men are eager to buy it with their very lives.[13] The man whose eyes have once been opened to see God's beauty in the universe is drawn to Him as wholly and as irresistibly as a man who falls in love at the first sight of a lovely woman. In many verses this parallel between the earthly and the divine beloved is explicit, and the verses may be interpreted in either sense or in both:

کس کی مسجد کیسے بت خانے کہاں کے شیخ و شاب

ایک گردش میں تری چشمِ سیہ کے سب خراب

Mosque and temple, shaikh and Brahmin, old and young and grave and gay—
Turn your eyes of black on them and see them fall beneath your sway.

(I.56.13)

طرزِ نگاہ اس کی دل لے گئی سبھوں کے

کیا مومن و برہمن کیا گبر اور ترسا

The way she looks has conquered all men's hearts—
Muslims and Brahmins, Christians and Jews.[14]   (II.212.22)

ہم ہوئے، تم ہوئے، کہ میر ہوئے

اُس کی زلفوں کے سب اسیر ہوئے

---

[12] Allusions to V.590.21, II.259.1, II.297.10, III.387.6–7.
[13] Allusion to IV.484.14.
[14] The original has not "Jews" but "Zoroastrians."

Yes, we and you and Mir are all her captives;
The beauty of her tresses binds us fast.   (I.172.1)

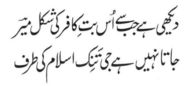

God knows what magic power her red lips hold;
Their still fire raises tumult in the world.   (II.308.10)

The worship of beauty is expressed symbolically in the language of
Hindu idolatry. The mistress (whether human or divine) is the idol; and
her house (the universe) is the temple in which the lover worships. And
it is this idolatry of beauty, and not Islam, which is the true religion:

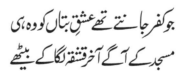

Since first I saw the form of that sweet infidel, my idol
I cannot find it in my heart to contemplate Islam.   (II.278.12)

جو کفر جانتے تھے عشقِ بتاں کو وہ ،ہی
مسجد کے آگے آخر قشقہ لگا کے بیٹھے

The very men who thought it blasphemy to worship idols
Sit now before the mosque and put the caste mark on their brow.
                                                    (II.348.13)

These verses are deliberately calculated to outrage the narrowly orthodox, but their real intention is to assert as forcefully as possible that true
religion, including true Islam, demands the love and worship of beauty as

an aspect of the love and worship of God, a point which Mir makes in the paradoxical verse:

ہیں مسلمان ان بتوں سے ہمیں

عشق ہے لا الہ الّا اللہ

> True Musalman am I, for to these idols
> I pledge my love. "There is no god but God." (III.432.20)

"There is no god but God" are, of course, the first words of the Muslim profession of faith. There could be no more forceful way of asserting that God and "these idols"—that is, God and beauty—are one and indivisible.

If all created things "declare the glory of God," none declares it so eloquently as man himself. To the Muslim, man is *ashraf ul makhlūqāt*, "the noblest of created things," greater even than the angels, for when God created Adam, He commanded the angels to bow down before him, and Satan (or Iblīs), the chief among them, was banished forever from God's presence because he refused to do so.[15] All men, Muslim or Hindu, fair-skinned or dark, rich or poor, learned or ignorant, are heirs to this greatness, and the humanism already implicit in the insistence on the oneness of all men who love God truly, whatever the form in which they worship Him, is made explicit in many verses. If the universe is a

[15] The story that the angels were ordered to prostrate before the new-created Adam, and that only Iblīs refused to do so, is told in the Qur'ān several times: 7.10, 17.63, 18.48, 20.115. It is one of the favourite stories of the mystics, who developed their anthropology and satanology out of it. The expression "the noblest of created things" does not occur in this exact wording in the Qur'ān. (A.S.)

As another classic proof of the greatness of man, Mīr refers (as the great Persian poet Hāfiz had four centuries before him) to a verse in the thirty-third chapter of the Qur'ān which reads—in the translation of A. J. Arberry, *The Koran Interpreted* (London, 1955), II, 129: "We offered the trust to the heavens and the earth and the mountains, but they refused to carry it and were afraid of it; and man carried it." What "the trust" was is not made clear, but to the poets the essential point is that God entrusted to man a burden which the heavens and the earth and the mountains dared not accept from Him, and that he alone had the courage and the strength to sustain it. Cf. VI.613.25, I.34.1, III.442.22. (This trust has likewise been a favourite topic of the modernists. Iqbāl, for instance, explains it as the power of individuation, which is man's prerogative and danger—A.S.) A. E. Housman has a poem of remarkably similar content: cf. p. 230 of *Collected Poems* (Harmondsworth, 1956). Āsī's footnote (to p. 442) quotes the most famous verse of Hāfiz on this theme. It is love that gives man the strength to sustain this burden. Cf. III.370.7.

mirror, the lustre which gives it both its own beauty and its power to reflect the beauty of God comes from man alone:

آدم خاکی سے عالم کو جلا ہے ورنہ

آئینہ تھا یہ ولے قابلِ دیدار نہ تھا

Man, formed of clay, gave lustre to this mirror:
None would have looked into it but for him.   (I.43.23)

آدمی سے مَلک کو کیا نسبت

شان ارفع ہے میرا انساں کی

What have the angels got to do with man?
The highest rank belongs to him alone.   (II.325.23)

Man was made from a handful of dust, but it is as though that dust were something very rare and precious, gathered by years of searching and sifting from ordinary dust:

مت سہل ہمیں جانو پھرتا ہے فلک برسوں

تب خاک کے پردے سے انسان نکلتے ہیں

Don't think us cheap: the heavens revolve for years
To bring forth man out of the veil of dust.   (I.98.22)

Such a creation as man is develops potentialities of its own:

ہیں مُشتِ خاک لیکن جو کچھ ہیں میرے ہم ہیں

مقدور سے زیادہ مقدور ہے ہمارا

Made from the clay—but what we are, we are.
Our power is greater than the power God gave us.

(I.28.23)

16 Cf. III.376.1.

And his aspirations are high as his origins are low:

گرچہ انسان ہیں زمیں سے ولے

ہیں دماغ ان کے آسمانوں پر

True, man was fashioned out of earth, and yet
His high resolve exalts him to the skies. (VI.641.12)

Mir represents mankind when he says:

ہیں گدا میر بھی ولے دو جہاں

کرکے ایک ہی سوال لیتے ہیں

Mir is a beggar, yes; but when he begs
He asks for nothing less than the two worlds. (III.419.21)

God created man, and found His creation good. But man himself cannot
be satisfied to be simply what God made him:

اب ایسے ہیں کہ صانع کے مزاج اوپر بہم پہنچے

جو خاطرخواہ اپنے ہم ہوئے ہوتے تو کیا ہوتے

Such as we are, God fashioned us close to His heart's desire:
If we had been what *we* had wished, what might we not have been!
(I.157.16)

The man who does not rebel against the role God planned for him is not
worthy of his human status:

الٰہی کیسے ہوتے ہیں جنھیں ہے بندگی خواہش

ہمیں تو شرم دامن گیر ہوتی ہے خدا ہوتے

Oh God, what sort of men are they who love to be Thy servants?
I would have been beset with shame even had I been God. (I.157.14)

This note of rebellion against God's will is heard recurrently in many forms. God himself exalted man above the angels. And yet man is now everywhere degraded and dishonoured, even by God himself, for nothing happens except by His will. There is a note of sarcasm in Mir's reflection on this:

خاک کو آدم کرکے اٹھایا جس کے دست قدرتنے

قدر نہیں کچھ اس بندے کی یہ بھی خدا کی قدرت ہے

Adam rose from the dust, formed by His mighty hand
To serve Him; now none honours him. Such is God's might!

(V.608.19)

If this was the fate God had in store for him, why did He create him? Why does God's word, the Holy Quran, stress his exalted status? And, most cruel mockery of all, why does God predestine all his actions and then call him to account as though he had acted of his own free will?

آنکھیں کھلیں تو دیکھا جو کچھ نہ دیکھنا تھا

خوابِ عدم سے ہم کو کاہے کے تئیں جگایا

My eyelids opened, and I saw what none should have to see;
I slept in nonexistence: why did You awaken me?   (II.249.24)

بہت سعی کریئے تو مر رہیئے میر

بس اپنا تو اتنا ہی مقدور ہے

The most that you can win is death at last.
Such is the power God has given you!   (I.179.8)

خوف قیامت کا یہی ہے کہ میر

ہم کو جیا بارِ دگر چاہیئے

If Mir fears Judgement Day it is because
He must rise up and start to live again.   (I.158.18)

ناحق ہم مجبوروں پر یہ تہمت ہے مختاری کی

چاہتے ہیں سو آپ کریں ہیں ہم کو عبث بدنام کیا

You call us free? You slander us unjustly.
Your will is done—and *we* must take the blame.   (I.4.10)

منھ نہ ہم جبریوں کا کھلواؤ

کہنے کو اختیار سا ہے کچھ

All that we "free" men do is under duress;
Mind that You do not force us to speak out!   (II.322.22)

God's very self-sufficiency is a ground for suspicion and complaint:

خدا کو کام تو سونپے ہیں میں نے سب لیکن

رہے ہے خوف مجھے وہاں کی بے نیازی کا

To God I have committed all my purposes—and yet
My heart misgives me; is He not a law unto Himself?

(I.53.6)

The same awareness of man's unique potentialities and of the unique honour he should enjoy in God's universe dictates the relations that should prevail between man and man. Mir believes that the essence of true religion can be summed up in the commandment not to injure your fellowmen, and that formal religion is unimportant by comparison:

در مسجد پہ حلقہ زن ہو تم

کہ رہو بیٹھ خانۂ خمار

جی میں آوے سو کیجیو پیارے

ایک ہونا نہ درپے آزار

Go to the mosque; stand knocking at the door—
Live all your days with drunkards in their den—
Do anything you want to do, my friend,
But do not seek to harm your fellowmen.

(I.68.24;69,1)[17]

کہتا ہے کون تجھ کو یہاں یہ نہ کر تو وہ کر

پر ہو سکے جو پیارے دل میں بھی ٹک جگہ کر

When have I said to you, "Do this!" or "Don't do that!" No, only try
To make more room within your heart: there is no other law, say I.

(I.70.21)

Many verses elaborate these general commandments. If you would obey
them, you must first change yourself, learning how to see "the fire that
stirs beneath the ruby"—that is, the potentialities that lie hidden beneath the surface in every man.[18] You must eradicate from your heart all
arrogance towards him, and bring in humility in its place:

جائے غیرت ہے خاکدان جہاں

تو کہاں منہ اٹھائے جاتا ہے

دیکھ سیلاب اس بیاباں کا

کیسا سر کو جھکائے جاتا ہے

Here in this world of dust look to your honour;
Head high in pride, you care not where you tread.
See how the flood, which makes this desert blossom
Moves ever on its path with lowered head.　　(II.353.8–9)

---

[17] This verse is almost an Urdū version of a couplet of Ḥāfiẓ.
[18] Allusion to III.445.11.

In Urdu the word for a humble, modest man means literally "like the dust," and Mir argues that to be "like the dust" is not to degrade one-self but merely to pay the dust the honour due to it, for it was from the dust that Adam, the ancestor of all mankind, was formed, and it is to the dust that all men one day return.[19] Pride and careless indifference can inflict inestimable harm:

بے لوگ تم نے ایک ہی شوخی میں کھو دیے

پیدا کئے تھے چرخ نے جو خاک چھان کر

One wilful act of yours, and he is lost
Whom heaven had sifted all the earth to find.   (I.74.1)

The "yours" may refer to God, to a cruel mistress, or to any man who fails in due regard for his fellowman, but in every case the stress is on the preciousness of man, and the need to act carefully so as not to hurt him. For man's heart is like a phial of delicate glass, which a single thoughtless action can shatter beyond repair.[20] In his autobiography Mir recalls the words of a mystic he had heard in his childhood: "Never on any account give pain to any man's heart, or break this phial with the stone of cruelty; for in the heart of man the Divine Beloved sits enthroned, and it is His special abode."[21] And often in his poetry, when he wants to stress the need to refrain from every action which can cause man pain, he uses this same metaphor of the phial or sometimes of the wineglass filled with the wine of the heart's blood and as beautiful as it is fragile. Or else in metaphors, which become all the more vivid when one recalls the con-ditions of the age in which Mir lived, the heart is a splendid city or a beautiful building that only a ruthless enemy would destroy:[22]

دل وہ نگر نہیں کہ پھر آباد ہو سکے

پچھتاؤ گے سنو ہو یہ بستی اُجار کر

The heart is not a city that can rise again from ruins.
Loot it, and—do you hear me?—you will live to rue the day.
(I.69.17)

[19] Allusions to IV.497.6 and I.103.21.
[20] Allusion to I.179.4.
[21] Cf. *Ẕikr i Mīr*, p. 39.
[22] Allusions to I.179.4, I.176.23, I.137.2–4.

دل سے خوش طرح مکاں پھر بھی کہیں بنتے ہیں

اس عمارت کو ٹک اک دیکھ کے ڈھایا ہوتا

No palace ever built could match the heart for grace and beauty.
Had you but glanced at it, could you have razed it to the ground?

(II.233.5)

The ideal is so to develop your sensitivity that you feel another's pain as
though it were your own. Often Mir compares man in his distress to a
songbird imprisoned in a cage, and says:

جی کھنچ گیا اسیرِ قفس کی فغاں کی اُور

تھی چوٹ اپنے دل کو گر قتارہم ہوئے

I heard the lamentation of the prisoner in his cage—
It was *my* heart that ached, and *I* that was held captive there.

(III.442.23)

If it were in his power, he would make all men happy:

میرے جنگل تمام بس جاوے

بن پٹرے ہم سے روزگار اے کاش

All the waste land would thrive and teem with life—
Alas! if only I controlled the means!   (IV.485.18)

If you can once fill your heart with the love of your fellowman, you
will inspire an equal love in his heart, and you will then see a miracle performed. For when love possesses it, that same heart which was once as
brittle as glass becomes so strong that no power can assail it. No longer
is it a fair palace defenceless against those who would destroy it. On the
contrary, when cities are destroyed, the building of the heart still stands:

یہ بنا رہتی سی آتی ہے نظر یہاں کچھ مجھے

اچّھی ہے تعمیر دل کی اس خراب آباد میں

The building of the heart alone is raised on strong foundations;
The heart alone will stand when ruin overwhelms the town.

(III.412.14)²³

ثباتِ قصر و در و بام و خشت و گل کتنا

عمارتِ دلِ درویشں کی رکھو بنیاد

Palace and gate and roof and brick and clay—none of them last;
So make the humble heart the strong foundation of your house.

(III.394.7)

دل میں رہ دل میں کہ معمارِ قضا سے اب تک

ایسا مطبوع مکاں کوئی بنایا نہ گیا

Live in the heart; make it your home; for the Great Architect
Has never built a dwelling so acceptable as this.   (I.27.13)

Verses like these depict the heart possessed by love as a power that stands immovable against every conceivable force. But it is something more than that; it is itself a force or irresistible power:

ماہیّتِ دو عالم کھاتی پھرے ہے غوطے

یک قطرہ خون یہ دل طوفان ہے ہمارا

دل کہ اک قطرہ خوں نہیں ہے بیش

ایک عالم کے سر بلا لایا

This heart which seems no greater than a single drop of blood
Is like a whirlwind mingling earth and heaven with its force.

(I.43.17; 33.16)

---

²³ Cf. V.591.10.

For the heart bears all, but conquers all. Physically small though it is, its capacities are as great as the ocean, as vast as the great expanses of the desert.[24] And this is why the heart, the seat of love, the throne of the Divine Beloved, the heart infinitely sensitive and yet infinitely strong, is man's surest guide in life:

طریقِ عشق میں ہے رہنما دل

پیمبرِ دل ہے، قبلۂ دل، خدا دل

Love was our faith, this heart our guide along the path we trod;
This heart was our preceptor, this our Prophet, this our God
(VI.647.6)[25]

—"our Prophet" and "our God" because the bidding of the heart *is* the bidding of the Prophet and of God.

Yet the man who would follow its dictates implicitly clashes inevitably with the pillars of society and with the man of the world. To the kings and nobles the good man is he who submits to their authority and obeys their will. To the shaikh, who is always the ally of the powers that be, he is the man who reveres him and looks to him for spiritual guidance. And neither king nor shaikh looks kindly upon one who rules his life not by their commands but by the voice of God, which speaks to his heart and tells him that love—love of God and love of his neighbour—must be the sole force which guides him. Neither the wealth of kings nor the learning of divines impresses him; both are quite irrelevant to man's task in life:

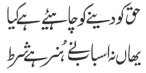

What do you need to render what is due ?
Nor wealth nor learning enters into it.   (II.276.11)

---

[24] Allusions to the ghazal in the fifth dīvan, pp. 579–580.
[25] Cf. III.405.10.

The clash with the man of the world is equally unavoidable. For the man of the world prides himself on his practical wisdom, on accepting the world as it is, on taking the view that high principles are all very well, but that a man has to make his way in the world, and in the practical business of life it is madness to bring principles into it. To this argument Mir replies, in effect, that if that way of life is sanity, then give him madness every time. For this madness is, once again, the madness of the lover, the way of life of the man so possessed by love for his mistress or his God or his ideals that he remains true to it no matter what men who lack the capacity to comprehend it may think of him or do to him. Such madness is a source of both joy and pride to him, for it teaches a wisdom incomparably higher than that produced in the hard heads of practical men, and any lapse into their sanity and good sense is something to regret:

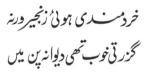

Good sense has come to fetter me. Before that
I knew the joy of life, for I was mad.   (I.98.15)[26]

He knows as well as the man of the world that this is the way not to wordly success but to poverty and destitution. The world does not treat kindly those who do not conform to its ways; Fate does not befriend such men, and it is the height of simplicity to expect it to:

It made and marred a thousand such as you.
Don't be so simple: Fate is not your friend.   (III.389.14)

The heavens extend like a vast table, with the gold and silver plates of the sun and the moon set out upon it, and you might expect to receive royal hospitality there. You would be wrong, for "both these plates are

[26] Cf. VI.661.7 and II.300.19.

empty."[27] But to the true lover his poverty is his badge of honour, the mark of his freedom and independence and determination to follow his own ideal. He is a *faqīr*—a word in which the senses of beggar and holy man are still closely associated in Urdu; he asks no man's favour, but trusts to God and to the generous impulses of his fellowmen to sustain him. And no status that the world can give a man can compare with his:

هو کوئی بادشاہ کوئی یہاں وزیر ہو

اپنی بلا سے بیٹھ رہے ہے جب فقیر ہو

> This may be king, and that be minister;
> What do I care? Am I not a faqīr?   (II.312.18)[28]

He owns nothing, so that when he lies down to sleep, he must pillow his head on his arm. That is why, Mir explains gravely, he cannot hold out his arm to beg; it has gone to sleep from the pressure of the head resting on it, and he cannot move it.[29]

Enough has already been said to show that "the religion of love," as Mir many times calls it[30] has its own commandments, and that these more often than not clash head-on with the commandments of orthodox Islam. It would be an understatement to say that no attempt is made to avoid this clash. The mysticism of the ghazal is the extreme, radical mysticism which the orthodox—the shaikh of the ghazal convention—abhorred, hated, and persecuted; and his loathing was most cordially returned. In the ceaseless warfare that followed, each side pushed its position to extremes. The mystic had started from the point that the prescribed Muslim duties of prayer, fasting, almsgiving, and pilgrimage were at best of limited value in helping the worshipper to cultivate the all-important love for God, and could be harmful if their ritual performance became a substitute for true religion and a source of self-righteousness. He now took the unequivocal view that they were always harmful, the source of bigotry and self-satisfaction, and nothing else; and not only must the mystic not perform them; he must openly flout them. Much the same is

[27] Allusion to I.101.3.
[28] Cf. I.43.7, VI.672.8, II.342.``
[29] Allusion to IV.521.16.
[30] I.24.13, V.570.11.

true for the Muslim prohibition on wine. Wine is not the enemy of the
true lover of God, but his helper, for it frees him from the crippling inhibitions of worldly wisdom and brings into play all the generous impulses of his heart. Moreover, intoxication with wine serves as a symbol
of that intoxication with the love of God which is the mystic's aim,
and thereby helps him to achieve that aim. Music and love—both of them
disapproved by the orthodox—fulfill a similar function, helping him
towards an ecstasy in which all consciousness of self is lost. Hence the
mystic is not only a lover but also a *rind*—a word in which the senses of
drunkard, happy-go-lucky, profligate, and rake are all present. He spends
his time in the taverns just as the ''godly'' man spends his in the mosque;
the deference which the godly man pays to the *imām*, or the man who
leads the congregation in prayer, the *rind* pays to the tavern-keeper;
what prayer and fasting and pious works are to the orthodox, wine and
music and revelry are to him. So that if he goes into the mosque, it is by
accident:

مستی میں لغزش ہو گئی معذور رکھا چاہئے

اے اہلِ مسجد اس طرف آیا ہوں میں بہکا ہوا

Worshippers in the mosque, it was an accident that brought me here.
My drunken feet have strayed this way: I trust you will forgive me!

(II.231.4)

In this setting the profligate's attacks upon his archenemy the shaikh
are more good-natured than in other contexts—rough, it is true, but not
bitter, as though he vaguely realises that after all it is not the shaikh's
fault, poor fellow, that he is like he is:

منکرِ حُسنِ بتاں کیوں کر نہ ہووے شیخ میر

حق ہے اس کی اور وہ آنکھوں سے ہے معذور تک

Of course shaikh won't concede to us the beauty of our idols.
There's something to be said for him, poor fellow. He is blind.

(II.280.1)

And sometimes Mir feels that even the shaikh, if only he can once be cajoled or bullied into exposing his heart to the full influence of wine and beauty, may yet be saved. One of the few ghazals of Mir which possesses continuity of theme expresses this mood:

شیخ جی آؤ مصلّیٰ گرو جام کرو
فرشِ مستاں کرو سجادہ بے تم کے تیئں
دامنِ پاک کو آلودہ رکھو بادے سے
نیک نامی و تقاوت کو دُعا جلد کہو
ننگ و ناموس سے اب گزر و جوانوں کی طرح
اُٹھ کھڑے ہو جو بُھکے گرد میں مینائے شراب
مطرب آ کر سے چنگ نوازی تو تم
سایۂ گل میں لب جوپہ گلا بی رکھو
آہ تا چند رہو خانقہ و مسجدیں

جنسِ تقویٰ کے تیئں صرفِ مے جام کرو
مے کی تعظیم کرو شیشے کا اکرام کرو
آپ کو منجھوں کے قابل دُشنام کرو
دین و دل پیش کش سادہ خود کام کرو
پرفشانی کرو اور ساقی سے ابرام کرو
خدمتِ بادہ گساراں ہی سر انجام کرو
پیرہنِ مستوں کی تقلید سے انعام کرو
ہاتھ میں جام کو لو آپ کو بدنام کرو
ایک تو صبح گلستان میں بھی شام کرو

Shaikh, pawn your prayer mat—for its price you'll get a glass of wine or so;
Yes, sell the gear of piety so that the rose-red wine may flow.
Or else unroll your worthless mat for drunkards to recline upon.
Sing praises to almighty wine! All honour to the bottle show!
Let the wine stain your spotless robe! Pester the pretty serving boys!
They'll swear at you, and that will be a fresh delight for you to know!
Come on now, say a quick goodbye to good repute. Your heart and faith
Present as an unworthy gift to her in whom all beauties glow.
Yes, let your good name go to hell. Be like the lads, and spread your
    wings.
Shout to the *sāqi*, "Bring more wine!"—and scold him if he comes too
    slow.

Stand up! The flagon bows its head to serve the revellers. You too
Proffer your services. You too in token of respect bow low.
The harpist comes to play and sing. You've nothing to reward him with?
Then be like us: take off your shirt and give him that. He won't say no.
Under the rosebush in the shade set down the wine jar by the stream.
Go on, take up your glass and drink. Disgrace yourself with high and low.
Too long the mosque and monastery have stifled you. One day at least
Set out at dawn and spend the day in gardens where red roses grow.

(I.130)

Verses in the same mood call on the recluse and the ascetic to follow
suit.

تو بھی رباطِ کہن سے صوفی سیر کو چل تک سبزے کی
ابر سیہ قبلہ سے آ کر جھوم پڑا میخانوں پر

Come on out, recluse! Leave your cell and see the green plants growing
And black clouds sent from Mecca swaying high above the taverns.

(V.559.3)

کہہ صوفی چل میخانے میں لطف نہیں اب مسجد میں
ابر ہے باراں باد نرمک رنگ بدن میں جھمکا ہے

Come to the tavern, recluse, now, for joy has left the mosque.
The rain falls, and the breeze blows soft, and all your body glows.

(IV.525.23)

طاعت کوئی کرے ہے جب ابر زور جھومے
گر ہوسکے تو زاہد اس وقت میں گنہ کر

Do people lead the holy life when clouds sway overhead?
In days like these, ascetic, you should see if you can sin.

(I.71.5)

The reference to the swaying clouds sets the scene in the rainy season, when after weeks of parching heat, rain falls torrentially and every green thing grows luxuriantly, and an atmosphere of relief and joy infects everyone. This season, and the nights of the full moon, are regularly associated in Urdu poetry with wine drinking, and the invitation to drink is therefore unmistakably implied. The tone of both verses is mocking. Thus in the first the point is stressed that the rain clouds come from Mecca, the holy city towards which Muslims turn to pray—and they do indeed come from that direction—so that the recluse may be more disposed to listen to their message. But the mockery is quite good-natured. The profligate's exhortation to the ascetic to see if he can sin stems from two convictions: first, that what the orthodox regard as sin is not sin at all, and secondly that if, by giving full rein to his best impulses, he does sometimes commit the sins of excess, this is still a far better thing than to live as the orthodox do, in mortal fear of sin, repressing every bold and generous instinct:

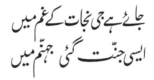

To save their souls they kill themselves with care.
A Paradise like that can go to Hell!　　　　　　　(III.419.7)

To lead such a life in the hope of heavenly reward is in any case unworthy of the true lover of God, who loves without any thought of benefit to himself. But is is also an insult to God in that it casts doubts upon His infinite mercy.[31] To mortify the flesh is to starve the soul as well and to do violence to the nature which God gave you. So Mir reassures his companions:

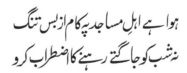

---

[31] Allusion to V.605.17.

خدا کریم ہے اس کے کرم سے رکھ کر چشم

دراز کھینچو کسو، میکدے میں خواب کرو

The people of the mosques are near to desperation. Why should you
Distress yourself to be like them and watch and pray throughout the
   night?
For God is merciful; His mercy is the hope to which we look.
Go to the tavern, lie full length, and sleep at ease till morning's light.

(IV.507.3–4)

ہم مذنبوں میں صرف کرم سے ہے گفتگو

مذکور و ذِکر یہاں نہیں صوم وصلوات کا

    It is God's mercy that we sinners speak of;
    Fasting and prayer are never mentioned here.

(II.210.10)[32]

In other images the point is driven home that it is the profligate and not
the shaikh who finds favour in God's sight. Thus it is he who is chosen to
lead the worshippers in prayer:

پھر میرؔ آج مسجدِ جامع کے تھے امام

داغِ شراب دھوتے تھے کل جانماز کا

Again today in the great mosque Mir led the worshippers—
He who but yesterday had washed the wine stains from his prayer mat.

(II.218.1)

Or, in another picture, the humblest of those who frequent the tavern is
worthy to be the guardian of the holy city of Mecca:

شریفِ مکّہ رہا ہے تمام عمر اے شیخ

یہ میراب جو گدا ہے شراب خانے کا

32 Cf. VI.638.9.

He has been all his life Sharīf of Mecca, shaikh—
This Mir who begs today outside the tavern door. (I.37.12)

If in this sort of context the shaikh is attacked with a sort of rough good
humour, elsewhere the tone is bitter and contemptuous. For if the shaikh
persecutes the mystic as a heretic and blasphemer, the mystic counter-
attacks with charges of worldliness, self-seeking, and hypocrisy.[33] In his
eyes the shaikh is a man whose guiding principles are derived not from the
religion he professes but from a despicable worldly wisdom which teaches
him to avoid unpopularity and shun conflict with the great and powerful,
or an even more despicable greed for wordly power which makes him
identify his interest with theirs. He is quick enough to fulminate against
others for real or imagined lapses from religious duty, but in secret he
himself does not observe even the plainest and most unambiguous commands of Islam, like the prohibition on wine. True, one cannot often
prove that he sins, but sin he does, and not in moderation. The shaikh is
to Mir what the Holy Willies and the ''unco guid'' are to his spiritual
brother and younger contemporary, Robert Burns; and like Burns, he attacks them with ridicule, bawdy, and invective. The shaikh boasts of his
other-worldliness, but God knows what pleasures he secretly prays for:

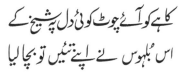

Shaikh never knew the ache of love. How could he?
He took good care to feel no more than lust.   (II.246.21)

His pretensions and those of his Pharisee friends to enjoy the privilege of
a special closeness to God contrast glaringly with his utter insensitivity
to what afflicts the hearts of God's servants, his fellowmen:

بندے کے دردِ دل کو کوئی نہیں پہنچتا

ہر ایک بےحقیقت یہاں ہے خدا رسیدہ

They cannot feel the grief that wounds His servant's heart,
Yet every worthless fellow here ''communes with God.''

(II.321.4)

33 Allusion to II.304.13.

For the sympathetic study of the human heart he substitutes the study of his books, until all hope of humanising him is gone:

کب اس عمر میں آدمی شیخ ہوگا

کتابیں رکھیں ساتھ گو ایک خربار

> What if he owns a donkey-load of books?
> Shaikh has got past the age to be a man. (I.69.13)

The implied comparison is clear, and is sustained in other verses. Mir pictures him with the staff which he always carries as the mark of his authority, and comments:

بن عصا شیخ یک قدم نہ رکھے

راہ چلتا نہیں یہ خر بے چوب

> Shaikh cannot walk a step without his staff—
> An ass that needs the rod to make him go. (I.57.3)

Give him wine and he at once reveals his true nature:

کچھ کم نہیں ہیں شعبدہ بازوں سے مے گسار

دارو پلا کے شیخ کو آدم سے خر کیا

> Our revellers are quite a match for any conjurer;
> They gave shaikh wine, and turned him from a man into an ass.
> (I.30.15)

Yes, he is an ass, and should be used as one:

قصدِ حج ہے تو شیخ کو لے چل

کعبہ جانے کو یہ بھی خر ہے شرط

> You're going to make the Pilgrimage? Then take the shaikh along;
> If you're to reach the Kaba, you must take an ass with you.
> (II.276.9)

His pretensions to insight and understanding are ridiculed, and Mir combines sarcasm on this score with a neat compliment to himself:

میر صاحب کا ہر سخن ہے رمز

بے حقیقت ہے شیخ کیا سمجھے

Mir's every word has meaning beyond meaning—
More than a worthless shaikh can understand.   (II.349.10)

شیخ تونے خوب سمجھا میر کو

واہ واہ اے بے حقیقت واہ واہ

Yes, shaikh, you understand Mir perfectly!
Bravo! you worthless dolt! Bravo! bravo!   (II.320.8)

Sometimes the shaikh's associate, the *vāiz*, or preacher, comes under fire. He is treated with the same sarcasm:

ہم نے یہ مانا کہ واعظ ہے ملک

آدمی ہونا بہت مشکل ہے میاں

I grant you, sir, the preacher is an angel.
To be a man, now—that's more difficult.   (II.306.6)

The comparison with the angels, who never fail in serving God, is here turned against the preacher by recalling how God commanded the angels to bow down before man. And another verse makes the same point. However angelic the preacher may be, he hardly qualifies for the honoured status of man:

برسوں تئیں جب ہم نے تردّد کئے ہیں تب

پہنچایا ہے آدم تئیں واعظ کے نسب کو

I worked at it for years, and only then
Could trace his lineage back to Father Adam.   (II.317.12)

Sometimes the tone is more serious:

شیخ کی تو نماز پر مت جا

بوجھ سر کا سا ڈال آتا ہے

> Shaikh says his prayers? Don't be deceived by that.
> Prayer is a load he lowers from his head.[34]   (I.178.1)

The more serious tone of a verse such as this brings one back to the essential basis of the conflict between the mystic and the shaikh. To the mystic the essence of religion is to love God with all your heart and soul and to love your neighbour as yourself. If you live by this religion, all other commandments are superseded; you may—indeed, you must— give full rein to every generous impulse within you, to everything which stimulates love and adoration; and if this sometimes leads you to excess, you can trust implicitly in God's infinite mercy to forgive you. The shaikh by contrast cannot even comprehend the meaning of loving God; to him religion means to obey Him, and this obedience he interprets in the narrowest sense, of formal compliance with prescribed rituals. He calls God "the Compassionate, the Merciful," but his whole attitude shows that in practice he conceives of Him as a ruthless, implacable tyrant. Because he observes the forms of religion, he exalts himself above his fellowmen; narrowness, intolerance, bigotry, and pride dominate his outlook, and he is as zealous in the condemnation and persecution of his fellows as he should be in love for them. And all too often he is a hypocrite, false even to that apology for a religion which he himself professes, and dominated by the lusts of the world.

Between him and the mystic, therefore, it is war to the end, and because the world and all its powers are on the shaikh's side, the prospect for the mystic is life-long persecution and, in the end, martyrdom. Where it is war to the end, any attempt to mitigate the harshness of the struggle is pointless. On the contrary, any word or action of the mystic that wounds the shaikh is a victory over him. Hence the ridicule and

---

34 In India loads are commonly carried on the head. The shaikh says his prayers not because devotion to God impels him to, but as an onerous duty that has to be discharged. The metaphor suggests also the ritual of Muslim prayer, in which one of the required postures is to lower one's forehead to the ground.

vituperation; hence the open violation of the prescribed ordinances of formal Islam; and hence the formulation of mystic doctrines in terms deliberately intended to outrage the orthodox. The type of the true mystic, in the eyes of the ghazal poet, is Mansūr al Hallāj,[35] who was crucified by the orthodox in A.D. 922 for crying out, ''Anā'l Haqq Anā'l Haqq''—''I am God! I am God!''—words which to the mystic express his sense of the complete merging of the individual soul with the Divine Beloved, but which to the orthodox are unspeakable blasphemy. Mansūr used to urge the absolute duty of standing by right, whatever the circumstances, by saying that he must take Satan as his model—Satan, who stood his ground and refused to bow down to Adam, even though this involved defiance of God's direct command, punished by the loss for ever of his pre-eminent position among the angels and by expulsion from heaven. Mir's position, and that of the ghazal poets in general, is Mansūr's position, and he takes it for granted that he will share Mansūr's fate.

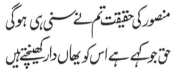

You must have heard what happened to Mansūr—
Here, if you speak the truth,[36] they crucify you.   (I.114.15)

And thus the parallel is completed between earthly and divine love. Persecution and perhaps death await alike the man who is constant in his love for his mistress and him who is constant in his love for his God and his ideals.

It has already been emphasised that the mystic extremism which the convention of the ghazal reflects was only one of the many forms that

35 Ḥusain ibn Manṣūr al Ḥallāj, the Woolcarder—mostly called after his father's name ''Manṣūr,'' the ''Victorious''—to whose fascinating personality the French orientalist L. Massignon has devoted fifty years of study, has been transformed, especially in the Indo-Pak environment, into the typical symbol of suffering love; but since he declared openly, ''I am the absolute Truth,'' he was accused of having disclosed the Divine secret—hence the stress laid by mystics upon ''hiding the secret, concealing the name.'' Cf. A. J. Arberry, Sufism (London, 1950), pp. 59–60; A. Schimmel, ''The Martyr-Mystic Ḥallāj in Sindhī Folk-Poetry,'' Numen, IX (1963), 3. (A.S.)
36 This is a play on words. Here Mir uses the word ḥaqq in the sense of ''the truth.'' But it is the same word as Manṣūr used in his cry ''Anā'l Ḥaqq!'' which there means ''God.''

mysticism took, and certainly not the dominant one in Islamic mysticism
as a whole. The identification of the ghazal poet with the mystic is a
conventional and not a literal one; and so is the identification of mysticism as a whole with the radical, extremist brand of it which the ghazal
presents. The actual historical picture is rather different. It shows that
the earlier mystics, far from attacking orthodox usages, were most particular to observe them, and while orthodoxy always distrusted the
mystic approach, it did not yet persecute it. Later mystics, of whom
Mansūr al Hallāj is the type, clashed sharply with the orthodox and seem
to have made no attempt to avoid doing so. Mansūr can hardly have failed
to realise how blasphemous his teachings must have sounded to orthodox
ears. Others were not less bold in their doctrines, but increasingly felt
the need to conceal them from the uninitiated, speaking of their mystic
experience only to those who had prepared themselves to receive and
understand it. A further parallel here arises with the situation of the
lover; like him, the mystic lover violates the code of love if he allows the
secret of his love to become known to a hostile society. If Mansūr
sinned, said later mystics, this was where his sin lay, and Mir is making
the same point when he writes:

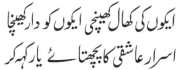

> Some they impaled upon the stake, and some they
> took and flayed alive.
> No lover yet betrayed the secrets of his love but
> had to die. (I.71.4)

After Mansūr came men who approach more closely the position that
the ghazal describes. One of them was the Persian Abu Sa'īd,[37] who
would not permit his disciples to make the pilgrimage to Mecca and
taught that the true mystic had no need to keep the commandments of
orthodox Islam. But the extreme position which the ghazal portrays, the
position of men who—deliberately, ostentatiously, and with intention to

---

[37] Abū Sa'īd ibn Abi'l-Khair (967–1049), one of the leading mystics of his time, lived in
Nīshāpūr. A number of mystical quatrains have wrongly been attributed to him. Cf. R. A.
Nicholson, *Studies in Islamic Mysticism* (Cambridge, 1921). (A.S.)

provoke the hatred of the orthodox—violated the law of Islam and the conventions of Islamic society, was probably never that of more than a small minority. In any case, long before Mir's day the bitter persecution of the mystics had ceased. If orthodoxy never wholly lost its distrust of mysticism, it had nevertheless come to accept it as a legitimate approach to God, provided that the commands and prohibitions of orthodox Islam were also observed; and the mystics on their side, whatever they might say or do within their own closed circle, were quite content to show these outward signs of conformity. What survived in the ghazal tradition were the types of the protagonists of the earlier struggle and the portrayal of all their practices, used as the symbols of something wider. Just as the ghazal adopts the language of Hindu idolatry as a striking way of asserting the worship of God through the worship of beauty, and the complete incompatibility of such worship with a soulless, ritualised "Islam," so too it adopts the language of mystic extremism as the most vivid way of asserting the spirit of mysticism as a whole.

But the gap between symbolic expression and literal reality may be even greater than this. The fact that the conventions of the ghazal prescribed the theme of love (in both the literal and the mystic senses) compelled every ghazal poet to present himself as a lover and a mystic, and we have to assess in each case from such factual knowledge as we possess to what extent he really was either. In an age when poetry was one of the polite accomplishments, the answer was quite often, "Not to any extent at all," for the rules of the ghazal, both in regard to form and theme, are so detailed, and its stock of traditional symbols and allusions so vast, that anyone who had the technical competence could make a ghazal out of them; and ghazals were written by men who show no sign of ever having been in love either with a woman or with their God.

But this is not the case with Mir. We know, both from his own masnavis and from external sources, that he had experienced love and had undergone the inevitable social persecution which this involved and which in his case actually drove him mad. But we know also that his mistress was not the cold, cruel mistress of his ghazals but, on the contrary, one who responded fully and tenderly to his love; and we may therefore legitimately conclude that the cruel mistress of the ghazals is the symbol of something else. To say that she stands for God, the Divine Beloved, would convey too narrow an impression to the modern reader.

In the terminology of the ghazal "real love"—that is, divine love—embraces not only the love of God in the sense in which the modern understands it, but a man's complete dedication to his ideals in life, ideals which he will serve to the end, no matter what suffering this may bring down upon him. The medieval man did not distinguish between the service of God and the service of his ideals, for he saw his ideals as prescribed for him by God and his devotion to them as an integral part of his devotion to God. But the modern distinction is relevant to an understanding of Mir, the more so because Mir was not himself a mystic, although he was deeply influenced by mysticism.

We can estimate the extent of its influence fairly accurately, mainly from his own direct testimony, which is to be found in a short work that he wrote in Persian prose entitled *Zikr i Mīr* (An Account of Mir). This is generally referred to as his autobiography, and indeed it is difficult to know what else to call it, though it is not what we understand by the term today, for Mir himself rarely comes into the foreground in it. Nowhere in the book does Mir claim to be a mystic, though he tells us that his father was, and the book begins with an account of his father and of the other mystics who were intimately associated with him. It continues with a very brief narrative of Mir's own experiences from the time of his father's death, during his boyhood, to the establishment of his reputation as a poet, and then goes on to tell the story of the decline of the Empire over a period of forty years—from 1748 to 1788—bringing in occasional references to the way in which the course of events affected his own fortunes. The quotations from Mir in Chapter 1 were taken from this book.

It is significant that the first part of the book, which covers little more than ten years out of the total span of about sixty, occupies more than a third of the whole. It consists, in the main, of stories of his father, of his father's young disciple Amānullah, whom Mir called "uncle," and of their mystic associates, and it is abundantly clear that their teachings made a life-long impression upon him. They treated him as a child mature beyond his years, and he has vivid memories of the things they said to him or to others in his presence. Scholars dispute over the extent to which the incidents he relates can be regarded as reliable, but whether they are reliable or not, they testify to Mir's deep interest in mysticism and show what aspects of it most strongly appealed to him. Chief among these was the mystics' stress on the all-pervading force of love. Mir quotes his father's words to him, urging him to love and to learn that love is the supreme force in the universe. And years later he begins one of his masnavis (*The Flame of Love*) [38] not with the lines in praise of God and the Prophet which convention prescribed, but with a hymn to love which virtually reproduces in Urdu verse these same words that his father had spoken to him. "Love brought forth light out of the darkness," it begins.

> Without love God could not have made Himself manifest. Love alone drives on the work of the world: without it the world would cease to move, and the heavens to revolve. It is love that gave heat to the sun, love that scarred the heart of the moon. Love can set fire to water. It is love for the candle's flame that draws the moth to burn to death, and that same flame of love that melts the candle away. It is love that opens the delicate mouths of the rosebuds to blossom in a smile, love that moves the rose to unfold her beauty before the nightingale, and love for the rose that inspires the nightingale's sweet, lamenting song. . . . It is love that sets man's heart aflame, that heart which, without love, is no better than a stone. It is love that inspires him to heroic deeds, love that makes him bow his neck gladly to receive the death blow from his beloved's sword, love that makes possible those things that, without love, man could not even conceive of. The whole firmament is filled with love, and earth and sky are brimming over with it.

The introduction to his own love story, *The Stages of Love*, is on similar lines, and his own experience must have strengthened his conviction of the truth of his father's words. He took also from the mystics their belief in the holiness of beauty, their humanism, their refusal to compromise their principles for the sake of worldly advancement, and their proud self-dedication to the highest ideals of life. The verses in praise of wine and extolling the man who violates the formal commandments of Islam seem, however, to be purely symbolic, for there is no evidence that Mir, so far as the externals of daily life were concerned, was in any marked way different from the average Muslim of his day.

Whatever Mir believed in, he believed in passionately, and he sought to express his beliefs in his poetry. He seems to have decided to devote himself to poetry from quite an early age, and indications in his autobiography suggest that he had already made his name by the mid-1740s—

[38] *Kulliyāt*, pp. 890–891.

that is, in his early twenties. His verse shows that one aspect of his humanism was his keen awareness that present generations inherit the achievements of men who have lived before them, that every man "builds his house with the clay of a hundred vanished forms" [39] or with the clay of men "whose mark is still to be seen on earth." [40] And with this goes the awareness that he too must make his contribution to mankind:

هميں کیا جو پوچھے کوئی ہم سے میّر

جہاں میں تم آئے تھے کیا کر چلے

What should I say if anyone should ask me:
"What did *you* do while you were in the world?"

(I.202.13)

Though Mir revered the mystics he did not follow those among them who withdrew from the world to live in solitary contemplation of God. He remembers how his father's young disciple, his "uncle" Amānullah, had shut himself up to devote himself to study and contemplation, and how when a year had gone by, his father had told him that he must return to live his life among other men.[41] And he writes:

بائے دنیا میں رہو غمزدہ یا شادرہو

ایسا کچھ کرکے چلو یاں کہ بہت یاد رہو

You must live in the world, where griefs and joys beset you—
And live to such effect that men may not forget you. (III.428.10)

Time is short, and death comes every day to thousands:

کارواں درکارواں یاں سے چلے جاتے ہیں لوگ

ہر طرف اس خاکداں میں دیکھتے ہیں گرد گرد

Caravan after caravan moves off to leave this world.
On every side you see their dust that rises in the air.

(III.394.18)

---

[39] Allusion to I.70.16.
[40] Allusion to II.264.12.
[41] Cf. *Zikr i Mīr*, p. 19.

You cannot afford to delay in doing what it lies in your power to do. Man's life is like a spark which flies up in the air and is gone; [42] all the more reason then why he should make good use of the short time allotted to him:

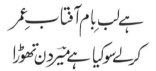

Time does not wait: too soon your eyes will close, Mir.
All that you have to do you must do quickly.   (IV.507.5)

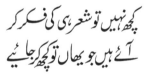

The sun of life sinks fast behind the roof.
Do what you have to do, Mir; night comes on.
                                                        (III.382.6)

Mir knew what he had to do, and it is characteristic of him that he could write with ironic understatement of what was in fact the most important thing in his life:

If nothing else, you can at least write poetry.
Now that you've come, do something while you're here.
                                                        (II.352.8)

Despite the fact that Urdu poetry was still in its infancy in northern India, Mir set himself ambitious aims. In a short work written before he was thirty, he defines rekhta (as Urdu poetry was called in his day) as "poetry on the Persian model, written in the language of . . . Delhi," [43] and goes on to describe his own practice in Urdu poetry in terms which

42 Allusion to I.113.13.
43 Nikāt ush Shu'arā, pp. 1, 187.

make it clear that he aimed to bring Urdu verse to the same pitch of
technical accomplishment as several centuries of development had produced in Persian. True, he enjoyed two great advantages: first, that the
whole literary heritage of Persian lay ready to hand, and secondly, that
he worked within a general trend towards supplanting Persian by Urdu as
the medium of poetry. The work just referred to is a brief account of his
contemporaries in Urdu poetry, and no less than 103 are spoken of in it.
Nevertheless, in this development Mir and Sauda—or "Mir and Mirza"—
were early recognised as being head and shoulders above the rest, and it
is remarkable in how short a time Urdu poetry developed to maturity in
their hands.

As we have said, Mir's main attention was devoted to the ghazal. In the
most recent edition of his collected verse, his six *dīvāns*, or collections of
ghazals, occupy 808 of the 1344 pages, and the first (and earliest) dīvān
contains some of the best. In general he works with apparent ease within
its somewhat strict conventions, but he also has no hesitation in breaking
them occasionally where he feels the need to do so. For example, two
ghazals on the same page in his first dīvān (I.50) consist of only three
couplets each (as against the generally prescribed minimum of five),
while at the other extreme, there is one in his second dīvān of no less
than thirty-two (where the most liberal of the prosodists allow only
seventeen), and that too with a single theme running throughout
(II.264–268). In another ghazal of exceptional length—nineteen couplets
—he anticipates criticism with a joke:

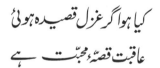

My ghazal's a qasīda? Well, what of it?
Is it not written on the theme of love? (I.193.4)

The words imply several arguments. If one takes rhyme scheme as the
salient characteristic of a particular form of verse, the ghazal and the
qasīda differ only in length, so that a ghazal which exceeds its prescribed
length does indeed become a qasīda. Mir therefore admits the charge,
and then goes on to justify what he has done. His poem is "on the theme
of love," he says; and this implies, first, that the main requirement of the

ghazal has thus been fulfilled; secondly, that because the themes of love are so inexhaustible, it is not always proper to curtail them by imposing an arbitrary and inflexible limit on the length of the poem; and thirdly, that the qasīda is by definition a poem of praise, and what could be more fitting than to write one in praise of love, the thing which beyond all others is most precious to the ghazal poet?

He allows himself a similar freedom with the laws of metre. Urdu metre, being based upon the Arab-Persian system, resembles that of the ancient classical languages, Sanskrit, Greek, and Latin, in that it is primarily based upon quantity.[44] But long and short syllables are some-what differently defined. In Urdu a short syllable consists of an initial short vowel, or a single consonant followed by a short vowel, while a long syllable consists of an initial long vowel, consonant-long vowel, or con-sonant-short vowel-consonant. The pattern of longs and shorts in a line determines the metre, and these patterns are, to modern ways of thinking, very rigidly prescribed. Thus if a poet selects for a poem the metre: ˘ — — | ˘ — — | ˘ — — | ˘ — (the metre of Mir Hasan's *Enchanting Story*), every line of that poem must reproduce this pattern exactly, without the sort of variation which is permitted, for example, in the Greek and Latin hexameter, where in many positions two shorts may be used as a variant of one long. Moreover, the Urdu poet is not, in general, permitted—as the ancient poets were—to run together all the words of the line for the purpose of scansion: every word must scan separately. In practice these restrictions are less severe than they might seem, because in Urdu the laws of quantity are modified by what one may call the "beat" of the rhythm. The effect of this is that many, though not all, consonant-long vowel units may, according to the poet's convenience, be scanned short, provided that they are not in a position where the beat of the rhythm also falls. In addition, there are a few metres, out of a very large total, that permit a measure of variation. That which Mir adopted for his own love story, *The Stages of Love*, is perhaps the commonest of this small group. Its basic pattern is — ˘ — — | ˘ — ˘ — | — — , but a short may replace the first long of the first foot; two shorts may replace the first long of the last foot; and other variations as well sometimes occur.

---

[44] The traditional science of prosody does not treat of the metre in these terms. But cf. R. Russell, "Some Problems of the Treatment of Urdu Metre," *Journal of the Royal Asiatic Society* (April 1960), pp. 48–58.

This much freedom was available to every Urdu poet, but Mir claims more than the general share. Thus, where it suits him, he will use colloquial Delhi pronunciations as the basis of his scansion, while elsewhere he uses the generally accepted ones. He also has a favourite metre in which the role of the musical beat is much more marked than in most, and the range of permissible variations much greater than the writers of textbooks on metre find comfortable. Its basic line consists of fifteen long syllables, with the beat falling on the first, third, fifth, and so on. But in any of the even syllables (second, fourth, sixth, etc.) except the eighth, which immediately precedes the caesura, two shorts may replace a single long. The effect is strikingly beautiful, and Mir seems to have grown increasingly fond of it in his later years, for in his fifth and sixth dīvāns it occurs again and again.[45]

But ghazals which break the accepted canons—whether of metre or length or form or theme—are exceptional in his work. He chose the ghazal form as his main medium because he felt it to be suited to his needs, because the themes that convention prescribed for it were precisely those on which he wanted to write, and because its intense and personal tone accorded well with his own temperament. The ghazal allowed him the unrestrained freedom to speak the truth about love and life as he saw it, and to attack the enemies of that truth in the sharpest terms. Society tolerated such frankness in poetry alone, and it was a freedom that Mir treasured:

عجب ہوتے ہیں شاعر بھی ہیں اس فرقے کا عاشق ہوں

کہ بے دھڑکے بھری مجلس میں یہ اسرار کہتے ہیں

What wondrous people poets are! They are the men I love;
In full assembly they speak out all that is in their hearts. (I.113.3)

اسرارِ دل کے کہتے ہیں پیر و جوان میں

مطلق نہیں ہے بندہماری زبان میں

I speak the secrets of my heart to old and young alike;
My voice is free and unrestrained; and none can curb my tongue.
(VI.652.25)

---

45 The ghazal given in the Appendix below is in this metre.

The great strength of his work lay in the fact that it told of things which he really felt with all his being. But he knew also that intensity of feeling alone was not enough; this was the raw material of poetry, but a mastery of the poet's craft was also needed before it could be made into a finished product, and he worked hard to acquire it. He wrote in his autobiography: "I exerted myself to the utmost in practising it [Urdu poetry], and the day soon came when the poets of Delhi acknowledged my mastery, and my verses became popular with high and low throughout the city." [46] His claims are borne out by a study of his verse, for some of his very best ghazals are in his first dīvān. In it he confidently prophesied the fame that he would win:

پڑھتے پھریں گے گلیوں میں ان ریختوں کو لوگ

مدّت رہیں گی یاد یہ باتیں ہماریاں

Men will recite my verses as they walk the city's lanes;
For years to come my words will live on in their memory.

(I.96.23)

And more boldly still:

جانے کا نہیں شور سخن کامرے ہرگز

تا حشر جہاں میں مرا دیوان رہے گا

My verse will live eternal down the years;
As long as the world lasts, so will my fame.   (I.5.12)

By the time he was compiling his second dīvān, he could record with pride how justified his confidence had been, how his fame had spread from northern India into the Deccan, and how he had evolved his own thoroughly distinctive style:

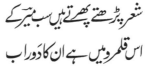

شعر پڑھتے پھرتے ہیں سب میرے کے

اس قلمرو میں ہے ان کا دور اب

It is Mir's verses that you hear on all men's lips;
In these dominions it is he who reigns today.   (II.251.3)

46 Ẕikr i Mīr, p. 67.

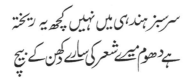

سرسبز ہند ہی میں نہیں کچھ یہ ریختہ
ہے دھوم میرے شعر کی سارے دکھن کے بیچ

My poetry grows green not only in the northern plains.
In all the Deccan too the praises of my verse resound.

(II.258.17)

نہیں ملتا سخن اپنا کسو سے
ہماری گفتگو کا ڈھب جدا ہے

My verse is not like any other poet's—
The way I speak to you is all my own.　　(II.355.16)

And later still, in his fourth dīvān he boasts:

دور تک رسوا ہوا ہوں شہروں شہروں ملک ملک
میرے شعر و شاعری کا تذکرہ گھر گھر ہے اب

In every region, every city, far and wide my fame is known;
The beauty of my poetry is spoken of in every home　(IV.471.23)

—and this not only in the cities but "in the country towns and the villages" as well (IV.475.18). Even if we allow for a measure of poetic exaggeration here, the truth behind it remains substantial. A nineteenth-century writer[47] tells us that Mir alone among Urdu poets had his verses taken along by men going on a journey to present to their host on their arrival.

It is worth attempting to illustrate some of the most notable aspects of his craftsmanship, though some cannot be adequately conveyed by translation. The first is his command of language. He naturalised with complete success many of the turns of phrase of the Persian ghazal, but this success is itself based upon the ease with which he made the speech of Delhi the basis of his diction. He once said that the basis of his poetry was

47 Āzād, *Āb i Ḥayāt*, p. 203.

"the steps of the Jama Masjid," [48] the great mosque in Delhi built a century earlier by the Emperor Shāhjahān. By this he meant that his language was that which the citizens of Delhi spoke when they conversed together on the steps of the great mosque; and he prided himself on his ability to use it poetically. His diction can be extremely simple, and yet extremely effective, exemplifying what in Persian and Urdu rhetoric is called "sahl i mumtana"—the forbiddingly simple. Ghālib, the greatest Urdu poet of the century following Mir's death, said that the term describes "the kind of writing which looks easy, but which you cannot match" [49]—the kind of line, for example, in which Mir describes how overwhelmingly beautiful his mistress' body appeared to him, saying that it was

قالبِ آرزو میں ڈھالا ہے

As though cast in the mould of my desire.   (921.9)

Or in which, writing years later, he describes his last parting from her:

یوں ہوا ان کے کوچے سے آنا

جیسے ہو وے جہان سے جانا

It seemed that as I came out of her lane
I went my way leaving the world behind.   (927.21)

He describes the lover, dying to speak his love and yet unable to utter a word in his mistress' presence:

کیا کہیں کچھ کہا نہیں جاتا

اب تو چپ بھی رہا نہیں جاتا

What can I say to her? No words will come.
And yet unless I speak to her, I die.   (II.235.20) [50]

The lover, hoping desperately that his proud mistress will just glance his way, says:

---

[48] Cf. below, p. 265.
[49] Cf. Ghālib, 'Ūd i Hindī (Lucknow, 1941), p. 200.
[50] Which, however, differs slightly from the traditional version here translated.

گر چہ کب دیکھتے ہو پر دیکھو

آرزو ہے کہ تم ادھر دیکھو

I cannot think that you could look at me,
Yet I will wish that you would look at me.   (I.124.22)

Years after he has lost her he imagines himself telling her:

رہتے ہو تم آنکھوں میں بستے ہو تمھیں دل میں

مدّت سے اگر چہ یہاں آتے ہو نہ جاتے ہو

My eyes still see you; *you* live in my heart,
Though years have passed since you would come and go.
                                            (II.312.8)

This extreme simplicity of diction often goes hand in hand with simplicity
of metre and form—used in short ghazals with a short unit line of eight to
ten syllables.[51]

His handling of the language is equally effective when he brings a
lighter touch to his themes. Many of his lines incorporate popular pro-
verbs and have a touch of humour about them:

شکوۂ آبلہ ابھی سے میرؔ

ہے پیارے ہنوز دلّی دور

Already you complain of blistered feet?
"It's a long way to Delhi yet," my son.   (I.71.22)

کرے کیا کہ دل بھی تو مجبور ہے

زمیں سخت ہے آسماں دُور ہے

What can I do? My heart is in her power.
"The earth is hard, the sky is far away."   (I.178.23)

---

[51] Two examples of such ghazals were given above, pp. 128 and 175.

That is, my present lot is hard, but every alternative seems unattainable. Another time the lover justifies his way of life to a critic not directly but by pleading that he acts under constraint:

لاعلاجی ہے جو رہتی ہے مجھے آوارگی

کیجئے کیا میرؔ صاحب بندگی بیچارگی

I roam about disgraced, but nothing can be done about it.
What is a man to do, Mir Sahib? "Service is servitude."

(I.145.22)

That is, when a man serves someone else he cannot do as he likes, for he is not his own master. And the someone else is in this case, of course, his mistress (or, his God). In a verse where the context is left to be inferred someone says to Mir:

میرؔ عمداً بھی کوئی مرتا ہے

جان ہے تو جہان ہے پیارے

No man goes to his death with open eyes, Mir.
"If you have life, then you have everything."   (I.180.9)

The speaker is probably the counsellor, the man who gives the lover well-meaning advice which common sense suggests to one who has no real inkling of what love is all about. And to those who know the ghazal and its values, the words themselves are enough to suggest their answer: that while other people do not adopt a course in life which they know will be fatal to them, the true lover does, and must, do precisely that.

Verses like these, in which Mir with such evident ease introduces the phrases of everyday speech, were and still are much appreciated. He makes similar use of the exclamations in Arabic which are still commonly used by Urdu speakers at solemn moments:

پیرِ مغاں سے ہے بے اعتقادی

استغفر اللہ استغفر اللہ

The tavern-keeper is nothing to you?
May God forgive me! May God forgive me!   (I.137.24)

"May God forgive me" is, in the Arabic phrase of the original, "astagh-firullāh!" It is used when someone has said or done something so shocking that only God can forgive it. Its use here conveys excellently the point of the verse: that if wine and all those associated with it are condemned by formal Islam, reverence for it and for those who dispense it is of the essence of true religion.

Mir sometimes uses even more homely idiom, though generally as something of a joke. One such instance is a verse in which he contrasts his own ill-fortune in love with the good luck of his rival, and which may be freely translated:

یہاں پلیتھن بکل گیا وہاں غیر

اپنی ٹکّی لگائے جاتا ہے

My rival is alright—he kneads the dough
—And I'm the flour he plonks it down upon.   (II.353.4)

Here the colloquialism used in the original is so homely that the present-day Muslim housewife would understand it, where in many cases her husband would not.

Mir is fond of that expressive repetition of words which is one of the characteristics of Urdu idiom, and which conveys either emphasis or distribution in time or space, or both. Thus where he says that his fame is known "In every region, every city . . . every home," the literal translation of the Urdu original would be simply "region region, city city . . . home home." Only occasionally can one hope to convey anything like the full effect in English. In a line which may be taken equally well either in the literal or in the mystic sense he says:

جیسے نسیم ہر سحر تیری کروں ہوں جستجو

خانہ بخانہ در بدر شہر بہ شہر کو بہ کو

I seek you like the morning breeze that with each dawn goes forth again
From house to house, from door to door, from town to town, from lane
   to lane.   (681.6)

Many other examples are quite untranslatable.

A similar liking for this style of expression is evident in the many verses where the whole force is achieved by piling word upon word:

هوش و صبر و خرد و دین و حواس و دل و تاب

اس کے اک آنے میں کیا کیا نہ گیامت پوچھو

She came but once, but do not ask what left me as she went:
My strength, and faith, and fortitude, and will, and heart and soul.

(I.133.19)

چشمک غمزہ عشوہ کرشمہ آن انداز و ناز و ادا

Her sidelong glance, imperious airs, her charm and grace and poise and
pride

(V.556.16)

گئی عمر میری ساری جیسے شمع باد کے بیچ

یہی رونا جلنا گلنا یہی اضطراب تجھ بن

The candle gutters in the draught, and my life too must waste away.
Like it I weep, and burn, and melt, and pine away, parted from you.

(I.117.24)

ثباتِ قصر و در و بام و خشت و گل کتنا

عمارتِ دلِ درویش کی رکھو بنیاد

Palace and gate and roof and brick and clay—none of them last.
So make the humble heart the strong foundation of your house.

(III.394.7)

And in a verse which has nothing to do with the major themes of the

ghazal, but speaks directly of the plight of the people of Delhi during the
1760s and 1770s:

چور اُچکّے سکھ مرہٹے شاہ و گدا ر زِ خواہاں ہیں

چھین میں ہیں جو کچھ نہیں رکھتے فقیری اک دولت ہے اب

Sikhs, Marāthas, thieves, pickpockets, beggars, kings—all prey on us.
Happy is he who has no wealth; this is the one true wealth today

(V.548.4)

—a verse in which the piling up of the words not only expresses the
multiplicity of demands to which the citizens of Delhi were subjected,
but also tacitly suggests that there is not much to choose between one and
another. It is worth noting incidentally that this verse occurs in Mir's
fifth dīvān, which consists of poems written long after he had left Delhi
forever to settle in Lucknow. It is one indication among many in his work
of how constantly he thought of the people of Delhi and how close a
kinship he felt with them. In the same dīvān it is of Delhi that he thinks
when he describes his sense of desolation:

دیدۂ گریاں ہمارا نہر ہے

دل خرابہ جیسے دلّی شہر ہے

Tears flow like rivers from my weeping eyes.
My heart, like Delhi city, lies in ruins now.   (V.621.6)

His intimate knowledge of the language of Delhi people, which has
already been discussed, is matched by a closeness to their lives and feelings, clearly evidenced in his use of simile and metaphor. Many of his
images are drawn from the experiences of invasion, pillage, and destruction, and to a Delhi audience he could have used none more meaningful.
Some have already been quoted; for example:

دل وہ نگر نہیں کہ پھر آباد ہو سکے

پچھتاؤ گے سُنو ہو یہ بستی اُجاڑ کر

The heart is not a city that can rise again from ruins.
Loot it, and—do you hear me?—you will live to rue the day.

(I.69.17)

دل سے خوش طرح مکاں پھر بھی کہیں بنتے ہیں

اِس عمارت کو ٹک اِک دیکھ کے ڈھایا ہوتا

No palace ever built could match the heart for grace and beauty:
Had you but glanced at it could you have razed it to the ground?

(II.233.5)

But the images recur again and again:

خرابئ دل کی کیا انبوہ درد و غم سے پوچھو ہو

وہی حالت ہے جیسے شہرِ لشکر لوٹ جاتا ہے

You ask me of the ruin of my heart by pain and grief:
It is a city looted by an army on the march.   (II.353.13)

شہرِ دل آہ عجب جائے تھی پر اس کے گئے

ایسا اُجڑا کہ کسی طرح بسایا نہ گیا

The city of my heart—alas!—was once a wondrous sight.
Her going razed it to the ground; none will live there again.

(I.27.18)

جل جل کے سب عمارتِ دل خاک ہو گئی

کیسے نگر کو آہ محبّت نے دی ہے آگ

Burnt in the flames till every building was reduced to ashes—
How fair a city was the heart that love put to the fire! (II.282.19)

In general his use of imagery is fresh and vivid. He sees beautiful women passing before him,

قامت لچکے ہے یوں ہوا میں

جس رنگ سے لچکتی پھولوں کی ڈالیاں ہیں

. . . their swaying walk as lovely
As flower-laden branches moved by the morning breezes.

(III.412.24)

He thinks of the radiance of his mistress' coming:

جس گھر میں تیرے جلوہ سے ہو چاندنی کا فرش

وہاں چادرِ مہتاب ہے مکڑی کا سا جالا

In that house where the moonlight of your radiance lies spread
The moonlight seems as lustreless as does the spider's web.

(I.39.16)

He recalls the days of his youth, when

لبِ ساغر پہ منہ رکھ رکھ کے ہر شیشہ بہکتا تھا

The bottle babbled to the cup, his mouth upon her lip.

(680.3)

کیا لطف تھا کہ مے کدے کی پشتِ بام پر

سوتے تھے مست چادرِ مہتاب تان کر

What days those were!—when I would drink and climb up to the tavern
  roof
And fall asleep, the white sheet of the moonlight over me. (II.270.13)

Or he describes the suppressed pain in his heart as the night of separation comes on:

شام سے کچھ بجھا سا رہتا ہے

دل ہوا ہے چراغ مفلس کا

> Since evening fell, the flame within my heart
> Burns dimly, as it were a poor man's lamp.   (I.6.14)

In his masnavi *The River of Love* the small boat crossing the great river appears like the crescent moon upon the night sky (907.8).

کشتی اک آن کر ہوئی موجود

ہو فلک سے ہلال جیسے نمود

In the same poem the waves encircle the limbs of the drowning lover like fetters being clamped upon them (907.23).

موج زنجیر ہو گئی پا میں

In the ghazal the imagery is often the more striking because it is so condensed:

عمر بھر ہم رہے شرابی سے

دلِ پُرخوں کی اک گلابی سے

> I passed my life in love's intoxication
> Drunk with the rose-red wine of my heart's blood.
>
>   (I.207.21)

آتشِ رنگِ گل سے کیا کہئے

برق تھی آشیان پر آئی

> Burn in the red fire of the rose in silence:
> Lightning must strike, and it has struck your nest.
>
>   (I.141.25)

میر تلوار چلتی ہے تو چلے

خوش خراموں کی چال ہے کچھ اور

Mir, *let* the bright sword flash—in dreadful beauty
A lovely woman's walk is something more.   (I.71.15)

Another metaphor, aptly suited to Mir's country and age, introduces also the use of conceits—a further very characteristic feature of his poetry and of ghazal poetry in general. In India a "wheaten" complexion—that is, a skin-colouring like that of wheat ready for harvest—is much admired. Mir laments the rarity of such beauty:

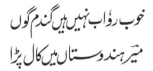

One sees no longer faces fair as ripened wheat;
It seems that there is famine now in Hindustan.   (I.32.18)

The train of thought is clear: from a dearth of wheaten faces to a dearth of real wheat and back again through the implied metaphorical use of this image. Mir's verse is full of such verbal conceits, and they had a great appeal for his audience. In one verse he says that the rose grows in the garden, her skirt all the time held fast in the grasp of the nightingale, and that the scene in the enclosed garden therefore foreshadows that of the Day of Reckoning.[52] The central idea is that on the Last Day the cruel mistress will have to answer to God for her cruelty to her lover. She is here, as so often, symbolised by the rose, and her lover is the nightingale. To grasp the skirt of someone's garment may mean one of two things: to claim his protection against a threatening danger, or to demand redress for a wrong he has done you. And the nightingale's grasp is here a metaphor for the calyx at the base of the flower, which, so to speak, holds the flower in its hand. Once again, the English-speaking reader has to go well back in his own literature to find parallels, back to the metaphysical poets and beyond, who relished such conceits as much as Mir.

[52] Allusion to I.13.10.

One may concede that the use of conceits is not one of the essentials of great poetry, but in a form like the ghazal, where brevity is often essential, they sometimes serve a real purpose. Thus Mir writes:

عشق کا شور کوئی چھپتا ہے

نالۂ عندلیب ہے گل بانگ

Do what you will, the lover's cry will yet be heard:
The nightingale's lament re-echoes everywhere.   (I.85.5)

The Urdu says: the nightingale's lament is a *gulbāng*, and the word has two meanings. First it *means* the song of the nightingale; and secondly, it means (to quote the standard Urdu-English dictionary) "fame, a loud shout, a war-cry." In addition *gul*, the first syllable of the word, means rose, and the Urdu reader relishes the suggestion it brings of the traditional association of nightingale and rose.

In other verses verbal conceit is only partly functional. The lover accused of stubborn persistence in his own ways replies, as though to justify himself:

نہ خود سر کیوں کہ ہم ہوں یار اپنا

خود آرا خود پسند و خود ستا تھا

Self-will is *my* trait—but then are not hers
Self-love, self-admiration, and self-praise?   (VI.627.19)

Here the play on the word "self" is the main thing in the couplet, and there is no real attempt at anything which could be called an argument. Similarly, in a much more complex example:

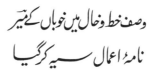

Praise of the form and features of fair women, Mir,
Has blackened all the record of your deeds   (I.54.14)

—a verse of which one can be practically certain that it is intended as something of a joke. Among other things, the deliberately very obtrusive alliteration indicates this. (The translation parallels the alliteration of the original: *vasf i khat o khāl men khūbān ke, Mīr.*) In translation we do get the general sense. Mir is quoting, without comment, the words which an orthodox Muslim might address to him, telling him more in sorrow than in anger that to spend his life in praising beautiful women is to acquire a record which will tell against him when he is judged. But all the points that the verse makes can be brought out only by reference to the original. "The record of your deeds" translates an Urdu phrase which bears a technical meaning. Your "record of deeds" is the complete account of all your actions in life, kept by recording angels to be produced before God on Judgement Day. The words translated "has blackened" also bear two possible meanings: first, that which the English suggests, and secondly, to "blacken paper" by writing on it, but with the same suggestion of prolific output as the English phrase "to cover reams and reams of paper" gives. The first line also conceals double meanings. "Form and features" translates the Urdu *khat o khāl*. These are, formally speaking, two separate words linked by the Persian *o* (meaning "and"), but are regularly used as a single word meaning "physical appearance." Yet the meanings of the individual words are also relevant to the verse. Khat again has two meanings: first, a letter, or piece of writing, and secondly, the black line of down on the upper lip. And khāl means a mole (on a beautiful woman's face). So the "blackening of the record," which it-self suggests two meanings, correlates also with the blackness of writing (khat in the first sense), the blackness of the line of down (khat in the second sense), and the blackness of the mole.

In other verses the verbal play fulfils practically no function at all, and is there for its own sake entirely. In the original of the verse:

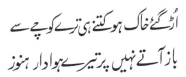

The wind has blown away the dust of men unnumbered from your lane;
Yet your true lovers are not daunted; men come to your threshold still

(I.76.7)

the Urdu word here translated ''true lovers'' is *havādar*; *dār* is a common suffix meaning ''possessing,'' and *hava*, which in this context means ''love,'' has the primary sense of ''wind.'' In short, the word *havādar* is here used simply because its first element has a purely verbal connection with the image of the first line. And this is very frequently done.

But if verbal play of this kind does not often appeal strongly to the modern reader, there are lines where its use does add appreciably to the poetic effect, as in a verse which Mir wrote as a little poem on its own, and not as part of a ghazal:

تری زلفِ سیہ کی یاد میں آنسو جھمکتے ہیں

اندھیری رات ہے برسات ہے جگنو چمکتے ہیں

Your long black tresses come to mind and glistening teardrops dim my sight.
And all is dark; the rains have come; the fireflies glimmer in the night.
(681.4)

The season of the rains, when alone in the Indian year the clouds cover the sky and the nights are really dark, has the same romantic connotations as spring does in Europe. But the second line not only evokes the atmosphere with a few vivid strokes, it also suggests the elements which make up the first line, for the long black tresses of the beloved are regularly compared with the long black night, and tears with rain, while the glistening tears and the glimmering fireflies (the two Urdu words used are equally close) also suggest each other. This is surely the use of words at its best, where every connotation is relevant and brings its contribution to the vivid intensity of the picture.

These are just some of the technical skills which Mir brings to the making of his poetry. They help to give it the many-sidedness which he proudly claimed for it:

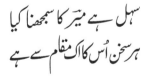

سہل ہے میر کا سمجھنا کیا

ہر سخن اُس کا اک مقام سے ہے

To understand Mir's meaning is no simple task:
Each at its level, meanings lie in every word.   (II.367.14)

But this many-sidedness derives mainly from the very nature of the dominant themes of the ghazal. One cannot explain these themes without taking them one by one, but to an audience that has been acquainted with them almost from childhood, a verse that is capable of interpretation on several levels is at once comprehended as such and appreciated the more deeply for being so. In any given verse it is a matter for surmise which meaning or meanings the poet had in mind when he composed it, but there are many which, whatever the precise intention of the poet, fit aptly into a wide variety of different contexts. This would be true of scores of verses quoted in the last two chapters. To give but one instance, in the verse:

اُڑ گئے خاک ہو کتنے ہی ترے کوچے سے

باز آتے نہیں پر تیرے ہوا دار ہنوز

The wind has blown away the dust of men unnumbered from your lane;
Yet your true lovers are not daunted: men come to your threshold still
(I.76.7)

the "you" referred to may be God or a human beloved or any ideal out of an almost infinite variety, in which a man believes so passionately that he will serve it even at the cost of his life. In the audience that hears such a verse recited, one will take it in one way, and one in another, according to the emotional and spiritual needs which each feels. The verse becomes the "little door that opens into an infinite hall where you may find what you please."

Much the same is true of the image of the cruel beloved, of whom Mir had no experience in literal reality. The image is the means of expressing the belief that true love is absolutely unselfish, giving its all without demanding the slightest return, and proof not only against indifference but even against hatred. In the mystic sense the cruel mistress is God—God who not only created all good but all evil too; God who may afflict His true servant with life-long pain and suffering, and yet whom His true servant loves with all his being. Or, in what one may call the quasi-mystic sense, she may symbolise a man's country or his people, whom he labours all his life to serve, regardless of personal hardship, even though they never cease to despise and reject him, and crucify him in the end.[53]

Mir's pride in the many-sidedness of his poetry is thus a pride in his ability to develop all the potentialities of the ghazal—the verse form which he had chosen as the major medium of his expression. The capacity of its verses for simultaneous interpretation on several levels appealed to him, for he himself felt that every aspect of his experience of life was relevant to every other. Many of his verses make this clear: besides those in which the use of imagery links, for example, the suffering of his heart with the suffering of eighteenth-century Delhi, there are others in which his view of his age and his view of his mistress (in whatever sense) are brought into direct relationship:

زبانیں بدلتے ہیں ہر آن خوباں

یہ سب کچھ ہیں بگڑے زمانے کی باتیں

Fair women break their word from hour to hour—
These are all signs of our degenerate age.   (III.414.17)

وفا لوگ آپس میں کرتے تھے آگے

یہ رسم کہن آہ تم ہی نے اُٹھا دی

People continued true to one another formerly.
This was the age-old custom—and now you have broken it.
                                                            (II.330.24)

[53] The range of possible identifications of "the beloved" is very wide. In sexual (albeit unfulfilled) love it may be a parda woman, a courtesan, or a boy. In the mystic or quasi-mystic sense it may be God or one's principles. In other human relations it may be a bosom friend. But it may also be a capricious, despotic king or noble—perhaps your patron—to whose service you are bound. For if the real beloved to whom you pledge your love and loyalty can be pictured as a cruel, capricious tyrant, symbol and reality may be reversed, and a cruel, capricious tyrant whom you must serve may be pictured as your beloved. There is no doubt that in the ghazal this is sometimes the case, and that the cruel mistress who slays her lovers with the sword of her proud glance stands for a real tyrant with a real sword. Thus the traditional story of Nādir Shāh's massacre in Delhi in 1739 (cf. above, p. 19) relates that when the massacre had continued for several hours, Niẓām ul Mulk went and stood silently before him, and when Nādir asked him what he wanted, replied by quoting a Persian verse: "Lay down your sword of pride, for none is left for you to slay / —Except you raise the dead to life that you may slay again." Nādir was touched, and gave orders for the killing to cease. Cf. Muḥammad Ḥusain Āzād, Qaṣaṣ i Hind, Pt. 2 (1872), (Lahore, 1961), p. 176.

But more than individual verses, his poetry as a whole makes clear his conception that not only are all aspects of his spiritual experience relevant to one another; they are all aspects of what is to him essentially the same experience, the experience of a man driven by the single spiritual force of love, manifesting itself simultaneously in love of women, love of God, love of his fellowmen, and love of a high ideal in life, as well as in the indomitable power to resist unbroken the persecution of the enemies of love in all these fields. It is this conception that unites all his poetry, makes it the expression of a single integral outlook, and gives it its powerful appeal.

CHAPTER SIX

Mir: The Man and His Age

WHERE A MAN'S POETRY proclaims high ideals of conduct, it is the tendency of some modern critics to compare his theory with his practice and criticise both the poetry and the poet if they find that the two do not correspond. This is perhaps not altogether fair, for the poet is not the whole man, and he may believe with all his heart in the ideals that his poetry declares, and yet lack the strength to bring his own life into conformity with them. Still Mir would have welcomed being judged in this way, and it is ironical that he usually had to face criticism from a standpoint which is almost the exact opposite of this. He found himself in a position where his poetry was universally praised, while his conduct was often disapproved; and yet that conduct was generally no more than the application in practice of the principles that his poetry upheld.

The fact is that the conventions of the ghazal worked in his favour in that they enabled him to speak "the secrets of his heart" with a voice that was "free and unrestrained";[1] but they worked against him as well, because his hearers were all too ready to assume that his verse was no more than an accomplished handling of the conventional themes, and only to the more sensitive among them did it occur that in his case the poetry really meant what it said. To the rest it was "only poetry," and remained so even though he told them:

[1] Cf. above, p. 213.

مجھ کو شاعر نہ کہو میر کہ صاحب میں نے
درد و غم کتنے کئے جمع تو دیوان کیا

Don't think me a mere poet—no, my verse
Is made of pain and grief more than you know. (III.370.5)

And,

اس پردے میں غم دل کہتا ہے میرا اپنا
کیا شعر و شاعری ہے یارو شعار عاشق

Under this guise of poetry Mir speaks the sorrows of his heart.
What poetry it is, my friends!—this lover's way of life. (II.279.1)

And,

کیا تھا زیختہ پردہ سخن کا
سوٹھرا ہے یہی اب فن ہمارا

Under this guise I spoke the message of my heart,
And all my practice now is to perfect this art. (I.28.14)[2]

For these verses too could be taken to be ''only poetry.'' He had to put
them into plain prose before people could see that he meant them—as
when he told a young nobleman who approached him with a request to
correct his verse: ''Young sir, you are a noble and the son of a noble.
Practice horsemanship and archery and the handling of the lance. Poetry
is a task for men whose hearts have been seared by the fire of love and
pierced by the wounds of grief.''[3] Whatever other men might think of
his attitude—and it was often resented and wrongly ascribed to arrogance
—Mir knew that the ''pain and grief'' of love, in all its senses, was the

2 Cf. III.423.23 and III.388.10.
3 Āzād, *Āb i Ḥayāt*, p. 215.

essential material of poetry, and that mere technical excellence could do nothing without it. At a distance of two hundred years most people can now see that he was right, and that his ghazals have outlived so many others precisely because they are the expression of an experience deeply and passionately felt.

What we know of his life [4]—and fragmentary though this knowledge is by modern standards, it is a good deal fuller than our knowledge of his contemporaries—shows how close was the relationship between his ideals and his practice. His capacity to suffer for his principles was put to the test while he was still a mere boy. His father had been married twice. By his first wife, a sister of the famous Persian scholar Khān i Ārzu, he had a son named Muhammad Hasan, and by the second, two sons, of whom Mir was the elder. Mir was clearly his father's favourite, and Muhammad Hasan bitterly resented this. When his father fell gravely ill, Mir was perhaps in his early teens. Despite treatment, his father's condition did not improve, and Mir describes in his autobiography how one day, sensing that death was near, he called his sons to his bedside and said: [5] "I am a faqīr,[6] and I own nothing. All I have is three hundred books. Bring them here and divide them between you." Muhammad Hasan said, "You know that I am a student, and that I spend most of my time on studies. What do my brothers want with these books? They will only tear them up to make kites and paper boats. It would be better to give them to me. But you must do as you please." His father replied, "You wear the cloak of unworldliness, but underneath it your nature is unchanged. You want to cheat these youngsters of their rights, and ill-treat them when I am dead. But remember that God is a jealous God, and befriends those who are jealous for their honour. I do not think that Muhammad Taqi [that is, Mir] will ever lay himself under obligation to you; and if you try to harm him, it will be he who will come off best. Men will never honour your name as they will this boy's. . . . People never trust a petty-minded man, and greed and jealousy will never reap

---

[4] The main sources for his life are *Ẕikr i Mīr* and his own poems, in which he often speaks more frankly than he does in prose. For *Ẕikr i Mīr* see above, p. 207. It is sometimes difficult to interpret, for though Mīr has an excellent memory for the sequence of the events he describes, he does not date them. One has to refer throughout to Sarkar's *Fall of the Mughal Empire* to provide the dating.

[5] *Ẕikr i Mīr*, pp. 59–60.

[6] Cf. above, p. 194.

anything but contempt and disgrace. Very well then. Take the books and take good care of them.'' Then he turned to Mir and said, ''My son, I owe three hundred rupees to the money-lenders, and I want you to promise that you will not bury me until you have paid it. All my life I have been true to my principles, and I never yet cheated any man.'' Mir replied, ''These books, which are now my brother's, were all our wealth. How can I pay our debts now ?'' Tears came into his father's eyes, and he said, ''God will provide, never fear. Even now money is on the way. I wish I could live until it comes, but death is near, and time is short; and I cannot wait.'' Then he gave Mir his blessing and commended him to God's care, and after breathing a little longer, died.

Mir says that by God's grace he carried out his father's commands without having to be beholden to anyone, although his stepbrother openly refused to accept any responsibility for the settlement of his father's affairs. Then he handed over charge of the household to his younger brother and set out to find himself some means of earning a living. But he could find no livelihood in Agra, and so he set out for Delhi to try his fortunes there. Again he could find no one to help him for quite a while. At length, however, he won the ear of a nobleman named Khwāja Muhammad Bāsit, the nephew of the great noble Samsām ud Daula, to whom reference was made in Chapter 1.[7] Samsām ud Daula at this time held one of the highest offices in the Empire—that of Imperial Paymaster and Marshal of the Nobility—and through Muhammad Bāsit, Mir was now able to gain an introduction to him.[8]

Samsām ud Daula had known and reverenced Mir's father, and when he was told whose son Mir was, he ordered that the boy should, for his father's sake, be paid a daily stipend from his treasury. During the interview an incident occurred which is highly characteristic of Mir. He asked that the order for the payment of his stipend be put into writing so that no difficulty could arise when he went to receive it. Muhammad Bāsit, thinking perhaps that this down-to-earth request might offend the noble lord, intervened and said, ''This is not the proper time for the inkstand.'' At this Mir, as though he had not already gone quite far enough, began to laugh. Samsām ud Daula looked at him in astonishment and asked, ''What

[7] Above, p. 16.
[8] *Zikr i Mīr*, pp. 62–63.

is the matter? Why are you laughing?" Mir replied: "I do not know what that means—'This is not the proper time for the inkstand.' If he had said 'The Navvāb cannot sign now,' or 'The inkstand-bearer is not here,' then I could have understood it. But this is a curious statement. The inkstand is not a living thing that can observe times and occasions; it is a piece of wood, which any of your servants will fetch whenever you order him." At this Samsām ud Daula laughed too, and made out the written order there and then.

Mir's good fortune did not last long. About a year after this, in 1739, came the invasion of Nādir Shāh, and in the disastrous battle of Karnāl, Samsām ud Daula was mortally wounded. Thus Mir was again without support. Whether he had remained in Delhi up to this point we do not know for certain, but we do know that, either before or after Samsām ud Daula's death, he returned to Agra; and here he soon had more bitter and painful experiences to undergo. In his autobiography he says only that all his relatives and friends turned against him, so that, as his poetic prose puts it, "men who had once made the dust of my feet the adornment of their eyes"[9] made his life so unbearable that he felt obliged to leave the city and go once more to Delhi.[10] His poetry, in which convention allowed him the freedom to describe experiences which would not have been acceptable in prose, provides the key to the mystery, and we may deduce with near certainty that the love affair which his masnavi *The Stages of Love* describes was the occasion of his persecution. Sooner or later this hostility made itself felt even in Delhi. Mir stayed for a time with his stepbrother Muhammad Hasan's uncle, Khān i Ārzu, but one day a letter from Muhammad Hasan came condemning Mir roundly and asking Khān i Ārzu not to assist him in any way. Mir writes sarcastically that the old gentleman, despite his pretensions, was one for whom considerations of worldly wisdom were paramount, and for this reason he acted on his nephew's request. "I never asked him for anything," writes Mir,[11] "but still he persecuted me, and if I were to write of all I suffered at his hands, it would fill a book." It was the cumulative effect of all this that drove him mad; the account which he gives in his autobiography tallies with that which forms the theme of the masnavi *Mir's Vision*, already described.

[9] *Zikr i Mīr*, p. 63.
[10] He did not see Agra again for more than 20 years.
[11] *Zikr i Mīr*, p. 64.

Thus Mir had indeed suffered "pain and grief more than you know" when he began to make his name as a poet; and it took him only a few years after he recovered his sanity to establish a reputation. Henceforth, for the rest of his long life, it was on his reputation as a poet that he depended for his livelihood. Most of his patrons were nobles highly placed in the imperial administration. The first was closely related to Qamar ud Dīn, Itimād ud Daula II, who was Vazīr of the Empire from 1724 to 1748. This man offended Mir, and he parted company with him. Soon after, he won the patronage of the eunuch Jāved Khān, who was all-powerful in the Empire from 1748 to 1752, when he was assassinated by his rival Safdar Jang. Mir, however, was taken under the wing of a noble close to Safdar Jang, until Safdar Jang's own downfall the following year again placed him in difficulties. It seems that for some years after this he was without any regular means of livelihood, until about 1757–1758, when Rāja Nāgar Mal, soon to become Deputy Vazīr of the Empire, became his patron. Except for a short break in 1760, Mir continued in his service for about fifteen years.

We can study more closely these twenty some odd years of Mir's life from the late 1740s to 1772, both in the histories of that period and in Mir's own brief account of them. A number of salient features emerge. The first is the ever-present insecurity which he must have felt, both from the repeated incursions of Abdāli from Afghanistan and from the armed strife between the different factions within India. His most powerful patron is assassinated; another is driven from Delhi after months of civil war; another time he himself is so distressed by conditions in Delhi that he wanders off on his own, "not knowing where he was going, but trusting in God to lead him." [12] So that if in 1772 he could look back on a period of twenty-five years during which he had rarely been without the patronage of an influential noble, it was nonetheless a period in which from day to day he had never felt secure.

The second striking thing is Mir's own close sense of involvement in the events of his day. His personal experience of Abdāli's invasions has already been described.[13] In addition, he tells us how he accompanied his first patron, Riyāyat Khān, in two campaigns in 1748, where he undertook a diplomatic mission of some importance on his behalf; how in 1750

[12] *Żikr i Mīr*, p. 90; cf. above, p. 33.
[13] Above, p. 32.

he suffered all the hardships of a forced retreat with Safdar Jang's defeated army after the fiasco of his military expedition to Rohilkhand and
Farrukhābād; and how in 1754 he was with the Emperor when he fled
before the forces of the Marāthas and of his own Vazīr Imād ul Mulk,
leaving his harem captive in their hands. But it is not only the events he
has personally experienced that remain clear in his mind. His autobiography gives the whole complicated story of the politics of imperial Delhi
during these years, for the most part crowding out all but the briefest
references to his own fortunes; and though he writes from memory many
years after most of these events had taken place, he is rarely at fault in the
account he gives. His belief that one must not withdraw from the life of
society, but "live in the world, where griefs and joys beset you,"[14] is
clearly one by which his own actions were guided.

Mir's attitude towards the great men upon whom he depended is also
worthy of note. He sees them in two roles, and judges them in each without reference to the other. As political figures, nearly all are judged
harshly, even scathingly. Thus Mir writes quite boldly of the eunuch
Jāved Khān that "[in 1748] the control of the Empire fell into his
hands,"[15] and by way of comment simply quotes a Persian verse to the
effect that power is perhaps a beggar that presents itself now at one man's
door, now at another's. Yet as a patron he found Jāved Khān generous,
and he praises him accordingly. Imād ul Mulk he considered in much the
same way. Mir describes the triumph of Imād and his associates with the
blunt words, "power came into the hands of worthless men,"[16] and
Imād's subsequent political crimes are related without any attempt at
palliation. But Mir also had dealings with him as a poet, and in this field
he found him a man of considerable accomplishments, and one who knew
the duties of a noble towards men of letters. And so a quite incidental
mention of him in connection with events that occurred in 1764–1765
prompts Mir to remark: "Despite his age he is still a unique figure in
these times, and has many accomplishments. He writes five or six styles
of script admirably, and composes good verse both in Persian and Urdu.
He is very good to me, and it has always been a great pleasure to visit

---

[14] Cf. above, p. 209.
[15] *Zikr i Mīr*, pp. 68–69.
[16] *Zikr i Mīr*, p. 74.

him." [17] A traditional, but quite credible, story of the two men shows that there was nothing in the nature of servility prompting this judgement. The story [18] is that one day Imād was sitting by the riverside amusing himself by watching the ducks and waterfowl. Mir happened to pass that way, and Imād called him across and proceeded to recite some qasīdas which he had composed. When he had finished, he asked Mir what he thought of them. "What need of my praise is there?" replied Mir. "See, every duck on the water is in ecstasy." Imād was much put out, as he clearly showed when he sent for Mir on the following day. When Mir entered, he found Imād seated, but there was no other seat in the room, and no carpet on the floor. Mir remained standing, expecting every moment that a chair or stool would be brought for him, but when none came, he understood that Imād expected him to stand in his presence. He at once folded his shawl, laid it on the floor, and sat down upon it. Imād then asked him to recite something. Mir recited this verse:

کل پاؤں ایک کاسۂ سر پر جو آ گیا

ناگہ وہ استخوان شکستوں سے چور تھا

کہنے لگا کہ دیکھ کے چل راہ بے خبر

میں بھی کبھو کسوؑ کا سرِ پُرغرور تھا

While walking yesterday I stumbled on a skull,
Which, as it crumbled into pieces, cried to me:
"O heedless one! Be careful where you set your feet!
I too was once the head of one as proud as you!"

There is nothing particularly outstanding about the verse, and the theme is the well-worn one that man should subdue his pride, remembering that death comes one day to level all men in the dust. The point of the verse is in the situation in which it was recited, and it would not be lost on Imād.

Mir himself relates an incident [19] of the period between 1753 and 1757, when he seems to have had no permanent security for his livelihood.

[17] *Zikr i Mīr*, p. 113.
[18] The story is quoted in Khwāja Aḥmad Fārūqī, *Mīr Taqī Mīr: Ḥayāt aur Shāʻirī* (Aligarh, 1954), pp. 291–292.
[19] *Zikr i Mīr*, p. 75.

He was sent for by Rāja Jugal Kishor, one of the wealthiest of the Delhi nobles and one who had held high office in a previous reign. He did Mir the honour of showing him his verses and requesting him to correct them. "I found," Mir writes, "that most of them were beyond correction, and scored them through." Such an action, which one of Mir's modern editors still finds shocking nearly two hundred years later, was not calculated to help him out of his material difficulties, but Mir would never allow such a consideration to weigh with him where he felt that his honour as a poet was concerned. And in fact the incident well illustrates the nature of the relationship between poet and patron that prevailed in Mir's day, for though Rāja Jugal Kishor must have been displeased, there was no breach in their relations. Only later did they part company, and Mir's account of the circumstances shows that for the noble it was a matter of honour to make adequate provision for a poet under his patronage, and a painful situation for him when he could not do so. At the time in question Mir was receiving so little support from him that he simply could not manage any longer on it, and one day in desperation he hinted this to him. "His face flushed with shame," writes Mir,[20] "and he replied, 'I am myself on the verge of poverty; otherwise I should not have been backward in helping you.'" One day shortly afterwards, Jugal Kishor visited Rāja Nāgar Mal and spoke to him about Mir. Later he told Mir to go and call upon Nāgar Mal. Mir did so, was kindly received, and was given to understand that permanent provision would be made for his support.

The fact that Mir lived for fifteen years under Nāgar Mal's patronage is the best testimony to his good opinion of him. There is little explicit comment on him in Mir's autobiography, but instances are given of his consideration not only for Mir but for the large numbers of others whom he took under his protection, and Mir's tone conveys the satisfaction he felt at this. There is also a notable absence of hostile comment on his political role. This could not have been a major one during the period of Mir's association with him, dominated as it was by the conflicts of far more powerful forces, but we know, partly from Mir and partly from other sources, that Nāgar Mal more than once mediated successfully between political rivals to avert armed clashes in which innocent people

[20] Zikr i Mīr, p. 78.

would have suffered, and there can be little doubt that this must have won him Mir's regard. All this notwithstanding, Mir was prepared to sever relations even with him when honour and self-respect seemed to demand it. The break came in 1771–1772, when the titular emperor Shāh Ālam, who had fled from Delhi thirteen years earlier to escape from the clutches of Imād ul Mulk and had ever since been a virtual captive—first of the ruler of Oudh and later of the British—decided to assert his right to return to the capital. Nāgar Mal, who had been living since 1761 in the Jāt kingdom, heard of this and sent Mir to smooth the way for him to join the imperial court. This Mir successfully did, but immediately after his return Nāgar Mal changed his mind and decided to throw in his lot instead with the Marāthas, who already occupied Delhi. Mir felt deeply humiliated, and though he accompanied Nāgar Mal on his journey to Delhi, as soon as they got there, he installed his wife and children in a suburb called Arabsarāi, and then parted company with him permanently.

He must have known how serious could be the consequences of the step he was taking. Nāgar Mal had been his mainstay for fifteen years, and for the last ten of them they had been away from Delhi. He was fifty years old, and had a wife and family to support. But the fact that Nāgar Mal had treated him dishonourably outweighed all these considerations, and though the next ten years were to prove some of the most difficult of his life, there is no indication in his writings that he ever regretted the course he took. He had long since determined not to submit to insult and dishonour—and long since realised what this resolve would cost him. He puts the point with wry exaggeration:

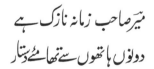

Mir Sahib, take care! The times are critical.
You need both hands to keep your turban on.[21]   (I.68.18)

The penalty Mir paid for such actions was not only material hardship and actual physical hunger; he had to endure also the disapproval of most of his contemporaries. It might be expected that though not themselves

[21] In the convention of Mughal society, to knock a man's turban off or to knock it crooked was a deadly insult.

prepared to make so drastic a sacrifice for their principles, they would at any rate respect one who was. But this was not the case. They had lived too long in an age when material self-interest was the overriding consideration guiding both the nobles and all those who depended upon them. A man must make his way in life, and that meant that he must change with every changing wind and not be too particular about principles. Poets were no exception: in their poetry they were lovers true unto death, eternally constant to their "beloved"—that is, to their mistress, to their God, to their ideals; but this was generally assumed to be a mere literary convention. It was in vain that Mir told them that he meant what he said. They could not understand that here was a poet who really believed with all his heart in the values which his poetry expressed, and did his best to practise them; and at a loss to comprehend the real motives of his actions, they attributed them to stubborn, foolish pride.

Mir knew well enough what they thought of him. In one of his verses he wryly addresses himself, as though in their words:

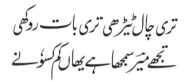

Your ways are awkward, and your speech is blunt.
None of us really understands you, Mir.   (II.343.22)

But their attitude was a constant source of pain to him, and after his break with Nāgar Mal, at the height of his difficulties, it was this, more than any material privations, that he felt most keenly. This is made clear in one of his most bitter poems, which must have been written at this time. We know from his autobiography to what straits he had been reduced. For a while another noble, less wealthy than Nāgar Mal, made such provision for him as he could, but a sudden change of political fortune deprived his new patron of his sources of income, and Mir was left with nothing. His autobiography says bluntly: [22] "I went out begging, calling at

---

[22] *Zikr i Mīr*, p. 122; the *mukhammas* on pp. 950–951 of the *Kulliyāt*. Khwāja Aḥmad Fārūqī (*Mīr Taqī Mīr*, p. 172) wrongly associates this poem with Mīr's visit to Kāmā in 1760–1761. The title given to the poem in the *Kulliyāt* is misleading, but Mīr was in Kāmā in 1771–1772 as well as in 1760–1761, and it is to the later period that the poem belongs. The poem is actually not about Kāmā at all, but about Mīr's experiences after his return from there to Delhi.

the door of every man of standing in the Emperor's camp; and because of my fame as a poet I was enabled to live somehow—as a dog or a cat might live.'' His poem gives a fuller account, describing how, weak with hunger, he made his way from one to another, with one hand on the wall to support himself; how he was rebuffed by men who had professed regard for him, and how he swallowed his pride to beg food and water from men whom in other circumstances he would have thought it beneath him to approach. He dwells bitterly on the lengths to which hunger forced him to go, and on the inhumanity with which he was treated, but these themes only lead up to the climax, and the poem ends with the words:

حالت تو یہ کہ مجھ کو غموں سے نہیں فراغ

دل سوزشِ دروُنی سے جلتا ہی جوُں چراغ

سینہ تمام چاک ہے ، سارا جگر ہے داغ

ہے نام مجلسوں میں مِرا میرِؔ بے دماغ

از بسکہ کم دماغی نے پایا ہے اشتہار

Grief assails me without respite, and my torn and wounded heart burns, as though in a flame that burns within my breast: and where men gather together they call me ''Mir the arrogant''—so widespread has my name for pride become.

Mir was universally acclaimed as a great poet, but he often felt that he met with no more understanding here than he did in other fields. He lived in an age when poetry was one of the polite accomplishments—as indeed to a considerable extent it still is in circles where Urdu is the language of culture—and most cultured men aspired to write it. Men of the world found no difficulty in praising their verse, particularly where its author was a man of influence. Mir, on the other hand, found considerable difficulty, because poetry was his life, and since most of this verse was not poetry, he could not bring himself to speak as though it were. It is an

accurate, though at the same time half-humorous, picture that he draws
of himself listening to a poet reciting his verse at a mushāira:

بات اپنے ڈھب کی کوئی کرے وہ تو کچھ کہوں

بیٹھا خموش سامنے ہوں ہوں کروں ہوں میں

Once let him speak a worth-while line, and he shall hear my praise.
Till then I'll sit here silent, greeting every line with "H'm!"

(III.423.24)

People attributed his attitude to the worst motives, and in this field too
thought him arrogant and overbearing.

  It is ironical that this view is still quite widely held among modern
Urdu critics, who do not seem to notice that their own judgements of
eighteenth-century poets are generally quite in accord with his. Thus he
and Sauda have always been recognised as the outstanding poets of their
day, and it is surely no grave fault in Mir that he knew this to be a sound
judgement, and said so. His assignment of the next place to the mystic
poet Mir Dard would also be generally accepted as just by most modern
critics. The judgement was not an arbitrary one, made on the spur of the
moment. In his earliest collection of verse he had written:

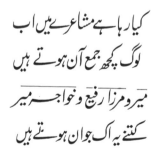

Though people still turn out to come to them
Mushāiras are dull affairs these days.
Mir, Sauda, Dard and just a handful more—
These stalwarts still deserve a poet's praise.

(I.110.13–15)

And according to a traditional story, which in essentials seems quite authentic, he repeated this judgement, with a significant modification, many years later.[23] "Who are the poets of today?" he was asked. He replied. "First, Sauda; next, your servant," and after a pause, "Mir Dard is half a poet." "And Mir Soz?" someone asked. Mir frowned and said, "Oh, is he a poet too?" "Well, after all," said the man, "he is the ustād of Navvāb Āsaf ud Daula." "Is that so?" said Mir drily, "Very well, then; make the total two and three quarters." We can only speculate what lay behind his assessment of Mir Dard as "half a poet," but it was certainly not arrogance or jealously, for we know that the two men liked and respected each other. Perhaps it was that Dard was one of the few Urdu poets who really were mystics, and Mir may have felt that his restriction of his poetry to mystic themes excluded him from the first rank of poets.

The latter part of the story illustrates perfectly the standards of judgement which his contemporaries applied and the contempt and ridicule with which Mir rejected them. To them the ustād of Āsaf ud Daula must be a great poet, because Āsaf ud Daula was a great man—ruler of Oudh and so one of the most powerful men in India. To Mir, as to us, this consideration is ludicrously irrelevant. (And we might add that nobody now thinks Soz a great poet.) He could indeed be scathing in his remarks about people who refused to recognise their limitations and imagined themselves to be the equals of Sauda and himself, and more than one of his comparatively few satirical poems are devoted to them. Once, during a prolonged absence from Delhi, he wrote of them:

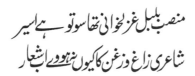

The nightingale held pride of place for song, but he is captive now.
What wonder, then, if crows and kites should now aspire to sing like him?

(II.265.2)

---

23 Āzād, *Āb i Ḥayāt*, p. 216. The story as Āzād gives it is not fully accurate, for he attributes it to the period when Mīr had settled in Lucknow. This cannot be correct, for the story implies that Saudā was still living. Yet he had died in 1781, a year before Mīr left Delhi for Lucknow.

And, more seriously:

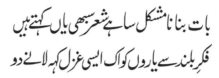

They won't find *saying* something all that easy.
As versifiers all of them are fine.
But let our friends show us their inspiration
By writing me a poem like this of mine.   (III.425.3)

This, however, is no proof of arrogance, particularly when one recalls
the satirical conventions of the age; and there is much weightier evidence
that points the other way. Thus throughout his life Mir acclaimed Sauda's
greatness in the warmest terms. He described him in *Nikāt ush Shuʻara* as
"outstanding among the poets of India . . . and fit to be acclaimed as
King of Poets."[24] More significant still in this connection in his unstinting praise of poets who never made a name for themselves but whose
work seemed to him to deserve it.

   The truth is that Mir's "arrogance" sprang from a steadfast adherence
to principle which in his degenerate age the average man was incapable of
understanding, and from a keen and growing sense of spiritual loneliness.
The attitudes of men around him were not new to him. Again and again
in his verse he had lamented the change that had come over his country,
a change so complete and all-embracing that it was as though he were in-
habiting a different world and a different universe:

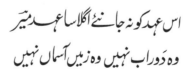

This age is not like that which went before it:
The times have changed, the earth and sky have changed.
                                                        (II.290.16)

24 Pp. 32–33; cf. above, p. 56.

He feels that an air of desolation pervades everything:

جس جا کہ خس و خار کے اب ڈھیر لگے ہیں

یہاں ہم نے انھیں آنکھوں سے دیکھیں ہیں بہاریں

Here where the thorn grows, spreading over mounds of dust and ruins,
These eyes of mine once saw the gardens blooming in the spring.

(I.115.5)[25]

اڑتی ہے خاک شہر کی گلیوں میں اب جہاں

سونا لیا ہے گود میں. بھر کر وہیں سے ہم

Here in this city where the dust drifts in deserted lanes
A man might come and fill his lap with gold in days gone by.

(II.289.25)

کل دیکھتے ہمارے بستے تھے گھر برابر

اب یہ کہیں کہیں جو دیوار و در رہے ہیں

These eyes saw only yesterday house after house
Where here and there a ruined wall or doorway stands.

(II.300.17)

The men who lived in these houses, the men whose achievements made
Mughal India great and prosperous, are gone, and no one remembers
them any more. Mir feels as though he had been present at a great assembly of talented men; just for a moment he had closed his eyes, and
when he opened them again they had vanished. All he can do is look at
the traces of their footprints in the dust, and weep for their loss. More
painful still, the people all around him have changed: he is living among
men to whom the old values mean nothing—values that have died with

25 Cf. I.116.18.

the men who believed in them; and yearn for them as he will, he feels
that they are gone beyond recall.[26] These days men live to themselves,
loving no one, loyal to no one, grieving for no one, finding no warmth in
one another's company, lacking the most elementary sense of common
humanity:

کیا زمانہ تھا وہ جو گزرا میؔر

ہمدگر لوگ چاہ کرتے تھے

What days were those!—the days that are no more,
The days when people loved their fellowmen.   (VI.673.17)

عہد ہمارا تیرا ہے یہ جس میں گم ہے ہمر و وفا

اگلے زمانے میں تو یہی لوگوں کی رسم وعادت تھی

Ours is a dark age; men have lost all trace of love and loyalty.
In former days it was not so; these things were second nature then.
                                                     (IV.530.9)[27]

سو ملک پھرا لیکن پائی نہ وفا اک جا

جی کھا گئی ہے میرا اس جنس کی نایابی

Roaming from land to land I sought for loyalty.
Grief tears my heart; it is not to be found.   (I.142.14)

تو جہاں سے دل اٹھایہاں نہیں رسم درمندی

کسی نے بھی یوں نہ پوچھا ہوئے خاک یہاں ہزار

Live out your life away from men's society,
For men no longer feel that you are one of them.
Thousands and thousands here were laid low in the dust
And no one even asked what had become of them.   (I.94.1)

---

[26] Allusions to III.456.11, I.145.23, II.349.14.
[27] Cf. II.275.24.

کیا کیا عزیز دوست ملے میرے خاک میں

نادان یہاں کسو کا کسو کو بھی غم ہوا

Such friends I had—and one by one they died and turned to dust.
I am a fool—nobody grieves for anybody now.   (I.26.3)

اب رسمِ ربط اٹھ ہی گئی ورنہ پیش ازیں

بیٹھے ہی رہتے تھے بہم احباب روز و شب

The custom now is quite extinct—and yet in days gone by
Friends would sit down and talk to one another night and day.
                                                              (I.55.22)

رسم اٹھ گئی دنیا سے اک بار مروّت کی

کیا لوگ زمیں پر ہیں کیسا یہ سماں آیا

The cult of human decency has vanished from the world.
What men are these upon the earth! What times we live in now!
                                                            (IV.466.11)

You cannot talk to them about the things that make up the meaning of
life; they are creatures in human form, but they are not human. And the
worst among them are the great men, the nobles who set the tone for the
rest of society. Mir feels deeply the injustice of an age in which good men
suffer, while wealth and power go to those who show the least scruple in
fighting for them, and having won them, use them for their own selfish
advantage alone. Such men destroy the peace and prosperity of society,
while those whose skill and talent should be rewarded are ruined instead.[28]

28 Allusions to I.113.18 and I.182.7.

Mir is at pains to dissociate himself from the rich and powerful, and to express his sense of oneness with those who suffer hardship and distress:

کیا اہلِ دولت سے ہے اے میرؔ مجھے نسبت

یاں عجز و فقیری ہے وہاں نازِ امیری ہے

What have you got to do, Mir, with men of wealth and substance?
On your side, all humility; on their side, boundless pride.

(III.439.6)

فرود آتا نہیں سر نازسے اب کے امیروں کا

اگرچہ آسماں تک شور جاوے ہم فقیروں کا

The nobles are so proud, they will not bow their heads to listen
Though we, the poor and humble, shake the heavens with our cry.

(II.243.8)

نہ مل میرؔ اب کے امیروں سے تو

ہوئے ہیں فقیر ان کی دولت سے ہم

Do not approach the great ones of the age, Mir;
It is their riches that have made us poor.   (II.289.16)[29]

Sometimes he expresses these themes with great bitterness, mingled with a fierce pride that if he is denied the conditions of comfort due to a great poet, at any rate his poverty clearly marks him off from a class of men whom he despises:

گو تو جھے سے زمانے کی جہاں میں مجھ کو

جاہ و ثروت کا میسّر سر و ساماں نہ ہوا

---

[29] Cf. I.187.13 and Āsī's footnote.

شکر صد شکر کہ میں ذلّت و خواری کے سبب

کسی عنوان میں ہم چشمِ عزیزاں نہ ہوا

Although the fortunes of the age have not shown favour to me
So that the ways of wealth and grandeur could not be my ways,
Praise be to God that I am poor and mean—for none can class me
With the great ones whom men delight to honour in these days.

(I.46.1–2)

But he knows that it is their values and not his which prevail in the
cultured society in which he moves, and he joins with Sauda in the
conclusion that "we are living in a special kind of age" [30] in which everything is the reverse of what it should be, an age that rewards vice and
punishes virtue, an age that seems to think it a grave offence to possess any
talent or skill and therefore ruins talented men and allows worthless
people to prosper, an age in which a great poet can expect a life of
hardship, just as the bird that sings most sweetly knows for that very
reason that it is he who will be trapped and shut in a cage:

یہ زمانہ نہیں ایسا کہ کوئی زیست کرے

چاہتے ہیں جو بُرا اپنا بھلا کرتے ہیں

What man would want to live in times like these?
When doing good means wishing yourself ill. (I.94.23)

صنّاع ہیں سب خوار ازاں جملہ ہوں میں بھی

ہے عیب بڑا اس میں جسے کچھ ہنر آوے

The craftsmen are all ruined now, and I am one of them.
It is a grievous sin to know your craft in times like these.

(I.167.3)

[30] Cf. above, p. 68.

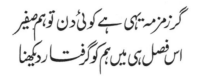

گر زمزمہ یہی ہے کوئی دن تو ہم صفیر
اس فصل ہی میں ہم کو گرفتار دیکھنا

If I sing on like this, my friend, I know the day will come
This very spring when you will see me captive in the cage.

(I.48.3)

اسیری کا دیتا ہے مژدہ مجھے
مرا زمزمہ گاہ و بے گاہ کا

The song I sing, in season, out of season,
Heralds the news of my captivity.   (III.373.20)

The world itself is like a great cage:

زیرِ فلک رکا ہے اب جی بہت ہمارا
اس بے فضا قفس میں مطلق ہوا نہیں ہے

Pent in between the earth and sky, we stifle
In this cage where no breath of air can come.   (II.360.21)

A man may wander from place to place and find no peace:

کہیں ٹھہرنے کی جا یہاں نہ دیکھی میں نے میر
چمن میں عالمِ امکاں کے جیسے آب پھرا

Here Mir could find no resting place; he must go on and on
Like running water flowing through the garden of the world.

(II.231.15)

Power and wealth are everything, and the man who has neither should
know better than to expect anyone to befriend him.

زور و زر کچھ نہ تھا تو بارے میر

کس بھروسے پر آشنائی کی

Power and wealth were not at your command, Mir.
How could you, then, make anyone your friend? (I.141.19)

پھر ایں صورت احوال ہر اک کو دکھا تا یہاں

مروّت قحط ہے آنکھیں نہیں کوئی ملاتا یہاں

I sought them one by one to show them how things stood with me.
Humanity is dead—not one would look me in the face. (IV.505.22)

It is not enough that they are incapable of giving their love to him or to
any other man; none of them is prepared even to accept the love that
others offer him. Love, which was once treasured as precious beyond
anything else that life could offer, is not wanted any more:

ہر جنس کے خواہاں ملے بازار جہاں میں

لیکن نہ ملا کوئی خریدار محبّت

Here in this market of the world all kinds of wares are in demand;
But one can find no purchaser: no one has come in search of love.

(I.58.17)

کوئی خواہاں نہیں محبّت کا

تو کہے جنس ناروا ہے عشق

Nobody here wants love; it seems they think
That it is tainted wares you offer them. (II.279.10)[31]

---

[31] Cf. I.33.15 and I.90.24–25.

And if Mir's reaction is to withdraw into himself, then he is "proud," "unapproachable," "reserved." The rare exception, who treats Mir with a love and respect to which he can respond, is asked in astonishment:

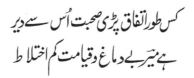

You've been with Mir? How did you manage that?
—So proud and unapproachable a man!   (II.276.18)

And this is a reaction which he hears so often that Mir sometimes imagines half-humorously that living with one's fellowmen must have needed some special skill, known to past generations, but now lost:

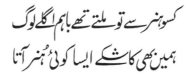

In former days men knew the way to live with one another.
Alas! if only I had learned to master some such skill! (III.380.23)

One is reminded of what Mark Rutherford wrote about himself:

> I have been accused [of] secrecy and reserve.... People would ordinarily set it down to self-reliance, with no healthy need of intercourse. It was nothing of the kind. It was an excess of communicativeness, an eagerness to show what was most at my heart and to ascertain what was at the heart of those to whom I talked, which made me incapable of mere fencing and trifling and so often caused me to retreat into myself when I found an absolute absence of response.... Only when tempted by unmistakable sympathy could I be induced to express my real self.[32]

---

[32] Mark Rutherford, *Autobiography*, 13th ed. (London, n.d.), pp. 23–24; cf. also pp. 109–110. Others who have expressed this feeling about themselves are T. E. Lawrence and A. E. Housman; cf. John Sparrow's Introduction to Housman's *Collected Poems* (Harmondsworth, 1956), p. 16.

The words fit Mir's case exactly. Men's reaction to him makes him feel as though he were a stranger in the land of his birth—

مسافر ہی رہے اکثر وطن میں

a foreign traveller in my own land. (I.98.14)

as though he and his countrymen did not speak the same language:

رہی نگفتہ مرے دل میں داستاں میری
نہ اس دیار میں سمجھا کوئی زباں میری

How could I tell my tale in this strange land?
I speak a tongue they do not understand   (I.150.9)[33]

—a simile that occurs again and again in his verse.

There are times when he regrets that he ever devoted himself to poetry:

ہر بحر میں اشعار کہے عمر کو کھویا
اس گوہرِ نایاب کی کچھ بات نہ پائی

I wrote in every metre, wasting all my years
Bringing up pearls for men who did not know their price.

(II.329.21)

پھر امت میرے سر اپنا گراں گوشوں کی مجلس میں
سنے کوئی تو کچھ کہیے بھی اس کہنے کا کیا حاصل

Why bother, Mir, to speak to this assembly of the deaf?
One speaks to those who listen: what's the good of speaking here?

(III.405.20)[34]

33 Cf. III.420.5 and VI.655.17.
34 Cf. III.395.23–24.

And he reflects that these are men who love a poet's immature flights of "poetic fancy," but give him good cause to regret it if once they feel he is trying to tell them something:

باؤلے سے جب تلک بکتے تھے سب کرتے تھے پیار

عقل کی باتیں کیاں کیا ہم سے نادانی ہوئی

I raved and ranted on, and so far everybody loved me.
I started talking sense—what folly I committed then!

(II.328.17)

He himself feels more and more the one survivor of a former race:[35]

کھا گیا اندوہ مجھ کو دوستانِ رفتہ کا

ڈھونڈتا ہائے جی بہت پراب انھیں پاؤں کہاں

My friends are dead and gone, and grief for them consumes my heart.
My soul seeks for them always, but where shall I find them now?

(III.409.21)

Men who knew the meaning of love and felt its torture with the same intensity as he are all dead. "Majnūn is gone from the desert and Farhād from the mountainside: the friends who brought some joy into my life are all dead."[36] And he tells himself that he should die too:

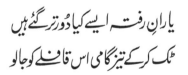

یارانِ رفتہ ایسے کیا دُور ترگئے ہیں

ٹھک کرکے تیزگامی اس قافلے کو جا لو

The dead friends that you mourn are not so very far ahead;
Quicken your pace a little; overtake the caravan.　(II.319.15)[37]

---

35 Allusion to I.136.20–21.
36 Allusions to I.184.5,8,9; II. 234.24.
37 Cf. IV.502.18.

Meanwhile, because he does not really belong to his own times and his contemporaries know it, they single him out for persecution, while they enjoy all the benefits that life has to give:

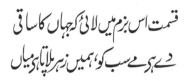

Fate brought me here, into a gathering where the cupbearer
Brings wine to all—and pours a deadly poison in my cup.

(III.419.1)[38]

In these conditions it is, once again, the qualities of the lover—using the word in all the senses that it bears in the ghazal—that give a man the strength to live, and to live to some purpose. The lover, the true worshipper of God, the man who is true to his high ideals, expects misunderstanding and hostility and hardship, and he is proud to show that he can bear them without wavering in his devotion.

During the hard years that followed his return to Delhi in 1772, Mir needed all these qualities to sustain him. For ten years he lived on there, apparently without any sort of permanent provision for his support, and this part of his autobiography makes painful reading. At one point he writes, "For the last three years I have lived in the most straitened circumstances, for none is left in the world who could be my patron. I have put my trust in God, for it is He who gives us our daily bread, and keep to my own house. There are a few men left . . . whom I sometimes visit and whom I can depend upon to help me when they can, and I receive occasional gifts from people who admire me as a poet or respect me as a good and unworldly man. I am usually in debt, and I live in great poverty." [39]

He comforted himself with the thought that since he had nothing, he would at any rate be spared the attentions of all those who harrass wealthier men.

38. Cf. I.139.20-21.
39 *Zikr i Mīr* (Rāmpūr MS), ap. Khwāja Aḥmad Fārūqī, pp. 207–208. This passage does not occur in the published edition of *Zikr i Mīr.*

غمِ زمانہ سے فارغ ہیں مایہ باختگاں

قمارخانۂ آفاق میں ہے ہاری ہی جیت

In times like these, those who have lost their all live free from care.
This is the sort of gambling house where only loss is gain.

(III.388.18)

He began to spend long periods in the seclusion of his own home. "Many
times the Emperor sent for me, but I did not go. Abul Qāsim Khān . . .
was very kind to me, and I occasionally used to visit him. From time to
time the Emperor would send me something. I still write a line of poetry
now and then, but that is all the world holds for me now." At another
point he speaks with high praise of the Deputy Vazīr, Hasan Raza Khān,
whom he describes as a good man, distinguished above all for his unstinting generosity. "Not only I, but many others, owe much to his
kindness."[40]

As the years went by he made up his mind that he would leave Delhi as
soon as opportunity offered. But as long as he had no money, this was out
of the question, and it was not until 1782 that the opportunity came. In
that year it was suggested to Āsaf ud Daula, who had succeeded Shuja ud
Daula as ruler of Oudh in 1775, that he should send Mir enough money to
cover the expenses of the journey and invite him to settle in Lucknow.
Āsaf ud Daula did so, and Mir at once set out. There he was kindly received by Āsaf ud Daula in person, and fitting provision was made for all
his needs. It is safe to say that nothing but the need to find conditions of
comparative security in his declining years (he was now sixty years old)
would have persuaded him to forsake Delhi. As it was, he was one of the
last to go. Sauda, who was by no means the first poet of note to migrate
elsewhere, had left twenty-five years earlier, and after Mir's departure
only one poet of major importance—the mystic poet Mir Dard—was
left there. One wonders how he would have fared if he had not left when
he did, for in the same year, 1782, there was a severe famine in the Delhi
district in which half of the total population died.[41]

40 *Ẕikr i Mīr*, pp. 135 and 136.
41 Spear, *India, Pakistan and the West*, p. 168. However, there seems to be some doubt
whether this date is correct. The same author's *Twilight of the Mughuls*, p. 116, gives the date of
the great famine as 1785.

Though almost all the famous poets of the day were now gathered in Lucknow, there is abundant evidence in Mir's poems of the deep regret he felt at leaving Delhi, the city which from his early youth had grown to be no less dear to him than Agra. Despite all the destruction, the city was still beautiful. To look at its lanes and side streets was like turning the pages in the album of a great painter, and wherever one looked, the scene that met one's eyes was itself a picture.[42] All the variety of the whole world was there:

هفت اقلیم ہر گلی سے ہے کہیں

دلّی سے بھی دیار ہوتے ہیں

> The seven climes are in its every lane.
> Does Delhi have its equal anywhere? (I.103.12)

The days of its greatest glory were past, but even now it seemed to him to preserve, more than any other place, the best values of Mughal India. It was the centre of the new Urdu poetry, the poetry which aspired to the heights already achieved by Persian, and the language of its people—"the language of the steps of the Jama Masjid"—was the raw material of that poetry. He felt a special warmth for the ordinary people of the capital and identified himself with them in their misfortunes:

صنّاع ہیں سب خوار ازاں جملہ ہوں میں بھی

> The craftsmen are all ruined now, and I am one of them. (I.167.3)

He valued the appreciation with which they received his verse, and sometimes felt that they understood him better than the nobility did. He makes the point both in the innocent-seeming verse:

جیسی عزّت میرے دیواں کی امیروں میں ہوئی

ویسی ہی ان کی بھی ہوگی میرے دیوان کے بیچ

> I will write verses showing that I hold the great
> In that same honour as the great have held my verses[43]

> (II.257.22)

---

[42] Allusion to I.146.19 and I.103.12.

[43] We have already seen the "honour" of the great that his verses express.

—and also quite directly, when he says:

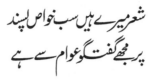

My verses are all liked by high society,
But it is to the people that I like to speak.   (II.367.11)

In his autobiography, which was concluded six years after he had left Delhi forever, it is still political developments at Delhi which form the main thread of the narrative.

The traditional account of his arrival in Lucknow[44] well shows the intense pride in Delhi which he felt and which he was to continue to feel until his death. On the evening of his arrival he went to take part in a mushāira. He was not known by sight to those present, and the gathering of fashionable, modern young gentlemen, complacent in the conviction that they represented the finest product of the culture of the age, smiled at one another as they noted the newcomer's old-fashioned dress. All this was not lost on Mir, and when it was his turn to recite he rose and recited this verse:

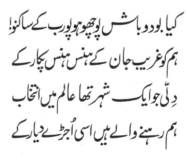

Why do you mock at me and ask yourselves
Where in the world I come from, easterners?
There was a city, famed throughout the world,
Where dwelt the chosen spirits of the age:
Delhi its name, fairest among the fair.
Fate looted it and laid it desolate,
And to that ravaged city I belong.

44 Āzād, *Āb i Ḥayāt*, p. 204.

After this his audience soon discovered who he was and hastened to make their apologies to him.

For some years after he had settled in Lucknow, a feeling of relief and thankfulness for his new-found security seems to have been uppermost in his mind, and in his autobiography, which takes us up to 1788, there is no indication that he was dissatisfied with his material position. Āsaf ud Daula gave him a stipend of three hundred rupees a month—considerably less than Sauda had received, if both figures are to be relied on, but more than that granted to most other poets, and, in any event, more than enough to provide for all his material needs.[45] In fact, Āsaf ud Daula is spoken of appreciatively in many passages. Mir accompanied him on hunting expeditions and wrote poems in which he gives an account of them. About one he writes in his autobiography,[46] "We went on a hunting expedition right to the foothills of the northern mountains [the Himalayas]. Although we experienced much hardship in covering so great a distance, we had never seen such game, or been in so lovely a setting or breathed such air. It was three months before we returned to the capital." He speaks highly of Āsaf ud Daula's skill as a poet, and seems to have felt it no burden in these years to fulfil his requests for the composition of particular poems.

But the words with which he ends his life story show that with all this he had not found peace in Lucknow. "The world is a place of strange vicissitudes," he writes.[47]

I have had eyes to see, and ears to hear, and what things have I not seen and heard! In this brief span of life this drop of blood which men call the heart has suffered all manner of blows, and is all bruised and bleeding. My temperament was unsuited to these times, and I no longer mix with people. I am sixty now, and old age is upon me.[48] I am generally ill, and for some time my eyes have been troubling me.... My failing powers, my sensitiveness, my weakness and grief and despondency, all tell me that my end is near, and the truth is that the times

---

[45] Cf. Khwāja Aḥmad Fārūqī, *Mīr Taqī Mīr*, p. 244. Sauda had been granted Rs.6,000 a year (according to accounts quoted by Shaikh Cānd in *Saudā*, pp. 61–62).

[46] *Zikr i Mīr*, p. 147.

[47] *Zikr i Mīr*, pp. 151–153.

[48] He was in fact more: perhaps 65 or 66.

are no longer fit to live in. It is time to withdraw from the world. I wish that I may come to a good end, but God's will must prevail.

The stylised, poetic prose which the fashion of the day dictated obscures to some extent the depth of feeling that lies beneath it, but his verse of this period—

"the guise in which he tells all that he has to tell" (II.365.24)—convinces one that he did indeed often feel that he had lived too long, and that death would be welcome. But another twenty-two years were to pass before his wish was to be realised, and as they dragged on, he came to feel an ever greater distaste for Lucknow and its whole atmosphere. For some years he seems to have received his stipend regularly and thus to have been free of any material worries. But he came more and more to feel that the treatment accorded to him was a mere formal rendering of what was conventionally due to a poet of his standing; for since Sauda's recent death in 1781, he was undisputedly the greatest Urdu poet living. His relations with Āṣaf ud Daula himself became strained, and one day an incident occurred which led him virtually to sever his connection with the court.

The tradition is [49] that on one occasion Mir, at the request of Āsaf ud Daula, was reciting one of his ghazals. They were standing by a fishpond, and as Mir recited, the Navvāb was playing with the fish, touching them with the end of a stick which he held in his hand. After one or two lines Mir stopped. "Go on, Mir Sahib," said the Navvāb. "If Your Majesty will give me his attention, I will," replied Mir. The Navvāb replied casually, "Any worth-while line will compel my attention." Mir was so displeased at this incident that he stopped coming to the court. A few days later he was walking along the street when he saw the Navvāb's carriage coming towards him. The carriage stopped by him and the Navvāb said, "Mir Sahib, you seem to have forsaken me altogether. You never come to see me now." Mir replied brusquely, "This is no place to talk about it. Gentlemen don't discuss these things in the street." [50]

[49] Āzād, Āb i Ḥayāt, p. 205.
[50] Cited by Khwāja Aḥmad Fārūqī, Mīr Taqī Mīr, p. 245.

This incident may well have made his breach with the court complete, though his stipend continued to be paid to him until Āsaf ud Daula's death in 1797 and, according to one authority, was still being paid three years later by Āsaf ud Daula's successor, Sa'ādat Ali Khān. But there seems to have come a time when even that ceased. At any rate the story is told[51] that one day Sa'ādat Ali Khān's carriage was passing through the streets and passed by a mosque near which Mir was sitting in a position overlooking the street. As the carriage drew level, everyone else stood up, but Mir remained seated. The poet Insha, a well-known younger contemporary of Mir, was in the Navvāb's immediate retinue, and the Navvāb turned to him and asked, "Insha, who is this man who is too proud to stand up?" Insha replied, "Sire, he is that proud pauper of whom we have often spoken to you. He is penniless, but see how proud he is! He has probably had nothing to eat all day." On his return Sa'ādat Ali despatched a palace servant to him with a ceremonial robe and a present of a thousand rupees. Mir would not take them. "I am not *so* poor," he said. "Give them to a mosque for charity." When this response was reported to Sa'ādat Ali, he was astounded. His courtiers explained the reason for Mir's reaction, and the Navvāb then instructed Insha to take the robe to Mir. Insha did so, urging him to accept it, if not for his own sake, then for the sake of his wife and family, adding, "It is a present from the ruling sovereign and you should accept it." Mir replied, "He is king of his own country, and I am king of mine. If a complete stranger had behaved as he has, it would have been understandable, and I would have had no cause to complain. But he knows who I am and what my present situation is. All this time he has shown complete indifference towards me, and then he sends some menial with a robe for me. I would rather stay poor and hungry than submit myself to such insult." Insha's eloquence persuaded him in the end to accept the gift, and thereafter he paid occasional visits to the court. But his relations with it remained tenuous for the rest of his life.

Mir's dissatisfaction was not only with the court. The cultural standards of Lucknow were changing, and in Mir's view changing very much for the worse. This was perhaps the inevitable result of the conditions of the time. When the eighteenth-century poets left Delhi in search of security

[51] Āzād, *Āb i Ḥayāt*, pp. 217–218.

elsewhere, it was natural that most of them should make for Oudh. It was remote enough from Delhi to escape involvement in the constant at-tacks of Afghans, Marāthas, Rohillas, Jāts, Sikhs, and others; and at the same time it was near enough for men to undertake the journey there—a perilous matter in those troubled times—more readily than they would have done to more distant centres. Oudh was one of the great powers in India, and after 1765 its security against attack by other Indian powers was further strengthened by alliance with the British, who were now felt to be a force to be reckoned with. The country was fertile and its rulers rich. Further, the rulers of Oudh consciously aspired to uphold in their dominions the values and traditions of Mughal India, including the tra-dition of generous patronage of literature and the arts. All these things attracted to their territories the emigrants from Delhi, and by the time Mir reached Lucknow, all the most famous poets had preceded him there. But Oudh was in fact a power already in decline. The British alliance had been imposed by force of arms, and though Shuja ud Daula seems to have tried to build up his resources with a view to ultimately reasserting his independence, the British saw to it that no such plan could be realised. When Āsaf ud Daula succeeded him, they imposed a new and more onerous treaty, and their inroads steadily increased until in 1856 Oudh was forcibly annexed to British territory.

Oudh's cultural decline was a logical consequence of this process. Whether from a sense of security in British "protection" or from a growing realisation that they were too firmly subordinated to British policies to play any independent role in Indian affairs, its rulers from Āsaf ud Daula onwards turned almost without exception to squandering their resources in all manner of ostentation. Their growing insignificance as political figures was matched by a growing self-conceit. Before Āsaf ud Daula's time they had been content to aim at continuing the best traditions of Mughal India; now they felt that Delhi's day was past, and that they could improve upon the old-fashioned ways of life which had been the standard there. One of Āsaf ud Daula's first acts was to move the capital from Faizābād to Lucknow, and here the change of cultural climate soon became very marked. Mir had a foretaste of it—if the traditional story is true—in the first mushāira he attended immediately after his arrival there.

There is no evidence that Mir grasped the causes of this cultural deca-dence, but he recognised it for what it was and reacted sharply against it. Lucknow had undertaken the task of (as it thought) giving polish and refinement to Urdu poetry. "Inelegant" words and loose grammar were henceforth to be excluded, and rules of diction, grammar, metre, and rhetoric were formulated to prevent the misguided from reverting to old, bad practices. Not all the work that Lucknow did in this respect was bad, but the spread of a literary taste which mistook technically accomplished versification for poetry was undoubtedly one of its results. Mir, who was now, since Sauda's death, undisputedly the greatest Urdu poet living, was angered by this presumption, and the stronger became Lucknow's conviction that Delhi's day was past and that Lucknow now set the standards, the more vigorously Mir asserted the contrary—that standard Urdu was the Urdu of Delhi, and the best models for poetry the work of the Delhi poets, including his own.

A traditional story of this period well illustrates the point.[52] On one occasion some prominent citizens of Lucknow went to call upon him, hoping to hear him recite his verses. The door was opened by an old maidservant, who, having enquired their business, went in, spread a piece of sacking on the floor, and asked them to be seated. She then prepared an ancient hookah for them to smoke and placed it before them, after which Mir came in. When the formalities of greeting were over, he was asked if he would recite. He was at first evasive, but being pressed, told them flatly that they would not understand his poetry. This of course they resented; but out of politeness they acknowledged their unworthiness, at the same time repeating their request. Mir again refused. At this one of them, unable to restrain his displeasure, said, "Come sir! We understand the poetry of Anvari and Khāqāni;[53] why should we not understand yours?" Mir replied, "Granted that you understand *them*; but there you have commentaries and vocabularies to help you; whereas one thing alone will help you to understand my verses—a knowledge of Urdu as you will hear it spoken on the steps of the Jama Masjid; and that knowledge you do not possess." He then recited one of his verses and said, "You will quote your books and tell me to give full weight to the *a* of *khayāl*, pointing out that in this line it is not taken into account. My answer to that is simply that I have used the word as the people of Delhi speak it."

---

[52] *Ibid.*, p. 217.
[53] Anvarī (d. 1169–1170) is considered the greatest panegyrist of Iran in the Seljuqid period. Khāqānī (d. 1199) is thought to be his peer in the art of qaṣīda. (A.S.)

The great prophet of "correctness" in poetry was the Lucknow poet Nāsikh, a man whose writings are generally agreed to be practically devoid of any deep feeling. There is a tradition,[54] which may well be true, that when Nāsikh began to write verse, he approached Mir with a request to accept him as his shāgird, and that Mir refused.

If empty formalism was one aspect of the Lucknow trend in Urdu poetry, another was an increasing emphasis on themes of sexual pleasure. The poet Jurat was the most accomplished poet of these themes, and was very popular in Lucknow. There is a story[55] that Mir was once present at a mushāira where Jurat was reciting, and being so loudly applauded that at times it was difficult to hear what he was saying. Perhaps carried away by this applause, he approached Mir, and in language of the utmost deference, invited him to give his opinion. Mir frowned and made no reply. Jurat asked him a second time, and Mir made some noncommital remark. But Jurat would not be content with this, and pressed him further, whereupon Mir said, "The fact is that you can't write poetry; just stick to your kissing and slavering." This judgement could be interpreted as an expression of traditional puritanism, but the character of Mir's own verse speaks against such an interpretation. It is more likely that he is condemning the kind of love poetry in which most of what the word *love* implied for Mir was ignored and the concept of love was restricted to one of mere sexual enjoyment.

Mir's aversion to Lucknow grew more and more intense with the years, and one can trace the development of his feelings through the last three collections of his ghazals—the fourth, fifth, and sixth dīvāns—all of which were compiled after he had settled there. In the fourth he writes,

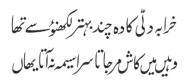

The ruins of Jahānābād were ten times better than Lucknow;
Oh, that I had stayed there to die—not come to live distracted here.
(IV.505.23)[56]

---

54 Āzād, *Āb i Ḥayāt*, p. 215.
55 *Ibid.*, pp. 237–238.
56 Cf. IV.463.7–8.

And in another verse, which does not mention Lucknow by name, he says that there is something wrong with a man who goes on living in a land that has no talented men.[57] The clear implication, that he still hoped even at this advanced age to find refuge in some more congenial place, is repeatedly made explicit in his fifth dīvān, compiled when, as one of his verses tells us, he had been living there "for years" (V.566.9). One whole ghazal in it is devoted to this theme. "Now I shall arise from here and go away; and never shall I come this way again," it begins (V.541.7). The city seems desolate, as though its human population had left it and the owls had moved into the empty city—so that "it is hard for a *man* [the word is deliberately emphasised] to live here any longer" (V.570.7). The word *owls* is deliberately and insultingly chosen, first because, as a bird that is commonly found in deserted ruins, it is a bird of ill-omen, and secondly because in colloquial Urdu it means a fool.

In the sixth dīvān this bitterness dies away. Rather, he laments his loneliness, which he feels more and more keenly as one by one his few remaining friends die, leaving him to long for death to release him from his imprisonment "within the four walls of the world." There is no more any sign that he still has hopes of leaving Lucknow, and in fact he never did.[58] Personal misfortunes added to the burden he had to bear. His health was failing and he was losing his sight. In three successive years he lost a son, a daughter, and his wife, to all of whom he had been deeply attached; and finally, he fell seriously ill with a painful disease of the bowels. But from this he never recovered, and in 1810, in his eighty-seventh or eighty-eighth year, he died.[59] In spite of all his afflictions, he had gone on writing poetry and attending mushāiras even in his last years. He writes:

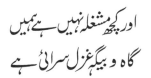

I have no other work to occupy me now.
In season, out of season, I recite my verse.   (V.622.25)

[57] Allusion to IV.529.21–22.
[58] Allusions to VI.640.22 and VI.649.21.
[59] Cf. Āsī's account in the Introduction to his edition of the *Kulliyāt*, pp. 32ff.

He knows that his time is drawing to a close, but he claims proudly:

کوئی دم رونق مجلس کی اور بھی ہے اس دم کے ساتھ

یعنی چراغ صبح سے ہیں، ہم دم بھی اپنا غنیمت ہے

Some moments more this gathering gains lustre from my name.
Night passes, and the lamp burns low; yet men see by its flame.

(V.608.16)

One of the most striking features of his last dīvāns is the number of
verses in which he continues to assert the same values that his poetry had
proclaimed ever since he first made his name. Some of these are expressed
in words almost identical with verses he had written many years earlier.
One short poem in the last dīvān of all can fairly be described as his last
testament as a poet.

باتیں ہماری یاد رہیں گی پھر باتیں ایسی نہ سُنیے گا

پڑھتے کسی کو سُنیے گا تو دیر تلک سر دُھنیے گا

سعی و تلاش بہت سی رہے گی، اس اندازِ کے کہنے کی

صحبت میں علما فضلا کی جا کر پڑھیے گِنیے گا

دل کی تسلّی جب کہ ہو گی گفت و شنود سے لوگوں کی

آگ بجھتے گی غم کی بدن میں اس میں جلیبے بجھنیے گا

گرم اشعارِ میر درد نہ داغوں سے یہ بھر دیں گے

زرد رُو شہر میں پھریے گا گلیوں میں گل چُنیے گا

A fairly free prose translation is: ''Remember well my verse; you will
not hear its like again. You will hear someone reciting it and long shake

your head as you sit and wonder at it. If you would write as I did, long and
earnestly must you seek. You must study in the company of men of
learning and culture, and ponder what you learn from them. And when
you have learned all you can from them, the fire of grief must kindle
within you, and in that fire you must burn. Then the burning verses of
Mir will sear all your heart, and you will roam pale and wan through the
city.'' The original poem is a ghazal of four couplets, unusual not only
because of its single, continuous theme but also because of its use of internal rhyme and the extreme freedom of its metre (VI.629.6). Its basic
pattern is that of the fifteen long syllables (seven spondees and a single
long at the end) of which he grew increasingly fond over the years.[60] But
the variations are, in this poem, almost unlimited, with ⌣ ⌣ — as well as
— ⌣ ⌣ alternating with the basic — —, as though Mir were forcefully asserting the right that his mastery gave him to establish his own norms
where he chose to do so. It deserves verse translation, but a comparable
effect in English verse cannot be achieved. In short, his message is what
it had been right from the start, that a poet must master his craft, but
only if he speaks out of the deep pain of a passionate spiritual experience
will he really be a poet.

Mir is buried in Lucknow. The graveyard in which he lies is a large
one. Many of the tombs have through years of long neglect lost all distinguishing marks, and moreover, part of the cemetery was destroyed
when the railway was built. At all events the site of Mir's grave is now
unknown. One as accustomed as he was to indifference and neglect
would perhaps not have minded too much, for he had long been convinced that he had raised his own memorial, and that it would be more
lasting than any tomb. In one of his first poems he had claimed:

جانے کا نہیں شورِ سخن کامرے ہرگز

تا حشر جہاں میں مرا دیوان رہے گا

My verse endures eternal down the years:
As long as the world lasts, so will my fame.   (I.5.12)

---

[60] Cf. above, p. 213.

And in one of his last he repeats the claim, more quietly, but just as confidently; for he knows that the poetry of his heart speaks to the hearts of his fellow men:

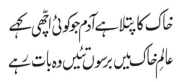

Man was first made of clay, and if the song you sing is good
This world of clay for years to come will listen to your voice.

(VI.675.5)

A Complete Ghazal of Mir

TRANSLATIONS of ghazals or of parts of ghazals have been given on pages 128, 148, 175, 177, and 196–197. That which is most nearly complete is that on pages 196–197, which omits only three couplets from the original poem of twelve. In the originals double rhyme has been used in every case, but only in the translation on page 128 have we found it possible to reproduce this feature in translation. In one important respect none of the ghazals translated is typical, for all of them possess a unity of theme or mood which the typical ghazal does not. We have found it impossible to reproduce in tolerable English verse, preserving the rhyme scheme of the original, any more fully typical Urdu ghazal than these. In default of this we give here a whole ghazal of Mir, followed by a full description and a literal prose translation with brief explanatory notes where these seem necessary.

اُٹّی ہوگئیں سب تدبیریں کچھ نہ دوائے کام کیا دیکھا اس بیماریِ دل نے آخر کام تمام کیا

عہدِ جوانی رو رو کاٹا پیری میں لیں آنکھیں مؤند یعنی رات بہت تھے جاگے صبح ہوئی آرام کیا

حرف نہیں جاں بخشی میں اس کی خونی اپنی قسمت کی ہم سے جو پہلے کہہ بھیجا سو مرنے کا پیغام کیا

ناحق ہم مجبوروں پر یہ تہمت ہے مختاری کی چاہتے ہیں سو آپ کریں ہیں ہم کو عبث بدنام کیا

سارے رند و باش جہاں کے تجھ سے سجود میں رہتے ہیں	بانکے ٹیڑھے ترچھے تیکھے سب کا تجھ کو امام کیا

سرزدم سے بے ادبی تو وحشت میں بھی کم ہی ہوئی	کوسوں اُس کی اور گئے پر سجدہ ہر ہر گام کیا

کس کا کعبہ، کیسا قبلہ، کون حرم ہے، کیا احرام	کوچے کے اس کے باشندوں نے سب کو یہیں سلام کیا

شیخ جو ہے مسجد میں ننگا، رات کو تھا میخانے میں	جُبّہ، خرقہ، کُرتا، ٹوپی، مستی میں انعام کیا

کاش اب برقع منہ سے اٹھا دے ورنہ پھر کیا حاصل ہے	آنکھ مندے پر اُن نے گو دیدار کو اپنے عام کیا

یاں کے پید و سیاہ میں ہم کو دخل جو ہے سو اتنا ہے	رات کو رو رو صبح کیا دن کو جوں توں شام کیا

صبح چمن میں اس کو کہیں تکلیف ہوا لے آئی تھی	رخ سے گل کو مول لیا، قامت سے سرو غلام کیا

ساعدِ سیمیں دونوں اس کے ہاتھ میں لا کر چھوڑ دیئے	بھولے اُس کے قول قسم پر ہائے خیالِ خام کیا

کام ہوئے ہیں سارے ضائع ہر ساعت کی ساحت سے	استغنا کی چو گنی اُن نے جوں جوں میں ابرام کیا

ایسے آہوئے رم خوردہ کی وحشت کھونی مشکل تھی	سحر کیا، اعجاز کیا، جن لوگوں نے تجھ کو رام کیا

میرے کے دین و مذہب کو اب پوچھتے کیا ہو اُن نے تو	قشقہ کھینچا، دیر میں بیٹھا، کب کا ترک اسلام کیا

The ghazal is from Mir's first dīvān.[1] It has fifteen couplets, and its themes include, among others, the life-long suffering which the lover must bear (couplets 1 and 2), God's injustice to man (4, 10), the poet's acknowledged pre-eminence among rakes and profligates—i.e., among mystics (5), the mystic's contempt for religious formalities and for those who uphold them (7, 8, 15), the great beauty of the beloved (11), and the beloved's timidity, elusiveness, fickleness, and inaccessibility (12, 13, 14). Thus there is no unity of theme in the ghazal as a whole; nor are the couplets on similar themes always grouped together.

[1] *Kulliyāt*, p. 4.

It is worth elaborating a little at this point the suggestion made earlier that the contrasting close unity of form and disunity of themes stems in great measure from the oral tradition of Urdu poetry. The ghazal was composed to be recited, not to be read, and where there was a prescribed line, fixing metre and rhyme for a whole succession of ghazals (cf. above, page 4), frequent variation of theme was a necessary measure to prevent monotony. Moreover, recitation with a pause after each couplet in order for the audience to react emphasised the completeness of each in a way which the printed page does not.

The rhyme scheme of the original is one syllable of qāfia (rhyme)— italicised in the transcription below—followed by three of radīf (end rhyme), thus:

First couplet:	*kām* (a)	kiya	A
	ta*mām* (a)	kiya	A
Second:	ānkhen	mūnd	B
	ā*rām* (a)	kiya	A
Third:	qismat	kī	C
	pai*ghām* (a)	kiya	A

and so on.

The metre is that described above, page 213—basically a line of fifteen longs (seven spondees followed by a single long syllable). There is a caesura after the fourth spondee, and the beat of the rhythm falls on the first, third, fifth, etc., syllables. But in the whole poem only one half-couplet (the first half of the fourth couplet) exemplifies this pattern:

nāhaq ham majbūron par yih tuhmat hai mukhtārī kī

Elsewhere two shorts may replace a long in any of the even syllables (second, fourth, sixth, etc.) except the eighth (which immediately precedes the caesura) and the fifteenth (the final syllable of the line). Thus the possibilities of variation are considerable. A full analysis gives the following figures:

First foot:	16 spondees;	14 dactyls
Second foot:	26 spondees;	4 dactyls

Third foot: 16 spondees;   14 dactyls
Fourth foot: 30 spondees;   0 dactyls
   (preceding the caesura)
Fifth foot: 16 spondees;   14 dactyls
Sixth foot: 24 spondees;   6 dactyls
Seventh foot: 12 spondees;   18 dactyls
Last single syllable always long.

It is noticeable that in the second, fourth, and sixth feet there is a heavy preponderance of spondees, and that it is in the first, third, fifth, and seventh feet that the dactyl most commonly replaces the spondee—in half the feet in question (60 out of a possible 120). This feature is emphasised by the fact that the rhyme-scheme necessarily produces the dactyl pattern in the seventh foot of every other half-couplet; but even if these feet are left out of account, 45 feet out of a possible 105 are dactyls.[2]

The first three couplets scan:

```
┌ — — │ — ∪ ∪ │ — — │ — — ‖ — ∪ ∪ │ — — │ — ∪ ∪ │ —
│ — — │ — — │ — ∪ ∪ │ — — ‖ — — │ — ∪ ∪ │ — ∪ ∪ │ —
┌ — ∪ ∪ │ — — │ — — │ — — ‖ — — │ — — │ — — │ —
│ — — │ — ∪ ∪ │ — — │ — — ‖ — ∪ ∪ │ — — │ — ∪ ∪ │ —
┌ — ∪ ∪ │ — — │ — ∪ ∪ │ — — ‖ — — │ — — │ — — │ —
└ — ∪ ∪ │ — — │ — — │ — — ‖ — — │ — — │ — ∪ ∪ │ —
```

The following is a literal translation of the ghazal. Each couplet is numbered and is followed by a brief explanation where necessary. Possible alternative interpretations are occasionally indicated, but these by no means exhaust the whole range of possible meanings:

1. All my plans have been overturned, and no medicine has had any effect. You see? This sickness of the heart [love] has killed me in the end [as I told you it would].

2. I passed the days of my youth in weeping, and in old age I closed my eyes. That is, I passed many nights in wakefulness, and when morning came I rested.

---

[2] However, in the first half of each couplet the seventh foot is a spondee in 12 cases out of 15.

There is a play on words here. The black hair of youth associated with the black nights, passed restlessly in the black despair of separation, contrasts with the white hair of old age, associated with the white light of dawn and peace and sleep.

3. I do not question her life-giving power. It is just the excellence of my fortune that the first message that she sent me was my sentence of death.

The beloved has power of life and death over her lover: one word from her can save him, and one word can kill him. It is his good fortune that her message, rejecting his love, is equivalent to sentence of death upon him. "Good fortune" may be ironical, or it could be literal, for it *is* good fortune to have the opportunity to die for one's love. The verse could also be interpreted in a mystic sense.

4. We act under constraint, and you slander us when you say we have free will. It is your will that is done, and we are blamed without cause.

A complaint against God.

5. All the rakes and profligates of the whole world bow down before you. The proud, the perverse, the awkward, the independent—all have acknowledged you their leader.

Mir addressing himself. He is the supreme profligate, the leader of all lovers of beauty—that is, of mystic worshippers of God.

6. If even in my distracted state I have been guilty of any want of respect [in daring to approach her], then it was little enough. For mile after mile as I made my way towards her, I fell down to worship her at every step.

Could be literal or mystical. The falling down perhaps also suggests the constant stumbling and falling as the lover makes his way through the thorns and briars of the wilderness of love.

7. What do we care for the Ka'ba, and the direction in which we should turn to pray, and the holy places and the robes of Pilgrimage? We who live in her lane have said farewell to all these things.

In the mystic sense. The constant lover never leaves the lane where his beloved lives. We who are constant in love for the Divine Beloved hold the formalities of religion as of no account.

8. If the shaikh stands naked in the mosque today it is because he spent the night drinking in the tavern, and in his drunkenness gave his cloak and gown and shirt and hat away.

Two points, perhaps. First a jeer at the shaikh's hypocrisy. And second, an expression of praise for the power of beauty, which even the shaikh cannot resist forever.

9. If only she would lift the veil from her face *now*. What will it profit me if when my eyes are closed [in death] she unveils herself for all to see?

Also could be taken in a mystic sense.

10. What can we do with the black and white of this world?[3] If anything, then only this, that we can see the [black] night out with constant weeping, and bear the toil of the [white] day until evening comes.

Perhaps a complaint to God, perhaps a more general lament on his sense of helplessness in the turbulent times in which he lived.

11. At morning in the garden she walked out to take the air. Her cheek made the rose her slave, and her graceful stature made the cypress her thrall.

So far did her cheek surpass the rose in beauty, and her stature the cypress in grace.

12. I held her silver-white wrists in my hands, but she swore [that she would come to me later], and I let them go. How raw and inexperienced I was to trust her word!

Not easily interpreted in a mystic sense.

13. Every moment I beseeched her, and this has brought all my efforts to nothing. Her proud indifference increased fourfold with every time I importuned her.

[3] I.e., what power have we to influence the course of events?

14. Such a timid, fleet gazelle does not easily lose her fear of man. Those who have tamed you have performed a wonder, as though by magic power.

Praise of his beloved's timid beauty, and envy of his successful rivals, who have won her favour when he could not.

15. Why do you ask at this late hour what Mir's religion is? He has drawn the caste mark on his forehead and sat down in the temple. He abandoned Islam long ago.

The worship of God through the worship of beauty, symbolised by Hindu idolatry.

BIBLIOGRAPHY
GLOSSARY
INDEX

BIBLIOGRAPHY

TEXTS OF THE POETRY

Saudā. *Kulliyāt*, ed. Mīr ʿAbdur Raḥmān Āhī. Delhi: Matbaʿ i Muṣṭafā, A.H. 1272 (A.D. 1856). Later editions are unsatisfactory. No reliable text of the complete poetical works has yet been published.

Maṣnavī i Mīr Ḥasan, ed. ʿAbdul Bārī Āsī. Lucknow: Newal Kishor, 1941.

Mīr Taqī Mīr, *Kulliyāt*, ed. ʿAbdul Bārī Āsī. Lucknow: Newal Kishor, 1941. This edition is slightly less complete, but more accurate, than the later edition of ʿIbādat Barelavī.

WORKS ON THE POETS

Shaikh Cānd. *Saudā*. Aurangabad: Anjuman i Taraqqī i Urdū, 1936.

Mīr. *Zikr i Mīr*, ed. ʿAbdul Ḥaq. Aurangabad: Anjuman i Taraqqī i Urdū, 1928.

Khwāja Aḥmad Fārūqī. *Mīr Taqī Mīr: Ḥayāt aur Shāʿirī*. Aligarh: Anjuman i Taraqqī i Urdū, 1954.

Qāẓī ʿAbdul Vadūd. Review of Fārūqī, *Mīr Taqī Mīr*, in two instalments in the periodical *Maʾāṣir*, Patna, August 1957 and January 1958.

Maḥmūd Fārūqī. *Mīr Ḥasan aur khāndān ke dūsre shuʿarā*. Lahore: Maktaba i Jadīd, 1953.

Muḥammad Ḥusain Āzād. *Āb i Ḥayāt*, 14th printing. Lahore: Shaikh Mubārak ʿAlī, n.d.

WORKS ON THE HISTORICAL SETTING

T. G. P. Spear. *India, Pakistan and the West*, 2nd ed. London: Oxford University Press, 1952.

Percival Spear. *Twilight of the Mughuls*. Cambridge University Press, 1951.

W. H. Moreland and Atul Chandra Chatterjee. *A Short History of India*, 3rd ed. London: Longmans, Green, 1953.

H. C. Rawlinson. *India: A Short Cultural History*. London: Cresset Press, 1952.

S. M. Edwardes and H. L. O. Garrett. *Mughal Rule in India*. London: Oxford University Press, 1930.

W. H. Moreland. *India at the Death of Akbar*. London: Macmillan, 1920.
William Irvine. *Later Mughals*, ed. Jadunath Sarkar. 2 vols. Calcutta: Sarkar, 1922.
Jadunath Sarkar. *Fall of the Mughal Empire*, 2nd ed. 4 vols. Calcutta: Sarkar, 1950.

SUGGESTIONS FOR FURTHER READING

Critical studies of Urdu literature, whether in Urdu or in English, tend to be unsatisfying. Old-style Urdu critics have followed the characteristically medieval tradition of evaluating poetry solely in terms of formal and technical accomplishment, without reference to the content of the poetry; and this tradition is still alive, though overshadowed now by more modern trends. Modern criticism came into existence a little less than a century ago, and was much influenced by nineteenth-century English writing—notably by Macaulay. This English influence unfortunately made its impact at a time when imaginative sympathy with medieval ways of thought and feeling was at a low ebb in Britain, and such lack of sympathy is still evident in both Urdu and English writings. There are three histories of Urdu literature in English:

T. Grahame Bailey. *Urdu Literature*. Calcutta: Association Press (Y.M.C.A.), 1932.
Ram Babu Saxena. *History of Urdu Literature*. Allahabad: Ram Narain Lal, 1927.
Muhammad Sadiq. *History of Urdu Literature*. London: Oxford University Press, 1964.

Bailey's is a very short sketch. Saxena's is fuller and more readable. Sadiq's is the best and fullest to be published so far.

The culture and literature of medieval and renaissance Europe has been studied with an insight and a sympathy not yet to be found in studies of Urdu. For this reason, and because the parallels with Urdu poetry are often strikingly close, it is worth while to read a number of them. Recommended are:

C. S. Lewis. *The Allegory of Love*. London: Oxford University Press paperback, 1958.
———— *The Discarded Image*. Cambridge University Press, 1964.
J. Huizinga. *The Waning of the Middle Ages*. Harmondsworth: Penguin, 1958.
J. M. Cohen. *A History of Western Literature*. Harmondsworth: Penguin, 1956. Chaps. 1–10.
J. B. Broadbent. *Poetic Love*. London: Chatto and Windus, 1964.

In other European languages are:

Joseph Garcin de Tassy. *Histoire de la littérature hindouie et hindoustanie.* 3 vols. Paris: Labitte, 1870–1871.

Alessandro Bausani. *Storia delle letterature del Pakistan.* Milan: Nuova Accademia Editrice, 1958. Chaps. 1 and 2 are relevant.

For those who know enough Urdu the best introductions to Urdu poetry are still Muhammad Husain Āzād's *Āb i Hayāt*, first published in 1879; and Altāf Husain Hālī's *Muqaddima She'r o Shā'irī*, first published in 1893. For a brief note on *Āb i Hayāt* see p. 7, n. 4. It is constantly being republished and is rarely out of print. Of Hālī's *Muqaddima* the first half is a general discussion of the canons of poetry, and leans heavily on Macaulay, but the second half, with all its limitations, is a good survey of the major forms of classical Urdu poetry. The edition of Vahīd Quraishī (Lahore: Maktaba Jadīd, 1953) reproduces the text of 1893, is excellently printed, and has many useful annotations.

A readable essay on Urdu love poetry is Firāq Gorakhpūrī, *Urdū kī 'Ishqiya Shā'irī* (Allahabad: Sangam Publishing House, 1945).

THE PERSIAN AND ISLAMIC BACKGROUND

Since Urdu poetry is in a direct line of descent from the Persian, works on Persian literature are also relevant to an understanding of Urdu; and Persian is much better served than Urdu by translations and interpretative studies. Some of the most important, together with some works on Islamic mysticism and on Islam in general, are:

E. G. Browne. *A Literary History of Persia.* 4 vols. Cambridge University Press, 1951. This is the classic survey.

A. J. Arberry. *Classical Persian Literature.* London: Allen and Unwin, 1958.

—————— *Sufism: An Account of the Mystics of Islam.* London: Allen and Unwin, 1950.

—————— *An Introduction to the History of Sufism.* London: Longmans, Green, 1942.

—————— *Fifty Poems of Hafiz.* Cambridge University Press, 1947.

R. A. Nicholson. *The Mystics of Islam.* London: Bell, 1914.

—————— *Studies in Islamic Mysticism.* Cambridge University Press, 1921.

—————— ed., *Jalāluddīn Rūmī's Mathnawī.* 8 vols. London: Luzac, 1925–1940. Edition of the text, with translations and commentary.

G. C. Anawati and Louis Gardet. *Mystique musulmane.* Paris: Vrin, 1961.

H. Ritter. *Das Meer der Seele.* Leiden: Brill, 1955. This gives the fullest account of classical Persian mysticism and its love-symbolism, and should be studied by everyone who wants to understand Persian, Turkish, or Urdu mystical poetry.

For the literary symbolism see:

F. Rückert. *Grammatik, Poetik und Rhetorik der Perser, herausgegeben von W. Pertsch.* Gotha: Perthes, 1874. (Reprinted 1967).

A. Pagliaro and A. Bausani. *Storia della letteratura Persiana.* Milan: Nuova Accademia Editrice, 1960.

H. A. R. Gibb. *Muhammadanism.* London: Oxford University Press, 1949.

R. Hartmann. *Die Religion des Islam.* Berlin: Mittler, 1944.

I. Goldziher. *Vorlesungen über den Islam.* Heidelberg: Winter, 1923.

SPECIALISED WORKS IN URDU

Important new work in Urdu on the eighteenth-century poets has been published since this book was written, including the following:

Khalīq Anjum. *Mirzā Rafi' Saudā.* Aligarh: Anjuman i Taraqqī i Urdū, 1966. This comprehensive study should supersede the pioneering work of Shaikh Cānd.

Delhi College Magazine, Special Mir Number. Delhi, 1962–1963.

Vaḥīd Quraishī. *Mīr Ḥasan aur un kā zamāna.* Lahore: Istiqlāl Press, 1959.

It is to be hoped that Urdu scholars will soon give their attention to producing definitive texts of the poets' works. *Kalām i Saudā,* ed. Khūrshīdul Islām (Aligarh: Anjuman i Taraqqī i Urdū, 1965), is a reliable text of a comprehensive selection of Saudā's verse. A definitive text of the collected verse is currently being prepared by Shamsuddīn Ṣiddīqī.

GLOSSARY

burqaʻ
: A loose, flowing garment worn in the Indian subcontinent by Muslim women who observe *parda* (purdah.) It envelops the whole body, from the crown of the head (which supports the garment) to the feet. Lace network, or a strip of thinner cloth across the eyes, enables the wearer to see while remaining fully protected from others' eyes.

dīvān
: A collection of ghazals.

faqīr
: Literally, a beggar; but the word has religious connotations also, and signifies one who spurns all worldly possessions and trusts in God to provide for him through the charity of his fellow men.

ghazal
: A short lyric poem consisting of couplets independent of one another in meaning, but bound by a strict unity of form, that is, a uniform metre and a rhyming scheme AA, BA, CA, DA, etc. The predominant theme is love, which may be either literal or figurative.

ḥakīm
: A physician who practises the traditional Greek system of medicine as modified by the Arabs.

jāgīr
: An assignment to a noble of the land revenue from one or more villages in lieu of salary.

kulliyāt
: The collected verse of a poet.

masnavī
: A lengthy poem in the rhyme scheme AA, BB, CC, etc. In Urdu it is generally a love story. The shorter masnavīs are generally realistic and tragic; the longer have a stronger element of fantasy and the story has a happy ending.

mukhammas
: A poem of five-line stanzas, rhyming AAAAX.

mushā'ira   A gathering at which poets assemble to recite their verse.

navvāb   Literally, one who exercises deputed power; in general
                   roughly equivalent to the British title of Lord.

parda (purdah)   The system of strict segregation of women traditionally
                   practised by Muslims in India and Pakistan (cf. p. 98).

parī   A supernatural being with magic powers, in the form of a
                   beautiful woman.

qaṣīda   A lengthy poem rhyming AA, BA, CA, etc.; generally a
                   panegyric ode.

shāgird   A pupil, or apprentice. A young poet in his capacity of
                   apprentice to his ustād.

shaikh   Literally, an old man; hence, an elder; hence, the pillar of
                   orthodox religion, always represented in poetry as a hypocrite
                   and a Pharisee.

takhalluṣ   The poet's pen-name, always introduced into the closing
                   couplet of the ghazal.

tazkira   A short account of poets, giving for each entry brief bio-
                   graphical details and a few specimen verses.

ustād   Literally, teacher, or master; the poet of established reputation
                   in his capacity of guide to his shāgirds.

vazīr   Minister, usually Chief Minister; the "Vizier" of the *Arabian
                   Nights*.

INDEX